W9-BFP-294

Hiking Washington's Mount Adams Country

A Guide to the Mount Adams, Indian Heaven,
and Trapper Creek Wilderness Areas of
Washington's Southern Cascades

Fred Barstad

FALCON®

GUILFORD, CONNECTICUT
HELENA, MONTANA

AN IMPRINT OF ROWMAN & LITTLEFIELD

A FALCON GUIDE ®

All photographs by the author unless otherwise noted.
Maps created by XNR Productions Inc. © Rowman &
Littlefield

Library of Congress Cataloging-in-Publication Data
Barstad, Fred.
  Hiking Washington's Mount Adams country: a guide to
the Mt. Adams, Indian Heaven, and Trapper Creek Wilder-
ness areas of Washington's southern cascades/Fred
Barstad.
    p. cm.
  ISBN 0-7627-3090-0
    1. Hiking—Washington (State)—Mount Adams
Wilderness—Guidebooks. 2. Trails—Washington (State)—
Mount Adams Wilderness—Guidebooks. 3. Mount Adams
Wilderness (Wash.)—Guidebooks. I. Title.

GV199.42.W22M64 2004
796.51'09797'34—dc22

                                        2004047199

Manufactured in the United States of America

Distributed by NATIONAL BOOK NETWORK

Contents

Mount Adams Country

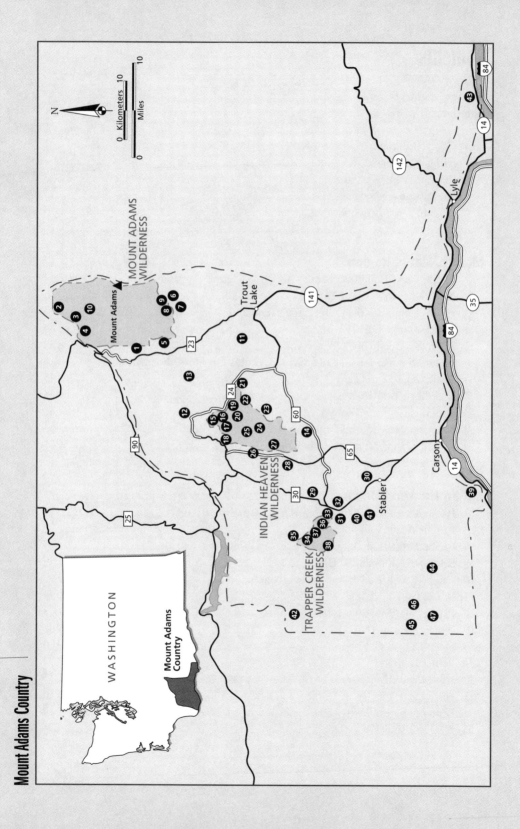

Trapper Creek Wilderness and the Region Near the Columbia River Gorge 151

Acknowledgments

Thanks to Jason Larvick, Eric Valentine, Dane Johnson, Dave Kaufman, Leif Bullock, Phil Bullock, Travis Dixon, and Drew Kelly for hiking and camping companionship. Thanks to Kerry Searls and Gary Fletcher for hiking, camping, and climbing the peaks with me. Thanks to Darrin Larvick and Dave Martin for hiking, scrambling, camping, and making car shuttles. Thanks to Lowell Euhus for providing information.

Many thanks to Tom Linde and Dean Robertson, Forest Service employees who reviewed my text. Thanks also to Jim Nieland of the Forest Service for reviewing text and furnishing historical information. Most of all, thanks to my wife, Suzi Barstad, for traveling, camping, and hiking with me and for editing the raw manuscript.

Introduction

Geology of the Mount Adams Region

In southern Washington, Oregon, and Northern California, the Cascade Range is mostly composed of uplifted sedimentary and ancient lava rock. These uplifted mountains are known as the Old Cascades. Built atop this foundation and, in some cases, slightly to the east of it is a string of huge, lofty stratovolcanoes, as well as lesser cones, vents, and subsequent lava flows. These peaks, called the High Cascades, are part of what is known as the "Ring of Fire" that encircles the Pacific Ocean. On a clear day one or more of these stratovolcanoes is visible from almost any elevated spot in the range.

The huge humped stratovolcanic cone of 12,276-foot-high Mount Adams dominates the view throughout much of the region covered in this book. By sheer volume, Mount Adams is one of the, if not the, largest peak in the Cascades. To the west of Mount Adams, slightly out of the area covered in this book, stands Mount St. Helens, the youngest stratovolcano in the region. When Mount St. Helens erupted in 1980, it dumped a layer of volcanic ash of varying depth over the entire area.

Climate

Rising a mile or more above the level of the Pacific Ocean in most places, the ridgeline of the Cascade Range creates a barrier to moisture-laden storms coming from the west. As it is pushed over the western slope of the range by the prevailing southwesterly winds, the air is forced to rise, and therefore cool. Cooler air can hold less moisture, so it precipitates out in the form of rain or snow; in some spots there is up to 150 inches of rainfall per year. At times low clouds (sometimes called a "marine deck") may fill the western canyons and valleys while the higher ridges and peaks are basking in sunshine. Because of this wet maritime climate, the western side of the mountains is covered with dense forest, except areas where logging or fires have disturbed it.

Along the crest, clouds sometimes get stuck and continue to drop precipitation even after the main storm has passed. Snowstorms and freezing temperatures can occur at any time of the year. The higher peaks, notably Mount Adams, at times make their own weather. Cloud caps can appear from an otherwise clear sky. In these caps, heavy wind, fog, and rain or snow can combine to make hiking miserable, difficult, and dangerous, if not impossible.

As the air passes the crest and begins to drop, it warms by compression (sometimes called the "Chinook effect"). This warmer air is able to hold more water, therefore the rainfall becomes much less, and in some cases the clouds just evaporate. Because of the drier climate, the forest gradually thins out as you descend the range's eastern slopes.

The range is also a temperature barrier. On the western slopes the ocean moderates the climate. It is rarely very hot in the summer, and the cold continental air from the interior only occasionally spills over the crest in the winter. East of the crest the winters are much colder and the summers hotter.

Human History

Native Americans used this region for both hunting and fishing. Trails across the mountains facilitated trade between coastal and inland tribes. The area in and around Indian Heaven Wilderness was a favorite spot for gathering huckleberries in late summer.

Big Watchable Wildlife

Blacktail deer are the most commonly seen large animal in the Mount Adams area. In fact, some people see them too closely when they hit them with a car. Blacktails *(Odocoileus hemionus columbianus)*, a slightly smaller and darker subspecies of mule deer *(Odocoileus hemionus hemionus)*, inhabit the damp western slopes of the Cascades as well as the Coast Range. Typical of a forest-loving animal, the antlers of a blacktail are much smaller than those of a mule deer. The namesake of a blacktail, its tail, is wider than that of a mule deer and completely black on its upper side. When alarmed a blacktail will generally run with its tail carried horizontally, but they occasionally flag (hold their tail straight up).

East of the Cascade crest is the range of the larger-antlered mule deer. The mule deer is easily distinguished from the blacktail by its white ropelike tail, which is tipped in black and generally hangs straight down even when alarmed. A mule deer's much-larger ears (hence its name) appear to be fuzzy on the edges and inside because of a thin covering of longer hair.

Two subspecies of elk (aka wapiti) roam the southern Washington section of the Cascade Range, but on the hikes described in this book the only one you are likely to encounter is the Roosevelt elk *(Cervus elaphus roosevelti)*. The wetter western slope of the Cascade Range is the home of this slightly larger and darker subspecies. Roosevelt bulls, which may weigh more than 1,000 pounds, are the largest animals to inhabit the Cascades. Roosevelts are common and may be expected almost anywhere on the western slopes of the mountains. On the eastern slopes of the range live the Rocky Mountain elk *(Cervus elaphus nelsoni)*. Be especially careful and vigilant while driving on the forest roads; hitting an elk can easily total your car and cause injuries.

Pure-white except for their eyes, horns, and hooves, mountain goats *(Oreamnos americanus)* are common on the northwest slope of Mount Adams. They range up to above 9,000 feet elevation along the North Cleaver Route and are often seen near High Camp. Hikes 3, High Camp via Killen Creek Trail, Trails 113, 10 and 10, Mount Adams North Cleaver Route are in this heavily populated mountain goat area.

Roosevelt bulls

Black Bears *(Ursus americanus)* are found throughout the Cascade Range. The densest population I have noticed is in and around Trapper Creek Wilderness. See the Be Bear Aware section in the Backcountry Safety and Hazards chapter of this book for more information about hiking and camping in bear country. Better yet, pick up a copy of the pocketsize Falconguide *Bear Aware,* by Bill Schneider.

Cougars *(Felis concolor),* also known as mountain lions, are also found throughout the region, though seldom seen by hikers. See the Be Cougar Alert section in the Backcountry Safety and Hazards chapter of this book for more information.

Backcountry Safety and Hazards

Being Prepared

There are a few simple things you can do that will improve your chances of staying healthy while you are on your hikes.

One of the most important things to do is to be careful of your drinking-water supply. All surface water should be filtered, chemically treated, or boiled before drinking, washing utensils, or brushing your teeth with it. The water may look clean and pure, and it may be, but you can never be sure. In a few cases there is no water along the trail, so you need to take along all that you will need. If you use a filter, be sure it has a fairly new cartridge or has been recently cleaned before you leave on your hike. Many of the trailheads do not have potable water.

Check the weather report before heading into the mountains. Stormy weather with wind, rain, and even snow is possible at any time of year. The opposite may also be the case at times. Hot sunny weather on the exposed slopes can cause quick dehydration. At these times a broad-brimmed hat, light-colored and loose-fitting clothes, and lots of sunscreen are what is needed. Keep well fed and drink plenty of liquids.

If you intend to make one of the mountain climbs or one of the short rock scrambles described in this book, be sure you have the climbing skills to do it safely. If you have not been on the route before, it is a good idea to go with a competent and experienced leader.

Inform friends or relatives of your plans and when you plan to return. If you are planning a long or difficult hike, or especially one of the mountain climbs, be sure to get into shape ahead of time. This will make your trip much more pleasant, as well as safer. Of all the safety tips, the most important one is to take your brain with you when you go into the wilderness. Without it no tips will help, and with it almost any obstacle can be avoided or overcome. Think about what you are doing, be safe, and have a great time in the outdoors.

Meeting Stock, Mountain Bikers, and ORVs on the Trail

Meeting stock traffic is a common occurrence on some of the trails in the southern Washington Cascades. So it's a good idea to know how to pass stock with the least possible disturbance or danger. If you meet parties with stock, try to get as far off the trail as possible. Horsemen prefer that you stand on the downhill side of the trail, but there is some question if this is the safest place for a hiker. If possible I like to get well off the trail on the uphill side. It is often a good idea to talk quietly to the horses and their riders, as this seems to calm many horses. If you have the family dog with you, be sure to keep it restrained and quiet. Dogs cause many horse wrecks.

Mountain bikers use some of the trails covered in this book. It is the responsibility of bikers to yield to other users, but in some rare cases they may not see a hiker quickly enough to prevent a collision. Bikes are quiet, so the hiker should keep a careful watch for their approach.

Motorbikes and ORVs (aka ATVs) use a few of the trails described in this book. Because these vehicles make a considerable amount of noise, they don't pose much of a safety concern for the hiker, but they are annoying to some people.

Read the Special Considerations section at the beginning of each hike to find out if the trail you are going to hike is open to these other users.

Following a Faint Trail

A few of the trails described in this book are faint, so good map-reading and route-finding skills are required to find your way. There are a few things you can do to make this route-finding job easier.

First read the entire description for the hike you are about to take before you start your trek. While hiking, try to keep track of your position on your map at all times. Learn to use your compass. Remember that a compass points toward magnetic north, which is not necessarily true north. In the southern Washington Cascades, the declination is from 18 to 21 degrees east. That means that the compass points that much east of true north. The USGS quad maps show the magnetic declination for that particular map.

An altimeter can be very useful for tracking your progress if it is properly used. Altimeters run on air pressure, which is always changing, so they must be set often. Any time you reach a point where you are sure of the elevation, set your altimeter, even if you set it only two or three hours earlier.

GPS coordinates for the trailheads, most major trail junctions, and key points are given at the end of each hike description. If you are proficient in the use of a GPS receiver, these can be very helpful, but remember that the government scrambles GPS signals. This may cause the readings to be a little off. Usually the reading you will get on your receiver will be within 30 yards of your actual location, but at times they may be much farther off than that.

While you're hiking watch for blazes cut into the bark of trees and rock cairns on the ground. Logs that have been sawed off also may be an indicator of the trail's route. Trees with the branches missing on one side may show that the trail passes on that side of the tree. Through thick woods, look for strips where the trees are much smaller or nonexistent; this could be the route that once was cleared for the trail.

All these things are not positive signs that you are going the right way, but, when taken together with good compass and map skills, they make it much easier to follow a faint trail.

Be Weather Aware

Thunderstorms are not very common in the Mount Adams region of the Cascades, but they do occur. On the high ridges and peaks, it is relatively easy to see and hear a thunderstorm before it reaches your location. But in the valleys and canyons, a storm can be on top of you with very little advance warning. If you get caught in a lightning storm, take special precautions.

- Remember that lightning can travel far ahead of the storm, so try to take cover well before the storm hits.
- Don't try to get back to your vehicle. It isn't worth the risk. Instead, seek the best shelter you can find. Lightning storms usually last only a short time, and from a safe spot you might even enjoy watching the storm.
- Stay away from anything that might attract lightning, such as metal tent poles, graphite fishing rods, and metal-frame backpacks.
- Be careful not to be caught on a mountaintop or exposed ridgeline or under a solitary tree.

- If possible, seek shelter in a low-lying area, ideally in a dense stand of small, uniformly sized trees.
- Get in a crouch position with both feet firmly placed on the ground; don't lean against a tree.
- If you have a pack without a metal frame or a sleeping pad with you, put your feet on it for extra insulation against electric shock.
- Don't walk or huddle together. Instead, stay 50 feet apart so that if someone does get struck the others can give first aid.
- If you are in a tent, it is usually best to stay there in your sleeping bag with your feet on your sleeping pad.

Be Bear Aware

The first step of any hike in bear country is an attitude adjustment. Being prepared for bears means having the right information as well as the right equipment. Unlike national-park bears, the black bears in the part of the Washington Cascades covered in this book are lightly hunted each year. This hunting doesn't seem to have much effect on the overall population of bears, but it does make them warier of people and less likely to approach humans. But they may pose a danger if you handle food improperly. At the very least, letting a bear get human food is contributing—directly—to the eventual destruction of the bear. Think of proper bear etiquette as protecting the bears as much as yourself. Black bears are especially common in and around Trapper Creek Wilderness but may be found on any hike covered in this book, except possibly Hike 43, Horsethief Butte Trail.

Camping in bear country

Staying overnight in bear country is not dangerous, but it adds an additional risk to your trip. The main problem is the presence of food, cooking, and garbage. Following a few basic rules greatly minimizes the risk to you and the bears.

Storing food and garbage. Be sure to finalize your food storage plans before it gets dark. It's not only difficult to store food in the dark but also easier to forget some juicy morsel on the ground. Also, be sure to store food in airtight, waterproof bags to prevent food odors from circulating throughout the forest. Store your garbage just as if it were food: It is to a bear.

Take a special bag for storing food. The bag must be sturdy and waterproof. You can get dry bags at most outdoor specialty stores, but you can get by with a trash-compactor bag. Regular garbage bags break and leave your food spread on the ground. You also need 100 feet of nylon cord. Parachute cord will usually suffice. The classic method of hanging food and gear smelling of food is to tie a rock or piece of wood to the end of your cord and toss it over a branch. And of course, don't let the rock or stick come down and hit you or someone else on the head. Attach the bag to the other end and hoist it 10 feet or more and well away from the trunk of any tree.

Camping on the summit of Mount Adams

What to hang. To be as safe as possible, hang anything that has any food smell. If you spilled something on your clothes, change before sleeping and hang the soiled garments with the food and garbage.

What to keep in your tent. You can't be too careful in keeping food smells out of the tent. Just in case a bear has become accustomed to coming into that campsite looking for food, it's vital to keep all food smells out of the tent. This usually includes your pack, which is hard to keep odor-free. Take only valuables (cameras, binoculars, clothing, and sleeping gear) into the tent.

Types of food. What food you have along is much less critical than how you handle it, cook it, and store it. Consider, however, the fewer dishes and or less packaging the better.

Hanging food at night is not the only storage issue. Also make sure you place food correctly in your pack. Use airtight packages as much as possible. Store food in the containers it came in or, when open, in ziplock bags. This keeps food smells out of your pack and off your camping gear and clothes.

Don't cook too much food and you won't have to deal with leftovers. If you do end up with extra food, however, you have only two choices: carry it out or burn it. Don't bury it, throw it in a lake, or leave it anywhere in bear country. A bear will most likely find and rip up any food or garbage buried in the backcountry.

If you end up with lots of food scraps in the dishwater, strain out the scraps and store them in ziplock bags with the other garbage or burn them. You can bring a lightweight screen to filter the food scraps from the dishwater, but be sure to store the screen with the food and garbage. If you have a campfire, pour the dishwater around the edge of the fire. If you don't have a campfire, take the dishwater at least 100 yards downwind and downhill from camp and pour it on the ground or in a small hole. Don't put dishwater or food scraps in a lake or stream. Do dishes immediately after eating, so a minimum of food smell lingers in the area.

Be Cougar Alert

If you have done much hiking in cougar country, you have almost surely been watched by a cougar and never even known it. Many people consider themselves very lucky to see this furtive animal in the wild, but the big cats, nature's perfect predators, are potentially dangerous. Attacks on humans are exceedingly rare, but it is wise to educate yourself before entering mountain lion country.

To stay as safe as possible in cougar habitat, follow this advice.

- Travel with a friend or group. There is safety in numbers.
- Don't let small children wander away by themselves. Small adults and children are more likely to be attacked than are larger adults.
- Don't let pets run unleashed.
- Know how to behave if you meet a cougar.

What to do if you encounter a cougar

In the vast majority of mountain lion encounters, these animals exhibit avoidance, curiosity, or even indifference that never results in human injury, but it is natural to be alarmed if you have an encounter of any kind. Try to keep cool and consider the following.

Recognize threatening cougar behavior. A few clues may gauge the risk of attack. If a mountain lion is 50 or more yards away and directs its attention to you, it may be only curious. This situation represents only a slight risk to adults but a more serious risk to unaccompanied children. At this point, you should move away while keeping the animal in your peripheral vision. Also look for rocks, sticks, or something to use as a weapon, just in case.

If the cougar is crouched and staring at you from less than 50 feet away, it may be assessing the chances of a successful attack. If this behavior continues, your risk may be high.

Do not approach a cougar. Instead, give the animal an opportunity to move on. Slowly back away, but maintain eye contact if close. Cougars are not known to attack humans to defend their young or a kill, but they have been reported to "charge" in rare instances, and they may want to stay in the area. If you come upon a cougar on a kill, it is best to take another route.

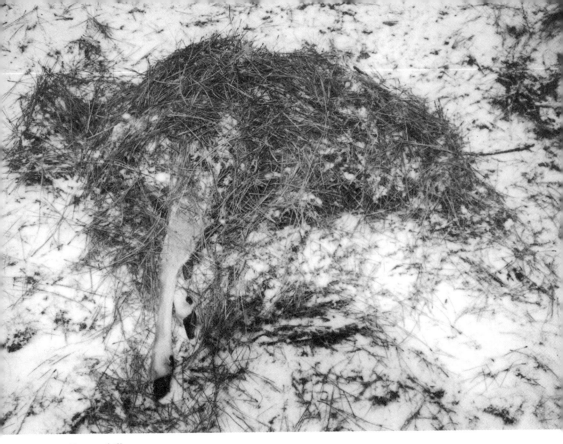

Cougar kill

Do not run from a cougar. Running may stimulate the animal's predatory response, and you may get chased.

Make lots of noise. If you encounter a cougar, be vocal; talk loudly and constantly and yell to make others in the area aware of the situation. Try not to panic.

Maintain eye contact. Eye contact shows the cougar that you are aware of its presence. However, if the lion's behavior is not threatening (for example, grooming or periodically looking away), maintain visual contact with your peripheral vision and move away.

Appear larger than you are. Raise your arms above your head and make steady waving motions. Raise your jacket or other object above your head. Do not bend over, as this will make you look smaller and more "preylike."

If you are with small children, pick them up. Bring the children close to you without bending over, maintaining eye contact with the cougar. If you are with other children or adults, band together.

Defend yourself. If attacked, fight back. Try to remain standing. Do not feign death. Pick up a branch or rock; pull out a knife, pepper spray, or other deterrent device.

Everything is a potential weapon; individuals have fended off cougar attacks with rocks, branches, and even cameras.

Defend others. In past attacks on children, adults have successfully stopped the attack. Defend your partners, but don't physically defend your pet.

Respect any warning signs posted by agencies.

Spread the word. Before leaving on your hike, discuss lions and teach others in your group how to behave in case of a cougar encounter.

Report encounters. If you have an encounter, record the location and details of the encounter and notify the landowner or land-management agency. In such areas as the southern Washington Cascades, where cougars are fairly common, a sighting doesn't constitute an encounter and may not get any action.

If physical injury occurs, it is important not to disturb the site of the attack any more than is necessary to rescue the victim. Cougars that have attacked people must be killed, and an undisturbed site may be critical in locating the dangerous cat.

See Falcon Publishing's *Mountain Lion Alert* for more details and tips for safe outdoor recreation in cougar country.

Be Rattlesnake Alert

Once you hear a rattlesnake buzz, it's a sound you will never forget. Forty-five of the fifty states are home to at least one species of rattlesnake. Unless you will be hiking only in Alaska, Hawaii, Rhode Island, Delaware, or Maine, you need to be aware of the possibility of encountering one. Within the rattlesnake states, some areas have only a very small population of these poisonous reptiles, and other areas have none at all. Local inquiry is the best way to assess your chances of meeting a rattler on the trail. Rattlesnakes may well be found along Hike 43, Horsethief Butte and at other places along the eastern part of the Columbia River Gorge. Elsewhere along the trails described in this book, they are very uncommon or nonexistent.

Rattlesnakes are members of the "pit viper" family. Pit vipers have heat-sensing organs (pits) in their faces that are used to detect heat. This heat-detection system is probably integrated with the snakes' visual senses, allowing the snake to *see* heat. This allows rattlers to easily strike in the dark.

Rattlesnakes inhabit a wide range of climatic zones. They are found from below sea level up to subalpine zones in the mountains of the western United States. However, they are seldom common above the transition (ponderosa pine) zone. Rattlers may be out at lower temperatures than is generally realized by most people. They are occasionally seen sunning themselves on warm rocks when the air temperature is only a few degrees above freezing. Conversely, the snakes seek shade or burrows when it is very hot. For a rattlesnake the perfect temperature is about eighty degrees.

Of the approximately 8,000 venomous snakebites in the United States each year, only 10 to 20 are fatal, and in many cases these fatalities can be attributed at least partly to other preexisting medical problems. Of these fatal bites, the diamondback rattlesnake, which ranges generally south of a line from Southern California to North Carolina, causes 95 percent. This is not to say that other species of rattlers do not cause much pain and an occasional death, but your chances of being killed by a snake diminish greatly as you travel north. Of the people who are bitten, about 35 percent are not injected with poison. These "dry bites" lead some people to wrongly believe that they are immune to rattlesnake venom.

Preventing bites

- Don't count on rattlesnakes to rattle at your approach; they are generally shy creatures in their encounters with humans. In most cases they will do their best to escape or to lie quietly and let the person pass without noticing them. In my personal experience only about half of the snakes have rattled before I saw them. Rattlers will sometimes strike before rattling.

- Don't place your hands or feet in places that you can't see clearly. About 65 percent of snakebites are on the hands or forearms, and another 24 percent are on the feet, ankles, and lower legs.

- In areas where there is a good chance of encountering a rattler, it may be advisable to wear protective clothing such as snake-proof gaiters or chaps and sturdy hiking boots.

- During hot weather be especially alert during the morning, evening, and night, as snakes are most active at those times.

- Don't handle any snake unless you positively can identify it as being nonpoisonous. Snakes that were thought to be dead have bitten many people.

- Inquisitive children have a higher than average chance of being bitten by a rattlesnake. Because of their smaller bodies, they are also more susceptible to the toxins in the venom. Warn your children of the danger and watch them closely when you're in snake country.

First aid for snakebite

The best first-aid treatment for snakebite is to get medical help as soon as possible, so that an injection of antivenom can be administered. Antivenom is the only proven treatment for snakebite. If you are within forty-five minutes of medical assistance, just get there as quickly as safety allows and don't bother with any other type of treatment.

Recommended first aid for snakebite when medical help is far away

If you are more than forty-five minutes from medical help, first-aid treatment may be of some advantage. If there are three or more people in your party, you may want to send someone for help as you are starting the first-aid treatment, but don't leave the victim alone at this point.

A snakebite kit is necessary to adequately perform the treatment. There are two main types of snakebite kits available on the market. The most common ones include two or three rubber suction cups and a razor blade. The more-advanced kits include a two-stage suction pump. The pump is capable of applying much more suction and is the preferred kit to carry. In addition to a snakebite kit, an elastic bandage is helpful in most treatments. If there is no disinfectant already in your snakebite or general first-aid kit, you should add some to it. If there is no safety razor included in your kit, one should be purchased and added to it. *Before putting your snakebite kit in your pack or pocket, open it, read the instructions, and familiarize yourself with its proper use.*

- Treatment must begin immediately after the bite occurs to be effective.
- If the wound is bleeding, allow it to do so for fifteen to thirty seconds.
- If the wound is on the hand, forearm, foot, or lower leg (which it probably will be), wrap the elastic bandage around the limb above the wound. *Wrap the bandage no tighter than you would for a sprain.*
- If you are using the pump-type kit, place the pump, with the appropriate suction cup attached, over the wound and begin the suction procedure. If a good seal cannot be achieved over the wound because of hair, it may be necessary to shave the area with the safety razor in your kit. The suction procedure needs to start within five minutes of the bite to be effective, and it should be left in place for thirty minutes or more.
- *It is best not to do any cutting on the victim,* but if you must use one of the kits that require it, first disinfect the wound area and the instrument that will be used to make the incisions. Make the incisions *no deeper than 3 millimeters (⅛-inch) and no longer than 5 millimeters (²⁄₁₀-inch)* across the puncture marks and along the long axis of the limb. If the bite is not in a large muscle, these cuts may need to be much shallower to prevent permanent tissue damage. Making these incisions too large is where you can get into trouble by cutting muscles and tendons, so be very careful to keep them small and shallow. They just need to bleed a small amount. After making the incisions, start the suction immediately.
- After getting the suction procedure going, check for a pulse below the wound. If none can be found, loosen the elastic bandage. *Remember that it is better to have no constriction than it is to have too much.*
- If possible, try to keep the bitten extremity at approximately the victim's heart level, and try to keep him or her as calm as possible.
- Do not give the victim alcohol.
- After completing the treatment, cover the bite as you would any other small wound. Be sure that any bandage you put on is not constrictive, as swelling will probably occur.
- Send someone for, or get the victim to, medical attention as soon as possible.

Campfire Regulations

Campfires are generally permitted on national forest lands during times of low fire danger. However, they are not encouraged. Building a fire above the Pacific Crest, Round the Mountain, and Highline Trails is prohibited in Mount Adams Wilderness. Check with any of the USDA Forest Service information stations for current campfire regulations.

Artifacts

The collecting of artifacts, including anything left by Native Americans or the miners or settlers that followed them, is strictly prohibited. Enjoy the artifacts but leave them where you find them.

Northwest Forest Pass, Wilderness Permit, and Cascade Volcanoes Pass

A Northwest Forest Pass is required to park at many of the trailheads. These passes are available at any Gifford Pinchot National Forest office and many retail outlets. A wilderness permit is necessary to enter any of the three wilderness areas covered in this book. Wilderness permits are self-issuing and can be obtained at most trailheads near the wilderness boundary. A Cascade Volcanoes Pass is required to climb above 7,000 feet elevation on Mount Adams. The Volcanoes Pass is available at the Trout Lake Ranger Station. The Volcanoes Pass takes the place of both the Northwest Forest Pass and the wilderness permit but is good for only one outing. If you plan on making more than one trip to the upper slopes of Mount Adams, you may wish to purchase an annual Cascades Volcanoes Pass. The annual pass is good for an unlimited number of climbs on Mount Adams and is also honored at Mount St. Helens subject to established quotas.

Forest Roads

Most of the roads leading to the trailheads described in this book are either paved or a reasonably good gravel surface. Rough roads requiring a high-clearance vehicle are noted in the Finding the trailhead section at the beginning of each hike.

Some of the paved roads are only one lane, with turnouts. Be very careful on these roads. Because of their smooth paved surfaces, many drivers drive much too fast on them. The edges of some of these roads have brush growing to the pavement edge, and sometimes this brush hangs out over part of the lane, severely limiting your sight distance.

How to Use This Guide

The author personally hiked these trails, many of them in both directions. The mileage was very difficult to gauge exactly. Mileage from Forest Service signs and maps were taken into account whenever possible, and times were kept while hiking. By knowing approximately what speed the author hikes across various types of trail, the mileage was calculated. The mileage printed in each hike description was figured by combining these means and in some cases by pacing off the distance.

Difficulty Ratings

The trails in this book are rated easy, moderate, or strenuous with the length or time involved not taken into account. Only the roughness of the trail, elevation change, and difficulty of following the route are considered.

The trails that are rated "easy" will generally have gentle grades and be easy to follow; however, there may be short sections that are rocky or eroded. Anyone in reasonable condition can hike easy trails given enough time.

Trails rated as "moderate" will climb or descend more steeply than easy trails. They may climb 500 or 600 feet per mile and have fairly long sections that are rough or eroded. Some route-finding skills may be required to follow these trails. If route finding is required for a particular hike, this information will be included in the hike description. A person in good physical condition can hike these trails with no problem. However, people in poor condition and small children may find them grueling.

Trails rated as "strenuous" are best left to expert backpackers and mountaineers. These trails may climb or descend 1,000 feet or more per mile and be very rough. Sections of these trails may be very vague or nonexistent, so excellent route-finding skills are a requirement for safe travel. In some cases there may be considerable exposure; falling from the trail or route can cause serious injury or even death. Many of these trails are not usable by parties with stock.

The difficulty and danger of the climbing routes is much greater than even that of the strenuous hikes. These routes require mountaineering skills to be completed safely. There may be considerable exposure in places, and the footing may be unstable. In some cases they may climb 2,000 feet or more in a mile. With experienced leadership a strong hiker can make these climbs, but they are difficult and dangerous for the novice. Mountain travel is typically classified as follows:

class 1—Trail or cross-country hiking.

class 2—Hiking across rough ground; may include the use of hands for stability.

class 3—Scrambling that requires the use of hands and requires careful foot placement. There may be moderate exposure in spots, and an inexperienced climber may need to be roped up.

class 4—Scrambling over steep and exposed terrain; a rope may be needed for safety.

class 5—Technical "free" climbing where terrain is steep and exposed, requiring the use of ropes, protection hardware, and related techniques.

Trail Mileage

For loop and shuttle hikes, distances are stated as one-way mileage, so this will be the entire distance you will hike. Out-and-back hikes are stated as round-trip, so you will hike the stated distance to make the complete trip. The additional hiking options are not taken into consideration when stating the total. Internal connector hikes are stated as one-way mileage.

Maps

The maps printed in this book are not intended to take the place of a topographic map. Take a good topographic map with you on your hikes; maps that cover the area are listed at the beginning of each hike description.

If you want one map to cover nearly the entire area, the map to get is the USDA Forest Service Gifford Pinchot National Forest map. The scale of this map, however, is 0.5 inch to the mile, making it too small to be of much use to the hiker on any but the best maintained trails. This map is the most valuable for finding the trail-heads.

The USDA Forest Service Mount Adams Wilderness Map, at a scale of 1 inch to the mile, is adequate for most hikes in the Mount Adams Wilderness. The wilderness map is a topographic and is quite accurate in most cases.

The USDA Forest Service Trapper Creek Wilderness and Indian Heaven Wilderness combined map is usually all that is needed for hiking in the Trapper Creek or Indian Heaven Wilderness areas. This map is a topographic at a scale of 2 inches to the mile, and it is quite accurate and up to date.

For hikes along or close to the Pacific Crest Trail, the USDA Forest Service Pacific Crest National Scenic Trail Southern Washington Portion map is a good one to use. The scale is 1 inch to the mile on this topographic map, and its accuracy is adequate.

If you are planning to hike the less-traveled and seldom-maintained routes described in this book, the USGS 7.5-minute quad maps mentioned at the beginning of most hike descriptions are a better choice. The larger 1:24,000 scale (about 2.7 inches to the mile) of these maps makes finding your exact location much easier. They are also much easier to coordinate with your GPS. For hikes outside the wilderness areas and not along the Pacific Crest Trail, these maps may be the only good choice.

Elevation profiles

This book uses elevation profiles to provide an idea of the length and elevation of hills you will encounter in each hikes. In all the profiles the vertical axes of the graphs show the total distance climbed in feet. In contrast the horizontal axes show the distance traveled in miles. This is an intentional exaggeration and allows the graphs to provide the information intended as well as fit on the page. Because the scale of the vertical axes of the graphs is exaggerated, the slopes depicted in the elevation profiles are not as steep as those shown. It is also important to understand that the vertical (feet) and horizontal (miles) scales can differ between hikes. Read each profile carefully, making sure you read both the height and distance shown. This will help you interpret what you see in the profile. Some elevation profiles may show gradual hills to be steep and steep hills to be gradual. Instead of interpreting the profile literally, look at how long the hill is and how high you climb. Elevation profiles are not provided for hikes with less than 250 feet of variation.

Map Legend

84	Interstate
35	State highway
64	Forest/county road
	Paved road
	Featured gravel road
	Gravel road
=====	Unimproved road
	Featured trail
---------	Other trail
	Railroad track
ㅍ	Bridge
▲	Campground
○	City
▬	Dam
•–•	Gate
◘	Overlook/viewpoint
P	Parking
)(	Pass
▲	Peak/elevation
■	Point of interest
•——•	Powerline
	Ranger station
⚲	Spring
START	Trailhead
∥	Waterfall

Mount Adams Region

Coming from the south on State Route 141, the imposing ice-clad slopes of Mount Adams dominate the view ahead. Most of the hikes in the region radiate around this huge volcanic cone. Hike 1, Pacific Crest Trail 2000, Mount Adams Wilderness Section and Hike 6, Round the Mountain, Cold Springs Trailhead to Horseshoe Meadow, Trails 183, 9 traverse the mountain's southern, western, and northwestern slopes just below timberline, passing through dozens of flowered meadows and crossing rushing glacial streams. Like the spokes of a wheel, Hike 2, Muddy Meadows Trail 13; Hike 3, High Camp via Killen Creek Trail, Trails 113, 10; Hike 4, Divide Camp Trail 112; Hike 5, Stagman Ridge Trail 12; and Hike 7, Shorthorn Trail 16 climb from trailheads around the flanks of the mountain to timberline to join Hikes 1 and 6.

The easiest way to reach the broad summit of Mount Adams is covered in Hike 9, Mount Adams South Climb Route, Trail 183. For people who don't necessarily climb their mountains via the easiest route, Hike 10, Mount Adams North Cleaver Route up the North Cleaver of the mountain is a far more challenging, if somewhat dangerous, alternative.

A short distance southwest of the wilderness, Hike 11, Sleeping Beauty Trail 37 takes you to the summit of Sleeping Beauty Peak and a view of the western slope of Mount Adams, where all the other hikes in the region are located.

Mount Adams Region

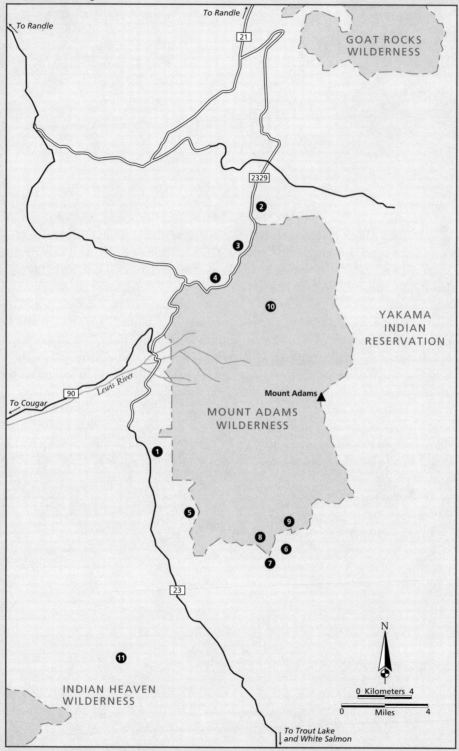

To Randle

To Randle

21

GOAT ROCKS
WILDERNESS

2329

2

3

4

10

YAKAMA
INDIAN
RESERVATION

Lewis River

90

To Cougar

Mount Adams

MOUNT ADAMS
WILDERNESS

1

5

9

8

6

7

23

11

INDIAN HEAVEN
WILDERNESS

N

0 Kilometers 4

0   Miles   4

To Trout Lake
and White Salmon

1 Pacific Crest Trail 2000, Mount Adams Wilderness Section

Hike across the western slopes of Mount Adams through fantastic flower-covered meadows and across rushing glacial streams.

Start: Pacific Crest Trail (PCT) 2000 trailhead on Forest Road 521.
Distance: 23.2-mile one-way shuttle 2- or 3-day backpack.
Difficulty: Moderate.
Seasons: Mid-July through September.
Fees and permits: Northwest Forest Pass and Mount Adams Wilderness Permit.
Parking and trailhead facilities: There is ample parking but no other facilities available at the trailheads at either end of this hike.

Maps: USDA Forest Service Mount Adams Wilderness or Pacific Crest National Scenic Trail Washington Southern Portion. Steamboat Mountain, Mount Adams West, and Green Mountain USGS quads also cover the area.
Trail contacts: Gifford Pinchot National Forest, Mount Adams Ranger District, 2455 Highway 141, Trout Lake, WA, 98650; (509) 395-3400; www.fs.fed.us/gpnf.

Finding the trailhead: Drive south from Seattle on I-5 to exit 133 at Tacoma and then follow State Route 7 for 55 miles to Morton. From Morton drive east on U.S. Highway 12 for 17 miles to Randle. From Randle drive south on State Route 131 (may be signed to FOREST ROAD 25) for 0.9 mile. Then turn left (east) onto Forest Road 23 and follow it east and south for 41.4 miles to the junction with FR 521. Turn left (northeast) onto FR 521 and go 0.3 mile to the trailhead.

From Portland drive east on I-84 to exit 64 at Hood River. Leave the freeway and head north across the Columbia River. At the junction with State Route 14 just north of the bridge, turn left and head west for 1.6 miles to the junction with State Route 141 Alternate, signed TO MOUNT ADAMS RECREATION AREA. Turn right at the junction and drive north for 2.1 miles to the junction with State Route 141. Turn left at the junction and continue north on SR 141 for 18.9 miles to Trout Lake. From Trout Lake drive north on FR 23 for 14.1 miles to the junction with FR 521. Turn right at the junction and follow FR 521 for 0.3 mile to the trailhead. The elevation at the trailhead is 4,020 feet.

To reach the trailhead on Forest Road 115 where this hike ends, drive back to the junction with FR 23 and turn right. Then drive north on FR 23 for 11.5 miles to the junction with Forest Road 2329. Turn right onto FR 2329 and follow it for 11 miles to the junction with FR 115. Turn right (east) onto FR 115 and go 0.3 mile to the point where the Pacific Crest Trail crosses the road.

The USDA Forest Service Gifford Pinchot National Forest map can be a great asset when trying to find your way to this out-of-the-way trailhead.

Special Considerations

This is a fairly long hike; be sure all the members of your party are in shape for it. Some of the glacial stream crossings can be difficult at times of high water. Use caution when crossing these cold, heavily silted, rushing waters. Glacial streams usually

Mount Adams from the Pacific Crest Trail. PHOTO: DARRIN LARVIK

have less flow in the cool of the morning than they do in the heat of the afternoon. In Mount Adams Wilderness no campfires are allowed above Round the Mountain, Pacific Crest, and Highline Trails.

The Hike

Leaving the trailhead the PCT climbs gently to the north beneath a canopy of old-growth fir and hemlock. Small huckleberry bushes and bunchberries cover the ground beside the path. In 0.2 mile the tread crosses a wooden bridge spanning a small but dependable stream. A nice campsite is located next to the stream. Past the bridge and campsite, the course climbs moderately for about 1.8 miles, climbing to 4,800 feet elevation. The route then flattens and leads southeast. A large spring gushes from the ground to the right of the trail 0.7 mile farther along. This spring, 2.8 miles from the trailhead, at 4,900 feet elevation, is the head of the White Salmon River.

Soon the route makes an ascending switchback to the left and quickly crosses a usually dry streambed. A quarter of a mile farther along, the route turns to the right (east) as you climb steadily toward the junction with the Stagman Ridge Trail 12.

The junction is reached 2.5 miles from the spring, at 5,790 feet elevation. Stagman Ridge Trail 12 descends 4.3 miles southwest to a trailhead on Forest Road 120.

Heading east from the junction, the PCT first climbs slightly then flattens before reaching the junction with the Round the Mountain Trail 9. The junction with Round the Mountain Trail is 0.5 mile from the junction with Stagman Ridge Trail, at 5,900 feet elevation on the edge of Horseshoe Meadow.

After making a hard left turn at the junction, the PCT climbs gently to the northwest. Cat's ear lilies line the trail and, high above to the right, White Salmon Glacier clings to the upper slopes of Mount Adams. The route crosses a spur ridge at 6,040 feet elevation, 0.4 mile from the junction. The trail is fairly level for the next 1.5 miles, passing rock outcroppings intermingled with small flower-covered meadows to another small ridgeline. As you cross the ridge, Mount Rainier comes into view to the north. Past the ridgeline the course descends slightly for a little more than 1 mile and then climbs over a rise before descending again to Sheep Lake. About 300 yards before reaching the lake, there is a small lava-tube cave on the right side of the trail.

Small and shallow Sheep Lake is a short distance to the left of the trail, at 5,768 feet elevation. There is a campsite between the trail and the lake; however, much of the summer the mosquitoes can make camping here very unpleasant. The trail crosses lightly silted Riley Creek 0.2 mile past Sheep Lake.

Just after crossing the creek, there is a small but less-buggy campsite next to the trail. From this campsite it is possible to take a short (0.5 mile) cross-country side trip to Crystal Lake. To get to Crystal Lake, recross Riley Creek and climb south-southeast to a ridgeline at 6,200 feet elevation. The beautiful alpine lake is on this ridgeline. There are several possible campsites on the low ridges around Crystal Lake.

The PCT reaches the junction with Riley Camp Trail 64 0.3 mile after crossing Riley Creek. Continue north from the junction on the PCT. After another mile of gentle hiking, the trail enters a lava flow. The route works its way through the jumble of lava boulders and soon reaches milky Mutton Creek, where there is another campsite. You climb along the silted creek for 0.2 mile and cross it at 6,000 feet elevation. Near the crossing Adams Glacier is in view to your right, high above on the slopes of Mount Adams. The trace continues to wind and climb through the lava flow for another 0.3 mile after crossing Mutton Creek. You then leave the lava and quickly cross a fork of the Lewis River. A small campsite is located on the right side of the trail just past the crossing. If you camp here, try not to trample the fields of lupine that nearly surround the site.

The tread soon crosses another small lava flow and then crosses a small stream whose banks are sometimes covered with monkeyflowers. The main stream of the Lewis River is crossed 0.7 mile after crossing the fork. Like its southerly fork, the Lewis River is quite milky with glacial silt. Divide Camp Trail 112 turns left off the PCT 0.4 mile after crossing the Lewis River.

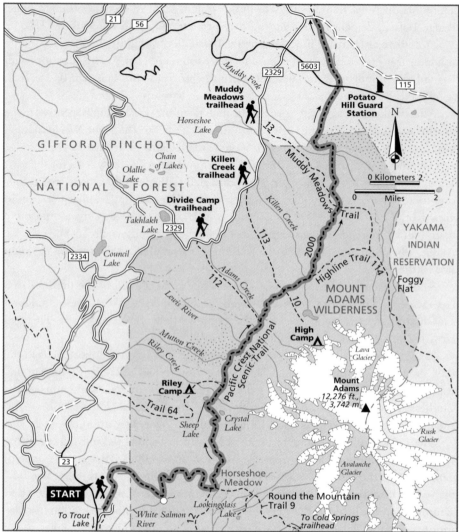

A short distance past the junction with Divide Camp Trail, the PCT passes a campsite and then fords the rushing, cold, silted waters of Adams Creek. This crossing can be very difficult at times. Besides the spring rain and snowmelt that can swell the stream and make crossing it safely nearly impossible, hot summer afternoons melt the glacial ice of Adams Glacier, which is the source of Adams Creek. During hot weather it is often better to cross this stream before late morning.

Shortly after crossing Adams Creek, the trail crosses a small clear stream. Beyond the clear stream you quickly enter beautiful meadows where gentian, lupine, and paintbrush bloom profusely between the scattered alpine trees and rock outcrops.

There is a pond below the trail to the left 1.1 miles past the junction with Divide Camp Trail. Another 0.2 mile brings you to the junction with Killen Creek Trail 113 and High Camp Trail 10. This junction, at 6,080 feet elevation, is 13.8 miles from the trailhead where this hike began.

The PCT heads northeast from the junction with Killen Creek Trail and climbs slightly to cross a low ridge. You then descend gently to reach Killen Creek 0.8 mile from the junction. There are a couple of good campsites next to Killen Creek. Another 0.2 mile of hiking brings you to the junction with the Highline Trail 114, at 5,900 feet elevation.

Highline Trail leads northeast from the junction and in 2.2 miles reaches a junction with the Muddy Meadows Trail. From the junction with the Muddy Meadows Trail, the Highline Trail continues past Foggy Flat and into the Yakama Indian Reservation.

Bear left at the junction with the Highline Trail and hike north–northeast, passing a pond in 0.4 mile. Past the pond the route climbs slightly and then traverses northeast, passing another tiny pond. Soon after passing the tiny pond, the tread turns north and begins a mile-long descent to the junction with the Muddy Meadows Trail 13. The junction with the Muddy Meadows Trail, at 5,200 feet elevation, is reached 17.2 miles from the trailhead on FR 521. This is a four-way junction with the Muddy Meadows Trail crossing the PCT.

After crossing the Muddy Meadows Trail, the PCT continues its gradual descent. By the time you reach the Muddy Fork, 1.6 miles from the junction with Muddy Meadows Trail, you have dropped to 4,750 feet elevation. The route crosses the Muddy Fork on a bridge and soon turns west to skirt around the bottom of a large lava flow. Before turning north–northeast again around the western margin of the lava flow, there is a good campsite next to a small stream. As you round the western tip of the lava flow, Lava Spring bubbles out from beneath the rocks. At the spring you have descended to 4,520 feet elevation.

As the route leaves the lava flow, it passes the Mount Adams Wilderness boundary, leaving the wilderness. The course then ascends gently for about a mile to the junction with Forest Road 5603, which is a paved road. The PCT crosses FR 5603 at 4,750 feet elevation and quickly reaches a small parking area and trailhead. Now the route heads northeast, climbing for a short distance before turning northwest to traverse around the base of Potato Hill. About 0.4 mile from FR 5603, the tread begins its final gentle descent to the trailhead on FR 115, which is reached in another 1.6 miles. The trailhead on FR 115 is at 4,500 feet elevation, 23.2 miles from the trailhead on FR 521 where this hike started.

Options

If you wish to continue north on the Pacific Crest Trail pick up a copy of another Falconguide, *Hiking Washington's Goat Rocks Country*. That book will guide you north

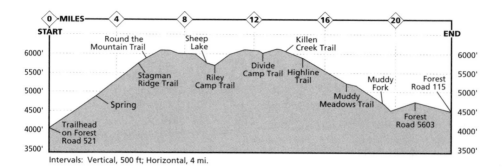

Intervals: Vertical, 500 ft; Horizontal, 4 mi.

along the PCT through the spectacular Goat Rocks Wilderness to White Pass on US 12. *Hiking Washington's Goat Rocks Country* is a comprehensive guide to the large trail system in Goat Rocks Wilderness, as well as the regions both east and west of it.

Miles and Directions

0.0 Pacific Crest Trail 2000 trailhead on FR 521 (GPS 46 10.242 N 121 37.581W).

2.8 Spring at the head of the White Salmon River.

5.3 Junction with Stagman Ridge Trail 12. Continue east on the PCT.

5.8 Junction with Round the Mountain Trail 9 (GPS 46 10.784 N 121 34.125 W). Make a hard left and climb northwest.

9.3 Sheep Lake.

9.8 Junction with Riley Camp Trail 64. Continue north on the PCT.

12.5 Junction with Divide Camp Trail 112 (GPS 46 14.434 N 121 32.740 W). Continue north on the PCT.

13.8 Junction with Killen Creek Trail 113 and High Camp Trail 10 (GPS 46 15.055 N 121 31.958 W). Continue northeast on the PCT.

14.8 Junction with Highline Trail 114. Bear left and hike north-northeast on the PCT.

17.2 Junction with Muddy Meadows Trail 13 (GPS 46 17.030 N 121 30.301 W). Continue north on the PCT.

21.2 Cross FR 5603 (GPS 46 19.541 N 121 30.365 W).

23.2 Pacific Crest Trail 2000 trailhead on FR 115 (GPS 46 21.047 N 121 31.081 W).

2 Muddy Meadows Trail 13

Traverse lush meadows and midmountain forest as you climb to the subalpine realm at the northwestern foot of Mount Adams.

Start: Muddy Meadows trailhead.
Distance: 8.6-mile out-and-back day hike or backpack.
Difficulty: Moderate.
Seasons: July through September.
Fees and permits: Northwest Forest Pass and Mount Adams Wilderness Permit.
Parking and trailhead facilities: There is adequate parking at the trailhead but no other facilities.
Maps: USDA Forest Service Mount Adams Wilderness or Green Mountain and Glaciate Butte USGS quads.
Trail contacts: Gifford Pinchot National Forest, Mount Adams Ranger District, 2455 Highway 141, Trout Lake, WA, 98650; (509) 395–3400; www.fs.fed.us/gpnf.

Finding the trailhead: Drive south from Seattle on I-5 to exit 133 at Tacoma and then follow State Route 7 for 55 miles to Morton. From Morton drive east on U.S. Highway 12 for 17 miles to Randle.

From Portland drive north on I-5 to exit 68 (68 miles north of the Interstate Bridge) and then follow US 12 east for 48 miles to Randle.

From Randle drive south on State Route 131 (may be signed TO FOREST ROAD 25) for 0.9 mile. Then turn left (east) onto Forest Road 23 and follow it east and south for 30.6 miles to the junction with Forest Road 2329. Turn left onto FR 2329 and follow it approximately 7.8 miles to the junction with Forest Road 087. Turn right (east) on FR 087 and go 0.4 mile to its end at the Muddy Meadows trailhead. The elevation at the trailhead is 4,400 feet.

The junction of FR 23 and FR 2329 also can be reached from Portland via Trout Lake. To get to Trout Lake, drive east from Portland on I-84 to exit 64 at the east edge of Hood River. Leave the freeway and head north across the Columbia River. At the junction with State Route 14 just north of the bridge, turn left and head west for 1.6 miles to the junction with State Route 141 Alternate, signed TO MOUNT ADAMS RECREATION AREA. Turn right at the junction onto SR 141 Alt and drive north for about 2.1 miles to the junction with State Route 141. Turn left at the junction and continue north on SR 141 for 18.9 miles to Trout Lake. From the Y intersection next to the Chevron station in Trout Lake, follow FR 23 for 25.6 miles north to the junction with FR 2329. The USDA Forest Service Gifford Pinchot National Forest map can be a great asset when trying to find your way from Trout Lake.

Special Considerations

This trail is heavily used by stock. Mosquitoes can be very bad before September. The trail is mostly sand in places between the trailhead and the PCT, making hiking a bit more strenuous.

Goat Rocks from near the junction with Highline Trail

The Hike

Mount Adams rises high above to your right as you leave the trailhead and hike east across Muddy Meadows. Shortly you enter the fringes of the lodgepole pine and spruce forest along the northern edge of the meadow. The track crosses a wooden bridge 0.3 mile from the trailhead and then follows the remains of a long-abandoned roadbed for some distance. The course begins to climb gently, passing a pond and crossing another bridge at about 1 mile. After crossing the second bridge, the route climbs several wooden "water bar" steps to yet another wooden bridge, at 4,600 feet elevation. Past the third bridge the trail has been reconstructed recently; the four new switchbacks ease the grade considerably. You reach the junction with Pacific Crest Trail 2000 1.5 miles after crossing the third bridge, at about 5,200 feet elevation.

The lupine-lined Muddy Meadows Trail crosses the PCT at the junction and continues to climb to the east. After about 0.5 mile the route turns south, climbing through narrow meadows that are covered with blooming lupine in late July. Soon views of Mount Adams show up ahead. The junction with Highline Trail is reached 1.6 miles from the PCT, at about 5,700 feet elevation. Between the groves of alpine

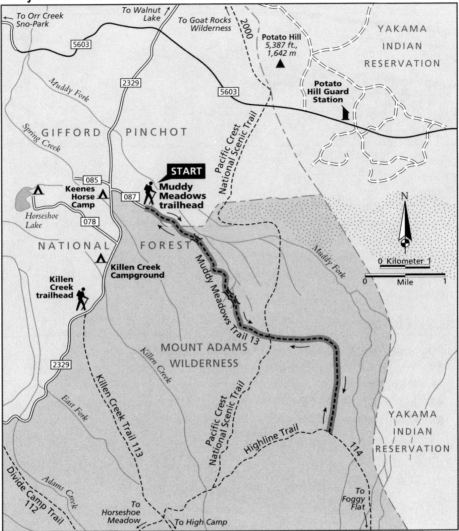

trees around the junction, paintbrush and heather cover much of the ground, and cat's ear lilies bloom around the first of August. Excellent views can be seen from the small rise just south of the junction.

This junction is the end of Muddy Meadows Trail, but if you turn left and follow Highline Trail it will lead you to Foggy Flat in less than a mile. From there the Highline Trail heads southeast and enters the Yakama Indian Reservation. A permit is required from the tribal headquarters in Toppenish, Washington, to enter the reservation.

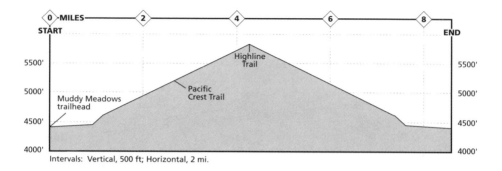

Intervals: Vertical, 500 ft; Horizontal, 2 mi.

Options

A lollipop loop hike can be done by combining Muddy Meadows Trail with short sections of the Highline and Pacific Crest Trails. To make the loop, turn right onto Highline Trail and hike southwest to the junction with the PCT. Turn right again onto the PCT and follow it to the junction with Muddy Meadows Trail mentioned above.

Miles and Directions

- **0.0** Muddy Meadows trailhead (GPS 46 18.488 N 121 32.364 W).
- **2.7** Junction with Pacific Crest Trail (GPS 46 17.030 N 121 30.301 W). Continue east on Muddy Meadows Trail.
- **4.3** Junction with Highline Trail (GPS 46 16.003 N 121 29.754 W). Turnaround point.
- **8.6** Muddy Meadows trailhead.

3 High Camp via Killen Creek Trail, Trails 113, 10

Hike to a windswept plateau high on the northwest slope of Mount Adams.

Start: Killen Creek trailhead.

Distance: 8.2-mile out-and-back day hike or backpack.

Difficulty: Moderate up to the Pacific Crest Trail (PCT), strenuous above there.

Seasons: Mid-July through Mid-October.

Fees and permits: Northwest Forest Pass and Mount Adams Wilderness Permit. If you plan to go above High Camp, a Cascade Volcanoes Pass is required. The Cascade Volcanoes Pass, which is required to climb above 7,000 feet elevation on Mount Adams, costs $15 for a Friday, Saturday, or Sunday start or $10 Monday through Thursday. The Volcanoes Pass takes the place of both the Northwest Forest Pass and the wilderness permit but is good for only one outing. If you plan on making more than one trip to the upper slopes of Mount Adams, you may wish to purchase an annual Cascades Volcanoes Pass. The $30 annual pass is good for an unlimited number of climbs on Mount Adams and is also honored at Mount St. Helens, subject to established quotas.

Parking and trailhead facilities: There is adequate parking at the trailhead but no other facilities.

Maps: USDA Forest Service Mount Adams Wilderness or Green Mountain and Mount Adams West USGS quads. The Mount Adams West quad covers the area around High Camp but doesn't show the trail.

Trail contacts: Gifford Pinchot National Forest, Mount Adams Ranger District, 2455 Highway 141, Trout Lake, WA, 98650; (509) 395-3400; www.fs.fed.us/gpnf.

Finding the trailhead: From Seattle drive south on I-5 to exit 133 at Tacoma and then follow State Route 7 for 55 miles to Morton. From Morton drive east on U.S Highway 12 for 17 miles to Randle.

From Portland drive north on 1-5 to exit 68 (68 miles north of Interstate Bridge) and then follow US 12 east for 48 miles to Randle.

From US 12 at Randle, drive south on State Route 131 (may be signed TO FOREST ROAD 25) for 0.9 mile. Then turn left (east) onto Forest Road 23 and follow it east and south for 30.6 miles to the junction with Forest Road 2329. Turn left onto FR 2329 and follow it approximately 6 miles to Killen Creek trailhead. The trailhead is on the right side of the road. The trailhead elevation is 4,660 feet.

The junction of FR 23 and FR 2329 also can be reached from Portland via Trout Lake. To get to Trout Lake, drive east from Portland on I-84 to exit 64 at the east edge of Hood River. Leave the freeway and head north across the Columbia River. At the junction with State Route 14 just north of the bridge, turn left and head west for 1.6 miles to the junction with State Route 141 Alternate, signed TO MOUNT ADAMS RECREATION AREA. Turn right at the junction onto SR 141 Alt and drive north for about 2.1 miles to the junction with State Route 141. Turn left at the junction and continue north on SR 141 for 18.9 miles to Trout Lake. From the Y intersection next to the Chevron station in Trout Lake, follow FR 23 for 25.6 miles north to the junction with FR 2329. The USDA Forest Service Gifford Pinchot National Forest map can be a great asset when trying to find your way from Trout Lake.

High Camp

Special Considerations

Before August the upper mile of this route may be at least partially snow covered some years.

The Hike

Leaving the trailhead the Killen Creek Trail climbs gently to the south. After about 0.6 mile you will encounter the first of several groups of wooden steps built into the trail. While not too high, these steps are too far apart to fit most people's stride. These steps are here to prevent erosion, not to make the climb easier. Above the first set of steps, much of the trail is sandy, which also makes walking a little more tiring.

Huckleberry bushes and mountain ash line much of the path as you hike through the conifer forest. Watch to your left (north) 1.1 miles from the trailhead for distant views through the trees of Goat Rocks and Mount Rainier. The route enters a meadow 2.2 miles into the hike. In the meadow at slightly more than 5,700 feet elevation, the tread crosses a small stream. This stream is the only water between the

High Camp via Killen Creek Trail, Trails 113, 10

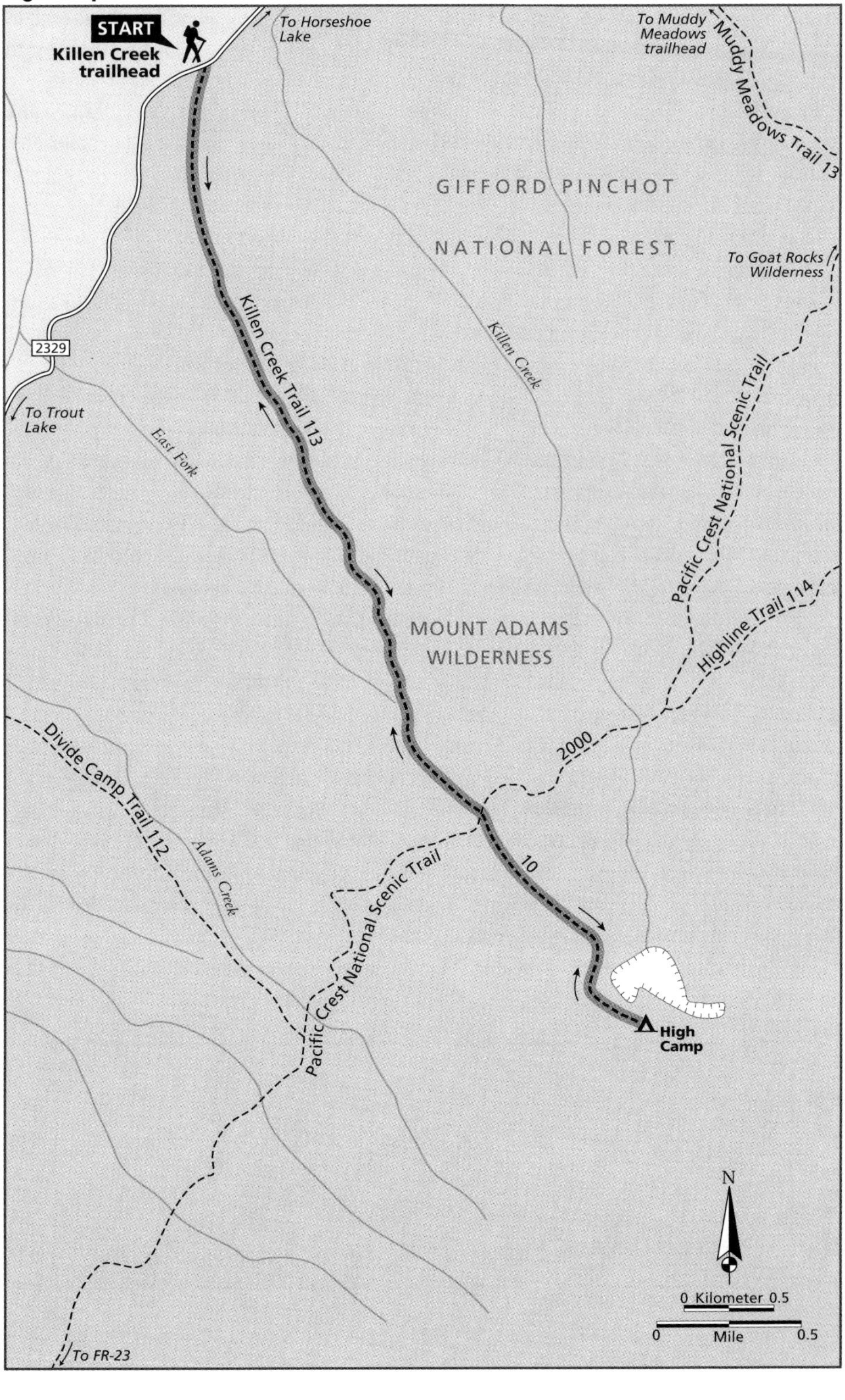

START
Killen Creek trailhead

To Horseshoe Lake

To Muddy Meadows trailhead

Muddy Meadows Trail 13

GIFFORD PINCHOT

NATIONAL FOREST

To Goat Rocks Wilderness

2329

To Trout Lake

East Fork

Killen Creek Trail 113

Killen Creek

Pacific Crest National Scenic Trail

MOUNT ADAMS WILDERNESS

Highline Trail 114

2000

Divide Camp Trail 112

Adams Creek

Pacific Crest National Scenic Trail

10

High Camp

N

To FR-23

0 Kilometer 0.5

0 Mile 0.5

trailhead and High Camp. Side paths here lead to several campsites along the fringes of the meadow. The route follows the stream and climbs gently southeast through the lupine-covered meadow for a couple of hundred yards. Then the trace begins to climb more steeply. As you climb, the timber becomes smaller and more alpine. The trail makes three switchbacks and then flattens out in a sandy area at 6,050 feet elevation. Hike southeast across the sand for 150 yards to the junction with the Pacific Crest Trail at 6,080 feet elevation, 3.1 miles from Killen Creek trailhead. In August the area around the junction is a garden of paintbrush and lupine.

Turn right onto the PCT and walk just a few feet to the junction with High Camp Trail 10. There are signposts at both junctions. Turn left (southeast) onto High Camp Trail. This steeper, rougher route immediately begins to climb. Rock cairns, a couple of them very large, mark much of the route. The tread becomes very rough and rocky as it crosses a talus slope 0.3 mile from the PCT. The route is also a little vague in spots. Once across the talus, the path crosses a small sand flat at 6,380 feet elevation, where it is lined on both sides with rocks. Now the route begins to climb in earnest. The track makes several switchbacks as it climbs a boulder-strewn, heather-covered slope. At the top of the slope, 0.7 mile from the PCT at 6,650 feet elevation, the route reaches a rocky ridgeline. Subalpine fir and whitebark pine elfinwood cling to the rocks beside the trail on this windswept spine.

Turn right onto the ridge and climb along it for a short distance. The track then bears left of the ridge to make a rocky ascending traverse for about 0.1 mile. Then the grade eases and you climb along a broad ridge through scattered whitebark pines. In another 0.1 mile the path bears slightly left off the now-rounded ridge and enters a broad plateau known as Adams Creek Meadows. On the plateau you hike along a small stream for the last 0.1 mile to High Camp, at 6,880 feet elevation.

There are several campsites available in the groves of stunted trees at High Camp. Gentian thrives in the wet meadows along the stream, and on drier slopes paintbrush, dwarf lupine, heather, and juniper cover the ground. Note that the stream generally has more water in the afternoon because of snowmelt. Watch for the many mountain goats that inhabit the area; you may notice their shed hair clinging to the stunted trees around High Camp. If you spend the night at High

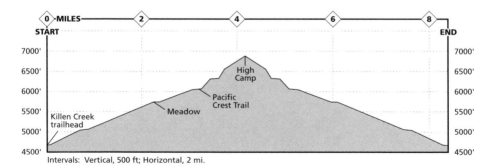

Intervals: Vertical, 500 ft; Horizontal, 2 mi.

Camp, please practice zero-impact camping; this is a delicate alpine area. Remember that there are no campfires allowed above the Pacific Crest Trail in Mount Adams Wilderness. From the low ridge just north of camp, cell-phone service is generally available. This ridge also offers an excellent view of Mount Rainier and the collapsed remains of Mount St. Helens.

Options

Use High Camp as a base camp for a summit climb of the North Cleaver. Killen Creek Trail, the first 3.1 miles of this hike, is a good access route to the PCT.

Miles and Directions

- **0.0** Killen Creek trailhead (GPS 46 17.294 N 121 33.140 W).
- **3.1** Junction with the PCT (GPS 46 15.055 N 121 31.958 W). Turn right onto the PCT, walk a few feet, and turn left (southeast) onto High Camp Trail.
- **4.1** High Camp (GPS 46 14.433 N 121 31.331 W). Turnaround point.
- **8.2** Killen Creek trailhead.

4 Divide Camp Trail 112

Divide Camp Trail first climbs through dense forest. Then the timber thins as you trek across the subalpine landscape beside Adams Creek on the northwest slope of Mount Adams to a junction with the Pacific Crest Trail.

Start: Divide Camp trailhead.
Distance: 5.6-mile out-and-back day hike or backpack.
Difficulty: Moderate.
Seasons: Mid-July through September.
Fees and permits: Northwest Forest Pass and Mount Adams Wilderness Permit.
Parking and trailhead facilities: There is

parking for several cars at the trailhead but no other facilities.
Maps: USDA Forest Service Mount Adams Wilderness or Green Mountain and Mount Adams West USGS quads.
Trail contacts: Gifford Pinchot National Forest, Mount Adams Ranger District, 2455 Highway 141, Trout Lake, WA, 98650; (509) 395-3400; www.fs.fed.us/gpnf.

Finding the trailhead: From Seattle drive south on I-5 to exit 133 at Tacoma and then follow State Route 7 for 55 miles to Morton. From Morton drive east on U.S Highway 12 for 17 miles to Randle.

From Portland drive north on 1-5 to exit 68 (68 miles north of Interstate Bridge) and then follow US 12 east for 48 miles to Randle.

From US 12 at Randle, drive south on State Route 131 (may be signed TO FOREST ROAD 25) for 0.9 mile. Then turn left (east) onto Forest Road 23 and follow it east and south for 30.6 miles to the junction with Forest Road 2329. Turn left onto FR 2329 and follow it approximately 3.5 miles to Divide Camp trailhead. The trailhead, which is on the right side of the road, is at 4,720 feet elevation.

The junction of FR 23 and FR 2329 also can be reached from Portland via Trout Lake. To get to Trout Lake, drive east from Portland on I-84 to exit 64 at the east edge of Hood River. Leave the freeway and head north across the Columbia River. At the junction with State Route 14 just north of the bridge, turn left and head west for 1.6 miles to the junction with State Route 141 Alternate, signed TO MOUNT ADAMS RECREATION AREA. Turn right at the junction onto SR 141 Alt and drive north for about 2.1 miles to the junction with State Route 141. Turn left at the junction and continue north on SR 141 for 18.9 miles to Trout Lake. From the Y intersection next to the Chevron station in Trout Lake, follow FR 23 for 25.6 miles north to the junction with FR 2329. The USDA Forest Service Gifford Pinchot National Forest map can be a great asset when trying to find your way from Trout Lake.

Special Considerations

Take your bug repellent; mosquitoes can be really bad in July and August.

Adams Glacier from the top of Divide Camp Trail ▶

Divide Camp Trail 112

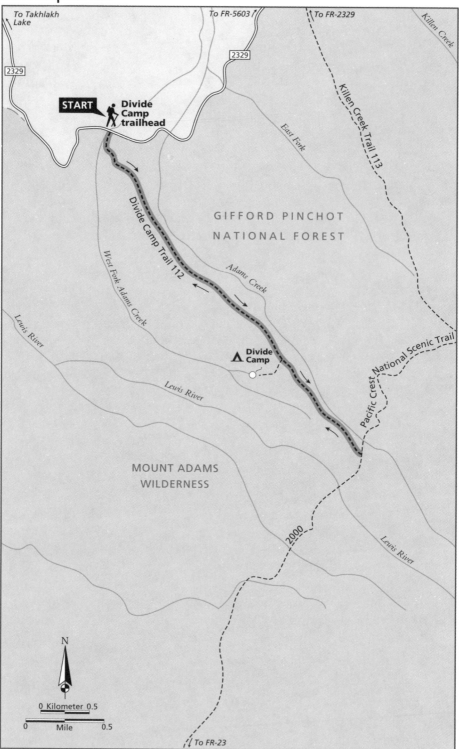

The Hike

The Divide Camp Trail begins as a roadbed. From the parking area take the left fork of the two roads heading south. In 150 yards the road ends, and you soon pass the Mount Adams Wilderness Boundary. Just after entering the wilderness, the route crosses a small stream as you hike through the thick woods. Soon the course starts to climb. You may hear the muffled roar of a rushing stream to your left 0.6 mile from the trailhead, but as yet you can't see Adams Creek. A quarter of a mile ahead, you get the first glimpses of the stream as you climb the sometimes rough and steep trail. Soon the tread begins passing through small openings in the forest, where lupine and avalanche lilies bloom in August.

A path turns to the left (east) off the trail 1.8 miles from the trailhead. This side path descends a short distance to the banks of Adams Creek. Paintbrush and false hellebore line the sides of the track as you continue southeast on Divide Camp Trail. Ahead, the heavily crevassed Adams Glacier tumbles from the summit of Mount Adams.

Another path leaves the trail to the right (southwest) 2.1 miles from the trailhead. This path is the trail to Divide Camp and a spring. In the meadows around this junction, at 5,680 feet elevation, lupine and paintbrush are in full bloom in early August. Heading southeast from the junction, the trail stays fairly close to the rushing, heavily silted Adams Creek for 0.7 mile to the junction with Pacific Crest Trail 2000. This junction is very close to timberline at 6,020 feet elevation. If you climb the rise a few yards southeast of the junction, Mount Rainer comes into full view to the north.

Options

Combine Divide Camp Trail with a short section of the Pacific Crest Trail and Killen Creek Trail to make a one-way hike. It is only about a 2.5-mile car shuttle between the Killen Creek and Divide Camp trailheads.

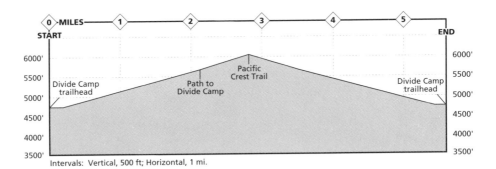

Intervals: Vertical, 500 ft; Horizontal, 1 mi.

Miles and Directions

0.0 Divide Camp trailhead, next to FR 2329 (GPS 46 16.140 N 121 34.722 W).

2.1 Junction with path to Divide Camp. Continue southeast on Divide Camp Trail.

2.8 Junction with Pacific Crest Trail (GPS 46 14.434 N 121 32.740 W). Turnaround point.

5.6 Divide Camp trailhead.

5 Stagman Ridge Trail 12

Hike this lightly used access route to the Pacific Crest Trail (PCT) and the flower-covered meadows on the southern slope of Mount Adams.

Start: Stagman Ridge trailhead.
Distance: 8.6-mile out-and-back day hike or backpack.
Difficulty: Easy to moderate.
Seasons: Mid-July through September.
Fees and permits: Northwest Forest Pass and Mount Adams Wilderness Permit.
Parking and trailhead facilities: There is parking for several cars, a picnic table, and a possibly dry campsite at the trailhead.

Maps: USDA Forest Service Mount Adams Wilderness or Mount Adams West USGS quad. The Forest Service map shows this trail more correctly than does the quad map.
Trail contacts: Gifford Pinchot National Forest, Mount Adams Ranger District, 2455 Highway 141, Trout Lake, WA, 98650; (509) 395-3400; www.fs.fed.us/gpnf.

Finding the trailhead: Drive east from Portland on I-84 to exit 64 at the east edge of Hood River. Leave the freeway and head north across the Columbia River. At the junction with State Route 14 just north of the bridge, turn left and head west for 1.6 miles to the junction with State Route 141 Alternate, signed TO MOUNT ADAMS RECREATION AREA. Turn right at the junction onto SR 141 Alt and drive north for about 2.1 miles to the junction with State Route 141. Turn left at the junction and continue north on SR 141 for 18.9 miles to Trout Lake.

From the Y intersection next to the Chevron station in Trout Lake, head north on Forest Road 23. In 1.4 miles you will reach the junction with Forest Road 80. Bear left (northwest) at the junction and stay on FR 23 for 7.7 more miles to the junction with Forest Road 8031. Drive northeast on FR 8031 for 0.4 mile. Then turn left (north) onto Forest Road 070 (signed TO STAGMAN RIDGE TRAIL) and follow it for 3.2 miles to the junction with Forest Road 120. Turn right (southeast) onto FR 120 and drive 0.8 mile to its end at Stagman Ridge trailhead. The road is gravel all the way from FR 23. The elevation at the trailhead is 4,190 feet. The road makes a small circle at the trailhead and does not continue past it as shown on many maps.

Special Considerations

Mosquitoes can be a problem in July and early August.

The Hike

The trail heads northeast from the trailhead for a few yards and then turns east to follow an abandoned roadbed. The roadbed (trail) climbs gently through a dense stand of young Douglas firs, the result of a clear-cut several years ago. Pearly everlasting grows in many places along the roadbed, which is slowly but steadily reverting to a trail. About 0.4 mile from the trailhead, the fir trees give way to stands of vine maple and other low bushes, and the views open up. As the track heads north,

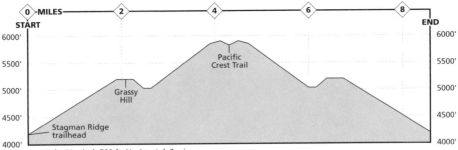

Intervals: Vertical, 500 ft; Horizontal, 2 mi.

look behind you to see Mount Hood towering over the Oregon Cascades in the distance. As you approach the upper edge of the old clear-cut about 0.5 mile from the trailhead, glimpses of Mount St. Helens can be seen to the west.

The old roadbed ends as the route leaves the clear-cut, at 4,490 feet elevation. A few yards farther along, you pass the Mount Adams Wilderness boundary. The track now climbs gently but steadily northeast through the virgin forest. One-half mile into the wilderness, the first views of Mount Adams show up through the trees ahead. Columbine, asters, and goldenrod add spots of color along the path as you climb.

The grade steepens in a few places, and the timber becomes more alpine as you near Grassy Hill. The tread crosses a small sloping meadow at 5,220 feet elevation, 2.1 miles from the trailhead. The short rise to your left here is Grassy Hill. The route traverses the meadow and then drops slightly to a saddle. In the saddle the tread turns to the left (northwest) and descends gently. After losing about 200 feet of elevation, the path crosses a couple of tiny meadows and a wet weather stream and then swings around to climb again to the northeast. The USGS Mount Adams West quad map is incorrect in this area. The USDA Forest Service Mount Adams Wilderness map is correct, however.

The trail climbs moderately for the next mile, heading northeast through woods and openings. Just as the route flattens to head west, you may notice the now-abandoned trail to Graveyard Camp turning to the right (northeast). After flattening out and descending slightly for the next 0.2 mile, the route turns north and begins its final climb to the junction with the PCT. The PCT is reached 4.3 miles from the trailhead, at 5,790 feet elevation.

Options

Stagman Ridge Trail is a good, lightly used way to access the PCT for an extended backpack through Mount Adams Wilderness. If you turn right at the junction with the PCT, it is only 0.5 mile to Horseshoe Meadow and the junction with Round

◀ *Along Stagman Ridge Trail*

Stagman Ridge Trail 12

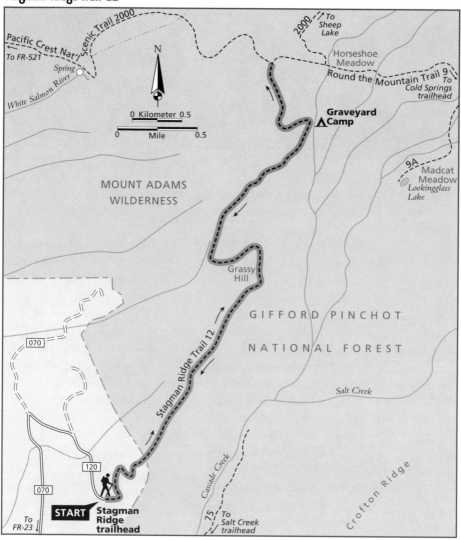

the Mountain Trail. The timbered fringes of the meadow make a great base camp from which to explore the southern slopes of Mount Adams.

Grassy Hill makes an ideal turnaround spot if this is to be a short day hike.

Miles and Directions

0.0 Stagman Ridge trailhead (GPS 46 08.402 N 121 35.844 W).

0.6 Mount Adams Wilderness Boundary.

2.1 Grassy Hill.

4.3 Junction with PCT. Turnaround point.

8.6 Stagman Ridge trailhead.

6 Round the Mountain, Cold Springs Trailhead to Horseshoe Meadow, Trails 183, 9

Climb gently to near the timberline of Mount Adams on the South Climb Trail and then contour the alpine southwest slope of the mountain to a junction with the Pacific Crest Trail (PCT) at Horseshoe Meadow.

Start: Cold Springs trailhead.
Distance: 14.6-mile out-and-back day hike or backpack.
Difficulty: Easy.
Seasons: Mid-July through early October.
Fees and permits: Northwest Forest Pass to park at Cold Springs trailhead and a Mount Adams Wilderness Permit.
Parking and trailhead facilities: There is plenty of parking, rest rooms, and campsites at the trailhead.
Maps: USDA Forest Service Mount Adams Wilderness or Mount Adams East and Mount Adams West USGS quads.
Trail contacts: Gifford Pinchot National Forest, Mount Adams Ranger District, 2455 Highway 141, Trout Lake, WA, 98650; (509) 395–3400; www.fs.fed.us/gpnf.

Finding the trailhead: Drive east from Portland on I-84 to exit 64 at the east edge of Hood River. Leave the freeway and head north across the Columbia River. At the junction with State Route 14 just north of the bridge, turn left and head west for 1.6 miles to the junction with State Route 141 Alternate, signed TO MOUNT ADAMS RECREATION AREA. Turn right at the junction and drive north for 2.1 miles to the junction with State Route 141. Turn left at the junction and continue north on SR 141 for 18.9 miles to Trout Lake.

From Trout Lake drive north on Forest Road 23 for 1.4 miles to the junction with Forest Road 80. Bear right at the junction and continue north on FR 80. In about 0.6 mile you will come to another junction. Turn left at this junction and continue north on FR 80 and Forest Road 8040 for 9.9 miles to Morrison Creek Campground and the Shorthorn trailhead. At the Shorthorn trailhead the road turns right and becomes Forest Road 500. Follow FR 500 for about 3 miles to its end at Cold Springs Campground and trailhead. Signs at each junction point the way to South Climb Trail. Forest Road 500 can be very rough at times, requiring a high-clearance vehicle. The elevation at the trailhead is 5,580 feet.

Special Considerations

The heavily silted creeks that this trail crosses could be difficult at high water. Remember that these glacial streams are usually higher in the afternoon and during periods of hot weather with a high freezing level. These streams are usually less silted in the morning. Campfires are prohibited in Mount Adams Wilderness above Round the Mountain, Pacific Crest, and Highline Trails.

Mount Adams from the southwest

The Hike

The first part of this hike follows the South Climb Route, which is a closed road that used to allow vehicles to drive to the now-abandoned and dismantled Timberline Campground. Leaving Cold Springs Campground and Trailhead, the route climbs generally north for 1.2 miles to the junction with Round the Mountain Trail 9, at 6,250 feet elevation. With the gain in elevation, the timber thins out, allowing distant views of Mount Hood to the south and Mount St. Helens to the west. As you approach the junction, the south side of Mount Adams comes into full, unobstructed view.

At the signed junction with Round the Mountain Trail, turn left (northwest) to begin your traverse around the southwest slopes of towering Mount Adams. Groves of hemlock, subalpine fir, and whitebark pine line the track, while lupine and asters cover the ground. Eight-tenths of a mile after leaving the South Climb Trail, you cross Morrison Creek. There are several possible campsites just past the creek crossing, and water can obtained here. After crossing Morrison Creek the trail passes through stands of larger whitebark pines and hemlocks. You may notice a path to the left 0.7 mile past Morrison Creek. This path leads a short distance to a viewpoint and possible dry campsite. The tread crosses seven more small streams (some of which may be dry late in the season) before reaching the junction with the Shorthorn Trail. Lewis monkeyflowers hug the banks of several of these creeks, and false hellebore grows where there is enough soil moisture to support it. Asters and paintbrush cover many of the drier slopes. The junction with the Shorthorn Trail 16 is reached 4 miles from the trailhead, on the top of Crofton Ridge, at 6,160 feet elevation.

Round the Mountain Trail crosses a spur ridge just past the junction with the Shorthorn Trail and then descends a few feet to cross a silted fork of Salt Creek in a small, eroded gully. A large spring is located to the left, below the trail 0.2 mile farther along, after crossing another eroded gully. A few yards past the spring, the course crosses a tiny stream in a small draw. Look to the right at the crossing for a view of a waterfall. One hundred fifty yards farther along, you cross a silted creek and then a small clear stream. Another 1.3 miles and the path reaches a heavily silted, foul-smelling (sulfur) fork of Cascade Creek. Just past the foul creek is a tiny clear stream, with banks covered with monkeyflowers.

Shortly, the trace crosses another silted stream, another fork of Cascade Creek, and quickly reaches the junction with Lookingglass Lake Trail 9A. The area around the junction, at 6,020 feet elevation, is dotted with small alpine timber and lots of boulders. Asters and lupine grow where they can between the boulders. To the right, Mount Adams looms high above, with White Salmon Glacier descending from near its humped but craggy summit.

Leaving the junction the trail descends very gently, heading northwest. After about 0.4 mile the route turns west to traverse an open south-facing slope. Then the tread re-enters the timber, where there will be a possible campsite a few yards to the left. Before long the trail enters Horseshoe Meadow at 5,880 feet elevation. There are several nice campsites around the fringes of the meadow in the timber. On the far side of Horseshoe Meadow is the junction with the Pacific Crest Trail 2000. This junction is 7.3 miles from Cold Springs trailhead, at 5,890 feet elevation.

Options

To continue around the west side of Mount Adams, follow the PCT north past Riley Creek, Adams Creek, Killen Creek, and the Muddy Fork to the PCT trailhead on Forest Road 115. The return hike can be done via Shorthorn Trail. This would require a short car shuttle between Cold Springs trailhead and Shorthorn trailhead.

Round the Mountain Trail also can be taken to the right (east) from the junction with the South Climb Route 1.2 miles from the trailhead. This section of the Round the Mountain Trail crosses rough lava flows with great views and reaches flower-covered meadows as you enter the Yakama Indian Reservation about 2 miles from the junction.

Round the Mountain, Cold Springs Trailhead to Horseshoe Meadow, Trails 183, 9

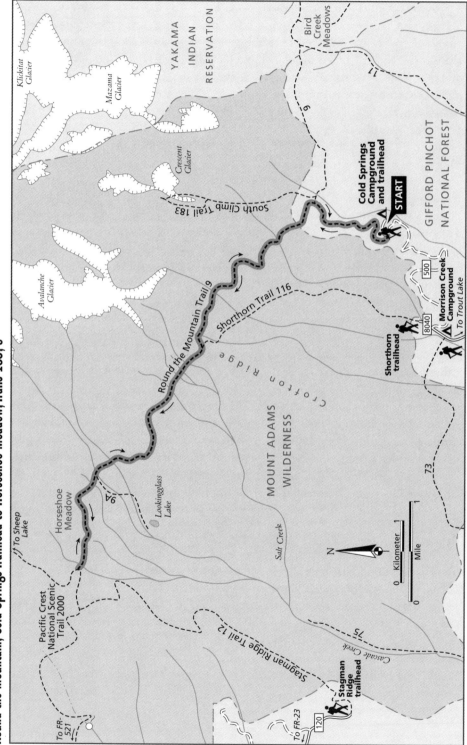

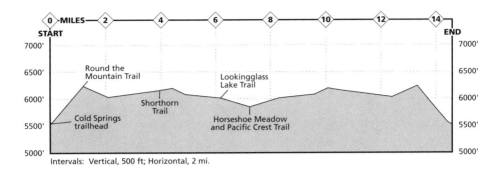

Intervals: Vertical, 500 ft; Horizontal, 2 mi.

Miles and Directions

0.0 Cold Springs trailhead (GPS 46 08.140 N 121 29.863 W).

1.2 Junction with Round the Mountain Trail 9 (GPS 46 08.772 N 121 29.421 W). Turn left (northwest).

4.0 Junction with Shorthorn Trail 16 (GPS 46 09.740 N 121 31.299 W). Continue west on Round the Mountain Trail.

6.2 Junction with Lookingglass Lake Trail 9A (GPS 46 10.691 N 121 33.013 W). Continue northwest on Round the Mountain Trail.

7.3 Junction with Pacific Crest Trail 2000, at Horseshoe Meadow (GPS 46 10.784 N 121 34.125 W). Turnaround point.

14.6 Cold Springs trailhead.

7 Shorthorn Trail 16

Hike through woods and tiny flower-covered meadows to a junction with Round the Mountain Trail near the timberline on the southwest slope of Mount Adams.

Start: Shorthorn trailhead.
Distance: 5.6-mile out-and-back day hike.
Difficulty: Moderate to strenuous.
Seasons: Mid-July through early October.
Fees and permits: Northwest Forest Pass and Mount Adams Wilderness Permit.
Parking and trailhead facilities: There is adequate parking at the trailhead. Rest rooms

and campsites are available close by.
Maps: USDA Forest Service Mount Adams Wilderness or Mount Adams West USGS quad.
Trail contacts: Gifford Pinchot National Forest, Mount Adams Ranger District, 2455 Highway 141, Trout Lake, WA, 98650; (509) 395-3400; www.fs.fed.us/gpnf.

Finding the trailhead: Drive east from Portland on I-84 to exit 64 at the east edge of Hood River. Leave the freeway and head north across the Columbia River. At the junction with State Route 14 just north of the bridge, turn left and head west for 1.6 miles to the junction with State Route 141 Alternate, signed TO MOUNT ADAMS RECREATION AREA. Turn right at the junction onto SR 141 Alt and drive north for about 2.1 miles to the junction with State Route 141. Turn left at the junction and continue north on SR 141 for 18.9 miles to Trout Lake.

From Trout Lake drive north on Forest Road 23 for 1.4 miles to the junction with Forest Road 80. Bear right at the junction and continue north on FR 80. In about 0.6 mile you will come to another junction. Turn left at this junction and continue north on FR 80 and Forest Road 8040 for 9.9 miles to Morrison Creek Campground and the Shorthorn trailhead. The trailhead is on the left side of the road just as it makes a hard right turn. The elevation at the trailhead is 4,650 feet.

Special Considerations

There are a few wet areas along this route, and the mosquitoes can be very aggressive. It also gets heavy stock use at times.

The Hike

Shorthorn Trail leaves the trailhead, climbing moderately. Slightly more than 0.1 mile into the hike, you pass the Mount Adams Wilderness boundary. Beargrass covers the ground beneath the lodgepole pines as you climb the sometimes steep and rough trace. Morrison Creek is below the trail to the right 0.8 mile from the trailhead; you get close to it 0.5 mile farther along. This trail was once used as a "stock driveway"; notice the signs on the trees.

The course crosses a small sandy, lupine- and phlox-covered meadow with a

Lupine, daisies, and monkeyflowers ▶

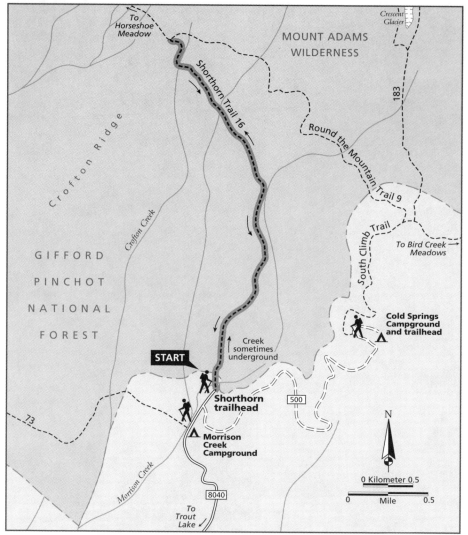

great view of Mount Adams 1.8 miles from the trailhead, at 5,680 feet elevation. The track flattens in the tiny meadow and crosses a small stream 0.3 mile farther along. Lewis monkeyflowers brighten the stream banks and lupine grows in the meadow. You soon cross another creek in a beautiful little wet meadow. Many varieties of flowers grow from the wet ground between the silver snags, and moss lines the stream banks. The trail is a little vague at the crossing, but it's marked with a cairn.

Leaving the meadow the trees soon get smaller and spaced farther apart. Between the volcanic rocks bloom paintbrush, lupine, and phlox. The route crosses Crofton Creek in a rocky bed 2.5 miles from the trailhead, at 5,900 feet elevation. Turn right up the streambed and follow it for a short distance. The trail then turns left and

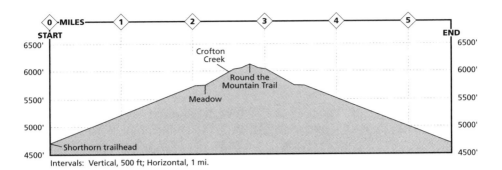

Intervals: Vertical, 500 ft; Horizontal, 1 mi.

climbs steeply out of the streambed to the rocky slope above. You then make two switchbacks as you climb the slope. Mount Hood is in the distance to the south. Above the switchbacks it's a short uphill walk to the junction with Round the Mountain Trail 9, at 6,160 feet elevation, on Crofton Ridge.

There is a fantastic view of the southwest side of Mount Adams from the junction. On the slopes above, Avalanche Glacier descending below The Pinnacle and a small waterfall is in view to the east-northeast. Trout Lake Valley is far below to the south, and to the southeast are the rolling, treeless hills near The Dalles, Oregon.

Options

Shorthorn Trail may be used as an alternate return route when hiking Round the Mountain Trail. Exiting the wilderness this way will require a car shuttle between the trailheads. During heavy snow years, when the road to Cold Springs trailhead still has a few drifts blocking it, the Shorthorn Trail may be a better way to access the Round the Mountain Trail.

Miles and Directions

0.0 Shorthorn trailhead (GPS 46 07.830 N 121 30.937 W).

2.8 Junction with Round the Mountain Trail 9 (GPS 46 09.740 N 121 31.299 W). Turn-around point.

5.6 Shorthorn trailhead.

8 Lookingglass Lake Trail 9A

Hike to an out-of-the-way lake that is filled with trout.

Start: Junction of Round the Mountain Trail and Lookingglass Lake Trail; the nearest trailhead is Shorthorn trailhead on Forest Road 8040.

Distance: 2.2-mile out-and-back day hike or backpack from the junction with Round Mountain; 12.2 miles round-trip from Shorthorn trailhead.

Difficulty: Easy to moderate.

Seasons: Mid-July through mid-October.

Fees and permits: Mount Adams Wilderness Permit. A Northwest Forest Pass is also required if you are leaving a vehicle at Shorthorn trailhead.

Maps: USDA Forest Service Mount Adams Wilderness or Mount Adams West USGS quad.

Trail contacts: Gifford Pinchot National Forest, Mount Adams Ranger District, 2455 Highway 141, Trout Lake, WA, 98650; (509) 395-3400; www.fs.fed.us/gpnf.

Finding the trailhead: Drive east from Portland on I-84 to exit 64 at the east edge of Hood River. Leave the freeway and head north across the Columbia River. At the junction with State Route 14 just north of the bridge, turn left and head west for 1.6 miles to the junction with State Route 141 Alternate, signed TO MOUNT ADAMS RECREATION AREA. Turn right at the junction onto SR 141 Alt and drive north for about 2.1 miles to the junction with State Route 141. Turn left at the junction and continue north on SR 141 for 18.9 miles to Trout Lake.

From Trout Lake drive north on Forest Road 23 for 1.4 miles to the junction with Forest Road 80. Bear right at the junction and continue north on FR 80. In about 0.6 mile you will come to another junction. Turn left at this junction and continue north on FR 80 and FR 8040 for 9.9 miles to Morrison Creek Campground and the Shorthorn trailhead. Hike north on the Shorthorn Trail for 2.8 miles to the junction with the Round the Mountain Trail. Turn left (northwest) onto Round the Mountain Trail and go 2.2 miles to the junction with Lookingglass Lake Trail. The elevation at the junction is 6,020 feet.

Special Considerations

Take along plenty of bug spray early in the season.

The Hike

Lookingglass Lake Trail descends from the junction with the Round the Mountain Trail through small meadows covered with lupine and asters. Shortly, the route begins to follow a stream and then crosses it at 5,900 feet elevation. At times this stream is heavily silted and yellow in color, and it smells of sulfur. Soon after crossing the silted creek, the track crosses a smaller, clear stream and passes a campsite. Look up and to your left here to spot a small waterfall. A few yards farther along, you cross another small clear creek and pass another campsite.

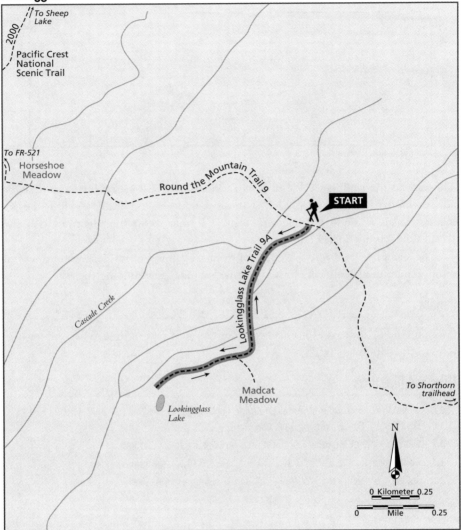

The route crosses another yellow–tan silted creek at 5,840 feet elevation, 0.6 mile from the junction with the Round the Mountain Trail. After crossing the sulfur-smelling stream, hike across a small, flower-covered meadow to an unsigned junction with a path to the left. This side path leads a short distance (250 yards) to Madcat Meadow, where there are some possible campsites. The meadow at the junction was once known as Meadow Camp; there is some evidence of its use in earlier times.

To continue to Lookingglass Lake, bear right at the junction and continue to descend along the left side of a small ridge. In a little more than 0.1 mile, the track crosses the small ridge. The trail appears to fork 150 yards after crossing the ridge.

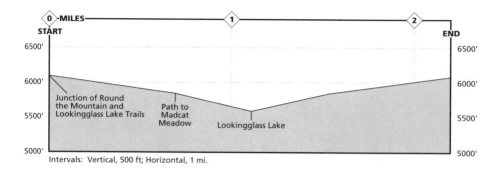

Intervals: Vertical, 500 ft; Horizontal, 1 mi.

The fork to the right once led to a spot called Graveyard Camp but now is abandoned and hard to follow. Bear left at the fork and descend fairly steeply to Lookingglass Lake, at 5,580 feet elevation and 1.1 miles from the junction with the Round the Mountain Trail.

The small lake seems to have lots of trout swimming in its clear waters. Several campsites are available in the fir and hemlock timber surrounding the lake.

Options

Lookingglass Lake makes an excellent side trip and or campsite when hiking the Round the Mountain Trail.

Miles and Directions

0.0 Junction of Round the Mountain Trail and Lookingglass Lake Trail (GPS 46 10.691 N 121 33.013 W). Follow Lookingglass Lake Trail.

0.7 Path to Madcat Meadow. Continue west on Lookingglass Lake Trail.

1.1 Lookingglass Lake (GPS 46 10.202 N 121 33.538 W). Turnaround point.

2.2 Junction of Round the Mountain Trail and Lookingglass Lake Trail.

9 Mount Adams South Climb Route, Trail 183

The South Climb Route is the easiest way to climb the second-highest peak in Washington.

Start: Cold Springs trailhead.
Distance: 11.2-mile out-and-back mountain climb.
Difficulty: Very strenuous by hiking standards. Easy climb by mountaineering standards.
Seasons: Mid-July through mid-September.
Fees and permits: Cascade Volcanoes Pass. The Cascade Volcanoes Pass, which is required to climb above 7,000 feet elevation on Mount Adams, costs $15 for a Friday, Saturday, or Sunday start or $10 Monday through Thursday. The Volcanoes Pass takes the place of both the Northwest Forest Pass and the wilderness permit but is good for only one outing. If you plan on making more than one

trip to the upper slopes of Mount Adams, you may wish to purchase an annual Cascades Volcanoes Pass. The $30 annual pass is good for an unlimited number of climbs on Mount Adams and is also honored at Mount St. Helens subject to established quotas.
Parking and trailhead facilities: There is plenty of parking, rest rooms, and campsites at the trailhead.
Maps: USDA Forest Service Mount Adams Wilderness or Mount Adams East USGS quad.
Trail contacts: Gifford Pinchot National Forest, Mount Adams Ranger District, 2455 Highway 141, Trout Lake, WA, 98650; (509) 395–3400; www.fs.fed.us/gpnf.

Finding the trailhead: Drive east from Portland on I–84 to exit 64 at the east edge of Hood River. Leave the freeway and head north across the Columbia River. At the junction with State Route 14 just north of the bridge, turn left and head west for 1.6 miles to the junction with State Route 141 Alternate, signed TO MOUNT ADAMS RECREATION AREA. Turn right at the junction onto SR 141 Alt and drive north for about 2.1 miles to the junction with State Route 141. Turn left at the junction and continue north on SR 141 for 18.9 miles to Trout Lake.

From Trout Lake drive north on Forest Road 23 for 1.4 miles to the junction with Forest Road 80. Bear right at the junction and continue north on FR 80. In about 0.6 mile, you will come to another junction. Turn left at this junction and continue north on FR 80 and Forest Road 8040 for 9.9 miles to Morrison Creek Campground and the Shorthorn trailhead. At the Shorthorn trailhead the road turns right and becomes Forest Road 500. Follow FR 500 for about 3 miles to its end at Cold Springs Trailhead and Campground. Signs at each junction point the way to South Climb Trail. Forest Road 500 can be very rough at times, requiring a high-clearance vehicle. The elevation at the trailhead is 5,580 feet.

Special Considerations

Be sure you are in shape before attempting this climb because if you are not, it will be grueling. Altitude sickness affects a fair percentage of the climbers on Mount Adams. Keeping well hydrated and moving at a moderate but steady pace lessens your chances of getting altitude sick, but it may happen anyway. The best cure for altitude sickness is to descend as soon as possible.

Mount Adams summit from Piker's Peak

If you are not an experienced mountaineer, it is best to join a party with experienced leadership. All members of the party should carry an ice ax and crampons. Don't wait until you need them to learn to put on your crampons. Get plenty of instruction and practice in the proper use of an ice ax before you attempt the climb. Carrying along this equipment and not knowing how to use it is just as dangerous as not having it at all.

Storms with hurricane-force wind (which you can't stand in) and blinding whiteout conditions are fairly common above timberline. Be sure you have the proper clothing to contend with these conditions. Sunglasses or goggles and sunscreen are a must.

If you plan to camp at Lunch Counter or on the summit, be sure your tent can stand the possible violent wind and your sleeping bag is up to subfreezing temperatures.

Water may be hard to find above Morrison Creek, so carry all you will need or take along a stove to melt snow.

The Climb

The South Climb Trail follows an abandoned roadbed as it climbs to the north from the west end of Cold Springs Campground. The roadbed used to allow vehicles to drive to the now-abandoned and dismantled Timberline Campground. The closing of this road has added nearly 2 miles and about 1,000 vertical feet to the climb, but it was needed to preserve the alpine wilderness.

After following the roadbed that is gradually reverting to a trail for 1.2 miles, you reach the junction with the Round the Mountain Trail 9, at 6,250 feet elevation. As you approach the junction, the south side of Mount Adams, including most of the route to the summit, comes into view.

From the junction continue along the roadbed to about 6,500 feet elevation, where the road becomes a trail. Beside the route asters nearly cover the volcanic ground; the best bloom is in August. Shortly after the roadbed quits, you ford Morrison Creek. Fill your water bottles here, remembering to filter or treat the water.

Above Morrison Creek the tread winds and switchbacks its way for 0.6 mile up to the snout of Crescent Glacier, at about 7,400 feet elevation. Sulfur was once mined near the summit of Mount Adams; the pack trail that was the access route to the mines turned to the southwest here and climbed the ridge to your left.

The route now crosses the lower end of Crescent Glacier, climbing steeply to the ridge on its west side. You may want to get out your ice ax here, as the glacier is fairly steep. On the ridgeline the route rejoins the old pack trail. Climb north on the ridge, making several switchbacks. Soon you pass the last whitebark pine elfinwood at about 8,000 feet elevation. These short, stunted trees attest to the rigors of this high-altitude climate. A little farther up, several rock windbreaks have been constructed along the trail. After passing the windbreaks the route crosses a snowfield to Lunch Counter. At Lunch Counter, a popular camping site at 9,100 feet elevation, many more windbreak tent shelters have been constructed. Water may be available here but don't count on it. There is generally good cell-phone service at Lunch Counter.

The route climbs northeast from Lunch Counter for a short distance and then turns north-northwest to climb the upper part of Suksdorf Ridge, the steepest part of the South Climb Route. As you start up the ridge, you have a choice to make. The snowfield can be climbed all the way to the False Summit or, just to its left, you can scramble up the boulders. If you have an ice ax and crampons, the snowfield is probably the easier route. However, at times this steep slope becomes very icy, and a long slide is possible. Climbing up the boulders is easier for some people, and it is the way to go if you are not equipped with an ice ax and crampons. Some of the boulders are loose, so climb cautiously.

Whichever way you climb, the False Summit is reached after a strenuous 2,400-foot climb from Lunch Counter. At 11,520 feet elevation, the False Summit makes a good rest stop after the strenuous climb. Many hikers are disheartened here because

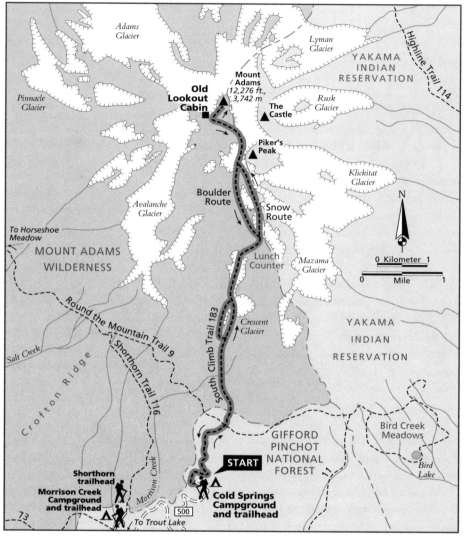

the summit still looks to be a long ways away. It is not as far as it looks, however, and the route is not as steep as what you have just climbed. From the False Summit follow the path northeast, passing below and left of Piker's Peak, a rounded hump on the ridgeline. Then cross a snowfield to the north to reach the base of the main summit dome. The snowfield may be deeply sun-cupped by August. Once across the snowfield climb the switchbacking trail to the northwest to just over 12,000 feet elevation. From here the path climbs west-northwest, crossing a stream that contains a considerable amount of sulfur and that should not be used

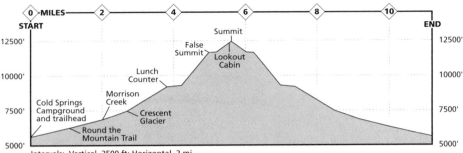

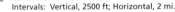

Intervals: Vertical, 2500 ft; Horizontal, 2 mi.

for drinking. After crossing the stream climb the last couple of hundred feet to the Summit Lookout Cabin.

The lookout cabin has not been used for many years; it is filled and partly buried with snow. The cabin's roof and south side are usually not completely snow-covered. If you wish to record your success, the summit register is next to the cabin. From the cabin the 12,276-foot-high summit is a little more than 0.1 mile to the northeast, along the rounded ridgetop. Cell-phone service is generally excellent from the summit area.

Options

For the hardy climber, camping on the summit is an exciting way to spend the night. At sunset if the weather is clear, a shadow of the mountain will gradually extend below you to the east across the plains of central Washington. In the early morning the opposite shadow shows up above the hills and sometimes fog-shrouded valleys to the west.

If you plan to camp on the summit, be sure to check the weather forecast first. It can quickly become very stormy, with wind so strong it is impossible to stand and whiteout conditions. In conditions like this, descent is very difficult if not impossible. Once when camped on the summit, we awoke to a combination of a dust storm and freezing fog, which built up a coating of thick tan frost on everything.

Tents used on the summit should be designed to stand up to these conditions, and sleeping bags should be rated to at least zero degrees. Much of the ground close to the summit is very acidic. If you camp here be sure to wash the floor of your tent when you return from the climb; if you don't, the floor material may be degraded.

Miles and Directions

0.0 Cold Springs trailhead (GPS 46 08.140 N 121 29.863 W).

1.2 Junction with Round the Mountain Trail 9 (GPS 46 08.774 N 121 29.424 W). Continue on the South Climb Route.

2.0 Morrison Creek.

2.6 Crescent Glacier.

3.7 Lunch Counter.

4.9 False Summit, near Piker's Peak (GPS 46 11.522 N 121 29.332 W).

5.5 Old Summit Lookout Cabin (GPS 46 12.090 N 121 29.565 W).

5.6 Summit (GPS 46 12.146 N 121 29.451 W). Turnaround point.

11.2 Cold Springs trailhead.

10 Mount Adams North Cleaver Route

Climb a challenging route to the highest point in the Washington Cascades south of Mount Rainier. Mountain goats are common up to 9,500 feet elevation along this spectacular route.

Start: High Camp; nearest trailhead is Killen Creek trailhead on Forest Road 2329.

Distance: 9.0-mile internal out-and-back mountain climb from High Camp; 17.2 miles round-trip from Killen Creek trailhead.

Difficulty: Very long and strenuous by hiking standards. The North Cleaver of Mount Adams is by far the most difficult route described in this book, and it should not be attempted even by strong hikers without experienced leadership. Much of this route is a class 2 climb with a few spots that are class 3 rock.

Seasons: Mid-July through mid-September. Before mid-July snow may cover much of this route some years, and by October lowering freezing levels may cause the rock to be iced.

Fees and permits: Cascade Volcanoes Pass. The Cascade Volcanoes Pass, which is required to climb above 7,000 feet elevation on Mount Adams, costs $15 for a Friday, Saturday, or Sunday start or $10 Monday through Thursday. The Volcanoes Pass takes the place of both the Northwest Forest Pass and the wilderness permit but is good for only one outing. If you plan on making more than one trip to the upper slopes of Mount Adams, you may wish to purchase the annual Cascades Volcanoes Pass. The $30 annual pass is good for an unlimited number of climbs on Mount Adams and is also honored at Mount St. Helens subject to established quotas.

Base camp facilities: There are several good campsites at High Camp, and water is generally available. If you camp here be sure to practice zero-impact camping, and please don't trample the flowers. Cell-phone service generally can be had from the low ridge north of camp.

Maps: USDA Forest Service Mount Adams Wilderness or Mount Adams East and Mount Adams West USGS quads.

Trail contacts: Gifford Pinchot National Forest, Mount Adams Ranger District, 2455 Highway 141, Trout Lake, WA, 98650; (509) 395–3400; www.fs.fed.us/gpnf.

Finding the trailhead: From Seattle drive south on I-5 to exit 133 at Tacoma and then follow Washington Highway 7 for 55 miles to Morton. From Morton drive east on U.S Highway 12 for 17 miles to Randle.

From Portland drive north on I-5 to exit 68 (68 miles north of Interstate Bridge) and then follow US 12 east for 48 miles to Randle.

From US 12 at Randle, drive south on State Route 131 (may be signed TO FOREST ROAD 25) for 0.9 mile. Turn left (east) onto Forest Road 23 and follow it east and south for 30.6 miles to the junction with FR 2329. Turn left onto FR 2329 and follow it approximately 6 miles to Killen Creek trailhead. The trailhead is on the right side of the road.

The junction of FR 23 and FR 2329 can also be reached from Portland via Trout Lake. To get to Trout Lake, drive east from Portland on I-84 to exit 64 at the east edge of Hood River. Leave the freeway and head north across the Columbia River. At the junction with State Route 14 just north of the bridge, turn left and head west for 1.6 miles to the junction with State Route

Sunrise below the North Cleaver. PHOTO: GARY FLETCHER

141 Alternate, signed TO MOUNT ADAMS RECREATION AREA. Turn right at the junction onto SR 141 Alt and drive north for about 2.1 miles to the junction with State Route 141. Turn left at the junction and continue north on SR 141 for 18.9 miles to Trout Lake. From the Y intersection next to the Chevron station in Trout Lake, follow FR 23 for 25.6 miles north to the junction with FR 2329. The USDA Forest Service Gifford Pinchot National Forest map can be a great asset when trying to find your way from Trout Lake. Hike Killen Creek Trail 3.1 miles to its junction with the Pacific Crest Trail (PCT). Cross the PCT and continue to the southeast on High Camp Trail 1 mile to High Camp, where this climb begins. The elevation at High Camp is 6,880 feet.

Special Considerations

Good map-reading and route-finding skills are necessary to follow this route safely, especially in a storm or darkness. Ice axes, crampons, and possibly a rope, as well as adequate clothing (including wind gear) should be taken along on this climb. Don't forget your sunglasses or goggles, sunscreen, and a flashlight or headlamp. Allow plenty of time; it is not unusual to take fifteen hours or more to make the round-trip. An early (3:00 or 4:00 A.M.) start is mandatory if you don't want to descend in the dark. Loose and/or falling rock are prevalent along the North Cleaver; they can be dangerous and even deadly. There is considerable exposure at many spots along the North Cleaver; a fall from any one of them could cause serious injury or even be fatal. Altitude sickness affects a fair percentage of the climbers on Mount Adams. Keeping well hydrated and moving at a moderate but steady pace lessens your chances of getting altitude sick, but it may happen anyway. The best cure for altitude sickness is to descend as soon as possible.

The stream at High Camp usually flows more in the afternoon, so fill your water bottles before you go to bed. There is usually no water available along the route above Iceberg Lake.

The Climb

There are two well-used routes from High Camp to Iceberg Lake. You can hike up the low rise on the right (southwest) side of the snow-filled gully where the stream that runs through High Camp originates, or the low ridge left of the gully can be climbed and followed. The low ridge is the more scenic route, so it is described here.

From High Camp, at 6,880 feet elevation, follow the vague path through groves of small, wind-shaped whitebark pines and stunted subalpine firs heading southeast to the top of the low ridge. Continue southeast along the ridge to a large flat area at 7,300 feet elevation, where you leave the small timber behind. Cross the flats and skirt a snowfield on its far side. Then turn south and climb through the boulders along the left side of a draw to Iceberg Lake, at 7,505 feet elevation and 1.2 miles from High Camp.

Several rock windbreaks near the east shore make this a possible campsite, but the heavily silted waters of the lake may make getting drinking water a problem. Silted water clogs filters quickly. An arm of Adams Glacier reaches the southeast shore of Iceberg Lake, and occasionally chunks of it break off to form the icebergs that float on the water.

Leaving Iceberg Lake the route first heads east, soon skirting the edge of a snow-field. About 0.2 mile from the lake, turn southeast, cross a narrow point in the snow-field (in early season), and climb gently. The route crosses a fairly flat area and then steepens, and you climb along a fairly well-used path toward the crest of the North Ridge. Before reaching the ridgeline the path makes several switchbacks, which ease the grade considerably.

The route reaches the North Ridge at 8,840 feet elevation. Above here the ridge steepens to become the North Cleaver. This is the turnaround point for most hikers. The next 2,600 vertical feet (1.3 miles) of the route require nearly continuous scrambling, and in several places there are short pitches of class 3 rock to be climbed. The path that you have been following to reach the ridge also becomes very vague as you head up the cleaver. Ideally, this point should be reached by sunrise to ensure adequate time for the rest of the climb and the descent.

Mount Adams North Cleaver Route

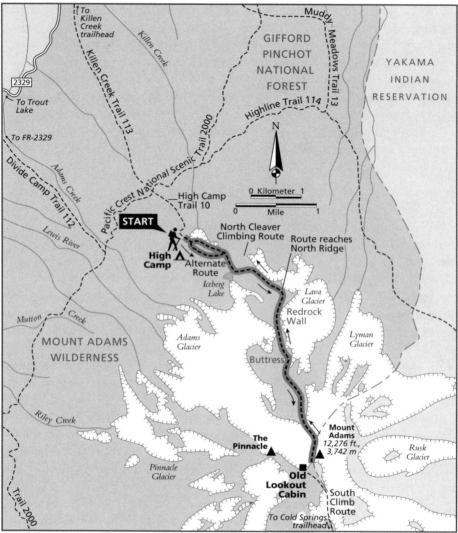

To continue, drop slightly off the ridgeline to the left and skirt the rock out-croppings for the first couple of hundred vertical feet, then regain the ridge. From here the route follows the ridgeline fairly closely, never getting more than a few feet below its crest. You will pass a small rock windbreak between two pinnacles just to the right of the ridgeline at 9,070 feet elevation. Just past the windbreak the route makes an exposed traverse (class 3) back to the ridge crest. A couple of hundred feet higher, the path appears to end just left of the ridgeline. To your right will be a redrock wall about 10 feet high. Turn right and climb up the wall to the crest of the

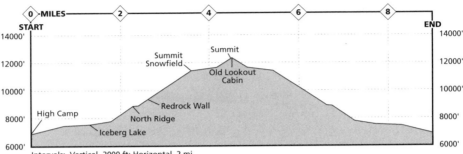

Intervals: Vertical, 2000 ft; Horizontal, 2 mi.

ridge (class 3). Climbing over this wall is essential to following the route. If you don't climb over it and instead try to traverse along the left side of the ridgeline here, you will get into an area of very loose, steep, and dangerous rock. Once at the top of the wall, traverse, descending slightly, just right of the ridgeline to the easier ground ahead. This wall and traverse, and the traverse below (just above the windbreak at 9,070 feet) are the most difficult spots of the entire climb.

Continue up the ridge, skirting left of a buttress between 9,600 and 10,000 feet elevation. The grade moderates as you reach 10,500 feet elevation, and by the time you get to the edge of the summit snowfield at 11,450 feet, it has become quite gentle.

Skirt the right side of the summit snowfield (really the top end of Lyman Glacier here), heading south. At 11,800 feet elevation, cross the snowfield, head south-southeast for 0.3 mile, and then climb the slightly steeper snow slope to the rim of the crater. This snowfield is an accumulation zone for both Lyman and Adams Glaciers and may have hidden crevasses. Once on the crater rim, you will be very close to (within a few yards of) the 12,276-foot-high summit of Mount Adams. From the summit most climbers will want to walk the nearly level 0.1 mile southwest to the abandoned lookout cabin and summit register. Try to allow enough time for a rest break at the ice-filled cabin, and take in the 360-degree panorama of the Cascades. There is excellent cell-phone service on the summit.

Descending the North Cleaver may take nearly as long as it did to climb it, so be sure you have enough remaining daylight hours. Noon is not too early to head down, even if you have not reached the summit, and 3:00 P.M. is too late to start your descent.

Options

If you can arrange a car shuttle, it is much easier to descend the South Climb Route than it is to climb back down the way you came. The descent via the South Climb Route usually takes only about one half the time it does to downclimb the North Cleaver.

Miles and Directions

0.0 High Camp (GPS 46 14.433 N 121 31.331 W).

1.2 Iceberg Lake.

2.3 Route reaches North Ridge (GPS 46 13.595 N 121 30.005 W).

3.6 Route reaches Summit Snowfield at 11,450 feet elevation.

4.4 Summit (GPS 46 12.146 N 121 29.451 W).

4.5 Old Summit Lookout Cabin (GPS 46 12.090 N 121 29.565 W). Turnaround point.

9.0 High Camp.

11 Sleeping Beauty Trail 37

Hike to an abandoned lookout site high on a jagged rock ridge above the Trout Lake Valley.

Start: Sleeping Beauty trailhead.
Distance: 3.4-mile out-and-back day hike.
Difficulty: Moderate, except for the last few yards to the old lookout site where you must scramble over exposed rock.
Seasons: Mid-June through October.
Fees and permits: None.

Parking and trailhead facilities: There is parking for several cars at the trailhead but no other facilities.
Maps: Sleeping Beauty USGS quad.
Trail contacts: Gifford Pinchot National Forest, Mount Adams Ranger District, 2455 Highway 141, Trout Lake, WA, 98650; (509) 395-3400; www.fs.fed.us/gpnf.

Finding the trailhead: Drive east from Portland on I-84 to exit 64 at the east edge of Hood River. Leave the freeway and head north across the Columbia River. At the junction with State Route 14 just north of the bridge, turn left and head west for 1.6 miles to the junction with State Route 141 Alternate, signed TO MOUNT ADAMS RECREATION AREA. Turn right at the junction onto SR 141 Alt and drive north for about 2.1 miles to the junction with State Route 141. Turn left at the junction and continue north on SR 141 for 18.9 miles to Trout Lake.

From the Y intersection next to the Chevron Station in Trout Lake, head west, staying on SR 141 for 1.7 miles to the junction with Trout Lake Creek Road. Turn right (northwest) onto Trout Lake Creek Road, which becomes Forest Road 88 at the Gifford Pinchot National Forest boundary 4.3 miles ahead. Follow FR 88 until you are 4.7 miles from SR 141 and then turn right onto Forest Road 8810. Follow FR 8810 for 6.3 miles northwest to the junction with Forest Road 040. Turn right onto FR 040 and drive northeast for 0.3 mile to the trailhead. There is a sign marking the trailhead. The elevation at the trailhead is 3,510 feet.

Special Considerations

This trail is maintained by Ralph and Virginia Preston under an agreement with the Forest Service. Sleeping Beauty Trail is open only to hikers from June 15 to November 15. Cliffs surround the summit area of Sleeping Beauty Peak on three sides, and the last few yards to the lookout site are an exposed rock scramble. This is no place to let children run ahead unsupervised.

The Hike

The wide, well-maintained trail winds up fairly steeply leaving the trailhead. In slightly less than 0.25 mile of climbing through the dense stand of second-growth Douglas fir, the route begins a series of five switchbacks, which take you up to nearly 4,000 feet elevation, 0.5 mile from the trailhead. Here the tread leaves the second-growth

Summit ridge of Sleeping Beauty

timber behind for much larger old-growth trees. Between the trees, vine maple and pearly everlasting add diversity to the flora.

The route continues to work its way up the slope for another 0.8 mile to reach a rounded ridgeline at 4,500 feet above sea level. On the ridge the track heads east for a short distance. It then bears slightly left off the ridge, climbing steeply. Soon the timber becomes smaller and changes to mostly hemlock, with beargrass growing between the short trees. One and one-half miles into the hike, the path makes a switchback below a large rock outcropping, which is part of the summit of Sleeping Beauty.

From here up to the summit the trail is a masterpiece of rockwork. The tread has been chipped out of the rock in places, and in other spots walls of flat rock have been laid to support it. As you reach the ridgeline after making many short switchbacks, there will be a path to the left. This short path leads to a viewpoint where Mount Hood can be seen to the south. A few yards farther along, the trail ends. To reach the site of the old lookout, you must scramble up the somewhat-exposed rocks to the

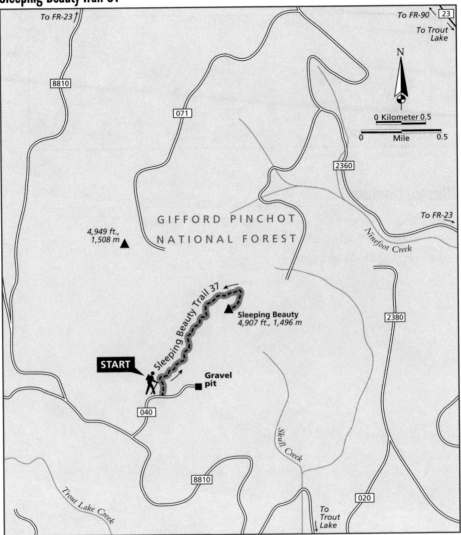

west for a few more yards. The viewpoint and the scramble could be dangerous, especially for children.

The old lookout site sits atop the 4,907-foot-high west end of Sleeping Beauty. Cliffs drop below the summit on the south, west, and north sides. To the east is the rugged summit ridge of Sleeping Beauty. To the northeast Mount Adams dominates the view, and to the north is the ice-covered summit of Mount Rainier. To the south the Trout Lake Valley is far below, and in the distance the sharp peak of Mount Hood rises above the Oregon Cascades.

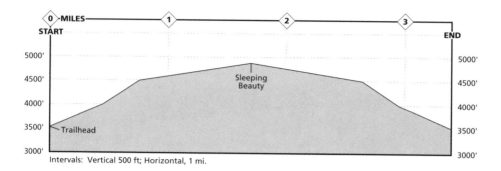

Intervals: Vertical 500 ft; Horizontal, 1 mi.

Miles and Directions

0.0 Sleeping Beauty trailhead (GPS 46 05.102 N 121 39.494 W).

1.7 Summit (GPS 46 05.570 N 121 38.997 W). Turnaround point.

3.4 Sleeping Beauty trailhead.

Indian Heaven Region

As the name indicates, Indian Heaven was once heavily used by Native Americans. Huckleberries were picked and dried here in late summer, and at times there was a party atmosphere. Hike 27, Indian Racetrack Trail 171 leads you to one of these people's favorite campsites, where horse races were once held.

Not as alpine as Goat Rocks or Mount Adams Wilderness areas, the Indian Heaven Region is a rounded plateau with a spine of somewhat higher buttes and peaks lined up from north to south along its middle. Hike 14, Pacific Crest Trail 2000, Indian Heaven Wilderness Section, follows this spine completely through the length of the wilderness. Close to the northern end of the wilderness, Hike 15, Sawtooth Mountain Trail 127, an alternate route to the Pacific Crest Trail, climbs into the more open country near the summit of Sawtooth Mountain.

Lakes are the dominant features in Indian Heaven. They are heavily scattered throughout the area, and nearly all of the trails reach one or more of them. Many of these lakes are shallow and do not support fish, but fishing can be very good at those that do.

From near the southwest corner of the wilderness, Hike 28, Falls Creek Trail 152 descends to the southwest deep into the Wind River Canyon. With the exception of Hike 13, Langfield Falls Trail 8, all the trails interconnect in some way. Roosevelt elk and blacktail deer are common throughout the area, as are black bears.

Indian Heaven Region

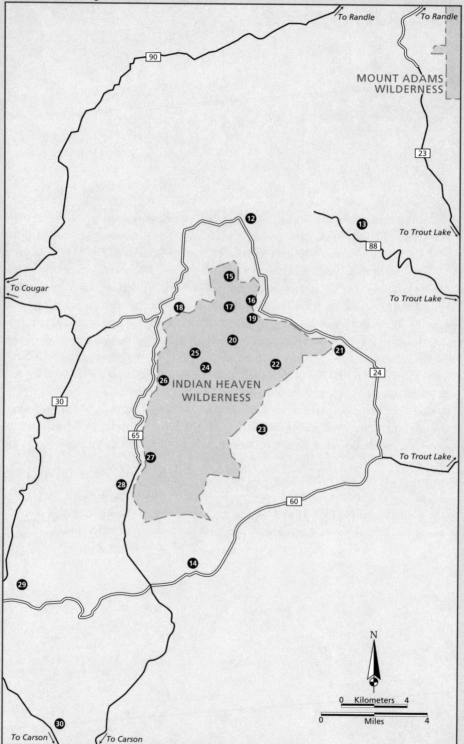

To Randle

To Randle

MOUNT ADAMS
WILDERNESS

90

23

12

13

To Trout Lake

88

15

To Cougar

18

17

16

19

To Trout Lake

20

25

21

24

22

24

26

INDIAN HEAVEN
WILDERNESS

30

65

23

27

To Trout Lake

28

60

14

29

N

0   Kilometers   4

0   Miles   4

30

To Carson

To Carson

12 Pacific Crest Trail 2000, Forest Road 24 to Forest Road 521

Hike the Pacific Crest Trail (PCT) through mostly moderate terrain between Indian Heaven Wilderness and Mount Adams Wilderness.

Start: PCT trailhead on FR 24.
Distance: 15.5-mile one-way shuttle day hike or backpack.
Difficulty: Moderate.
Seasons: July through mid-October.
Fees and permits: Northwest Forest Pass.
Parking and trailhead facilities: There is parking for several cars at the trailhead on FR 24 but no other facilities.

Maps: USDA Pacific Crest Trail Washington Southern Portion.
Trail contacts: Gifford Pinchot National Forest, Wind River Ranger District, Mile Post 1.26 Hemlock Road, Carson, WA 98610; (509) 427-5645.
Mount Adams Ranger District, 2455 Highway 141, Trout Lake, WA 98650; (509) 395-3400; www.fs.fed.us/gpnf.

Finding the trailhead: Drive east from Portland on I-84 to the Cascade Locks (exit 44). Leave the freeway and cross the Bridge of the Gods over the Columbia River. Turn right at the north end of the bridge (east) onto State Route 14. Drive east on SR 14 for about 7 miles to the junction with Wind River Road, signed TO CARSON.

If you are coming from the east on I-84, leave the freeway at Hood River (exit 64). Cross the bridge over the Columbia River and turn west onto SR 14. Follow SR 14 west for 15 miles to the junction with Wind River Road.

Turn north through Carson and follow Wind River Road for 30.2 miles to Lone Butte Sno-park. From the sno-park, head northeast on Forest Road 30 for another 7.8 miles to the junction with FR 24. Turn right onto FR 24 and follow it 0.6 mile southeast to the trailhead at the point where the PCT crosses the road. The elevation at the trailhead on FR 24 is 4,270 feet.

To reach the trailhead on FR 521 where this hike ends, drive south from Seattle on I-5 to exit 133 at Tacoma and then follow Washington Highway 7 for 55 miles to Morton. From Morton drive east on U.S. Highway 12 for 17 miles to Randle. From Randle drive south on State Route 131 (may be signed TO FOREST ROAD 25) for 0.9 mile. Then turn left (east) onto Forest Road 23 and follow it east and south for 41.4 miles to the junction with FR 521. Turn left (northeast) onto FR 521 and go 0.3 mile to the trailhead.

Special Considerations

Late August and September is huckleberry picking time in the Sawtooth Fields, at the beginning of this hike. Remember that the berries on the east side of FR 24 (along the PCT described here) are reserved for Indians. Black bears are common all along this trail.

The Hike

The Pacific Crest Trail heads north through the huckleberry bushes, leaving the trailhead on FR 24. Here on the east side of FR 24, the Indians have exclusive rights to the berries, by treaty. Soon entering the forest, the route descends gently and turns to the northeast. You will have lost about 200 feet of elevation when you reach a saddle 1.4 miles from FR 24. From the saddle the tread climbs around the western slope of East Twin Butte to a broad saddle, at 4,270 feet elevation, between East and West Twin Buttes. Leaving the saddle the course descends generally to the northeast. As soon as the snow melts here, avalanche lilies push up their white showy heads from the forest floor, between the old-growth hemlocks. After crossing a tiny stream, the trail reaches Forest Road 8851, at 3,890 feet elevation, 3.9 miles from FR 24. There is a small parking area here a few yards north on FR 8851.

The PCT crosses FR 8851, continues to descend east, and soon crosses the outlet stream of Big Mosquito Lake (a fork of Mosquito Creek). As noted by the names, the mosquitoes can be very thick here. Leaving the creek the route climbs gently and works its way around a spur ridge. You will cross a roadbed at about 4,100 feet elevation 2.5 miles after crossing FR 8851. This road leads a short distance north to Forest Road 8854. The PCT continues northeast, descending into a small draw, with a stream that may be dry by late summer, in another 0.4 mile. In the draw is the junction with a side trail that heads north to Steamboat Lake. The PCT climbs slightly leaving the draw. It then quickly descends to another stream crossing before climbing a short distance to a rounded saddle and the junction with another side trail to Steamboat Lake. The side trails meet at Steamboat Lake Campground, so they can be used as an alternate, slightly longer route. Steamboat Lake Campground is quite small and has very limited facilities.

The PCT then winds through the forest, descending gently for 1.2 miles to the crossing of Forest Road 88 at 3,470 feet elevation, 8.8 miles from FR 24. Head north for a short distance on the road to pick up the trail on the far side. As you walk along the road, Mount Adams is in full view ahead. Leaving FR 88 the trail climbs slightly and then descends to Trout Lake Creek, at 3,310 feet elevation, 0.4 mile from FR 88. Shortly after crossing Trout Lake Creek, the route crosses Grand Meadows Creek. Across the creek the tread climbs to a ridgeline, crossing a roadbed about one third of the way up. You descend slightly to cross a small streambed, and then the route climbs steadily to reach Forest Road 8810, at 4,120 feet elevation, 2.1 miles from Trout Lake Creek and 11.3 miles from FR 24.

The trail crosses FR 8810 and continues to climb for another 0.6 mile east to a rounded ridgeline. Then you turn to the north-northeast and descend along the eastern slope of the ridge slightly below the crest for another 0.6 mile. Here the route recrosses the ridgeline, passing through a small opening called Dry Meadows.

◀ *Beargrass*

Pacific Crest Trail 2000, Forest Road 24 to Forest Road 521

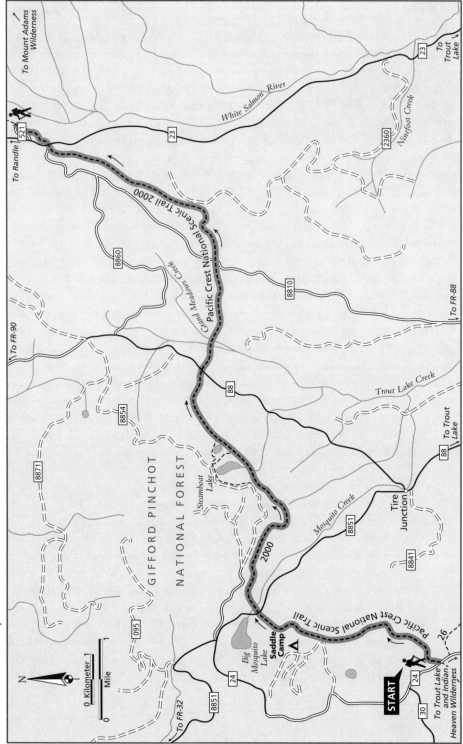

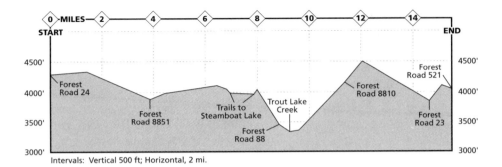

Intervals: Vertical 500 ft; Horizontal, 2 mi.

Then the trace descends the forested western slope of the ridge for 1.4 miles to the abandoned roadbed of Forest Road 120. Across FR 120 the track continues to descend for 0.7 mile to FR 8810. Turn right onto FR 8810 and walk a few yards to the junction with FR 23. The junction with FR 23 is 14.6 miles from FR 24, at 3,850 feet elevation.

The PCT crosses FR 23, soon crosses a stream, and climbs generally north, reaching 4,090 feet elevation before descending to the trailhead on FR 521. This trailhead, at 4,020 feet elevation, is 0.9 mile from FR 23 and 15.5 miles from FR 24 where this hike started.

Options

It is possible to continue north along the PCT on the east side of Mount Adams past Crystal Lake and Sheep Lake, below High Camp, and through Muddy Meadows to the PCT trailhead on Forest Road 115 for a 23.2 mile extension of this hike.

Miles and Directions

   0.0 PCT trailhead on FR 24 (GPS 46 05.505 N 121 45.960 W).

   3.9 Cross FR 8851 (GPS 46 07.490 N 121 45.194 W).

   8.8 Cross FR 88 (GPS 46 08.096 N 121 41.403 W).

   9.2 Trout Lake Creek.

  11.3 Cross FR 8810 (GPS 46 08.034 N 121 39.685 W).

  14.6 Cross FR 23.

  15.5 Trailhead on FR 521 (GPS 46 10.242 N 121 37.581W).

13 Langfield Falls Trail 8

A short hike to a beautiful waterfall.

Start: Langfield Falls trailhead.
Distance: 0.3-mile out-and-back day hike.
Difficulty: Easy.
Seasons: June through October.
Fees and permits: Northwest Forest Pass.
Parking and trailhead facilities: There is parking for several cars at the trailhead but no other facilities.
Maps: Sleeping Beauty USGS quad covers this area, but a topo map is not really necessary

for this short trail. The USDA Forest Service Gifford Pinchot National Forest map is a help when trying to find the trailhead.
Trail contacts: Gifford Pinchot National Forest, Wind River Ranger District, Mile Post 1.26 Hemlock Road, Carson, WA 98610; (509) 427-5645.
Mount Adams Ranger District, 2455 Highway 141, Trout Lake, WA 98650; (509) 395-3400; www.fs.fed.us/gpnf.

Finding the trailhead: Drive east from Portland on I-84 to exit 64 at the east edge of Hood River. Leave the freeway and head north across the Columbia River. At the junction with State Route 14 just north of the bridge, turn left and head west for 1.6 miles to the junction with State Route 141 Alternate, signed TO MOUNT ADAMS RECREATION AREA. Turn right at the junction and drive north for about 2.1 miles to the junction with State Route 141. Turn left at the junction and continue north on SR 141 for 18.9 miles to Trout Lake.

From the Y intersection next to the Chevron station in Trout Lake, head west (left), staying on SR 141 for 1.7 miles to the junction with Trout Lake Creek Road. Turn right (northwest) onto Trout Lake Creek Road, which becomes Forest Road 88 at the Gifford Pinchot National Forest boundary 4.3 miles ahead. Follow FR 88 until you are slightly more than 12 miles from SR 141 at Tire Junction. There is a large equipment tire in the center of the junction with flowers growing out of it. Turn right at Tire Junction and drive 0.1 mile northeast (still on FR 88) to Langfield Falls trailhead. The trailhead is on the right side of the road at 3,480 feet elevation.

Special Considerations

Children should be kept under close supervision on this trail, as falling from it is possible. This is a hikers-only trail.

The Hike

The wide, well-maintained trail descends east from the trailhead through a fairly large hemlock and Douglas fir forest. Just about 100 yards from the trailhead, the falls comes into view to the right as the path traverses a steep, wooded slope. Shortly, the route makes a right turn, descending some wooden steps. To your right is an informational sign and to the left a bench. Now, heading directly toward the beautiful falls, the tread continues to head down, soon reaching another bench, and ending a few feet farther along. The total elevation loss to the end of the trail is only about 70 feet.

Langfield Falls Trail 8

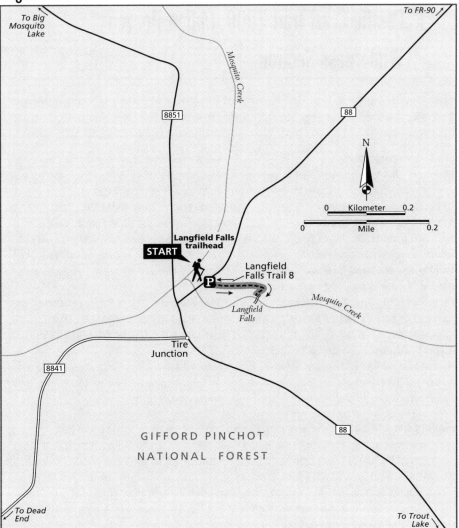

The second bench is at a viewpoint near the pool at the base of the falls. Early in the season (June), the force of the falls causes considerable mist, which carries well past this bench. A use path leads on down the last few feet to the edge of the pool, but much of the time it is muddy and slick.

Miles and Directions

0.0 Langfield Falls trailhead (GPS 46 05.936 N 121 43.209 W).

0.15 End of trail. Turnaround point.

0.3 Langfield Falls trailhead.

14 Pacific Crest Trail 2000, Indian Heaven Wilderness Section

Hike the Pacific Crest Trail (PCT) through the length of Indian Heaven Wilderness. Much of this trail is not very scenic, but it gives access to many side trails that are.

Start: Crest Camp trailhead.

Distance: 16.4-mile one-way shuttle, two- or three-day backpack, or long day hike.

Difficulty: Easy to moderate.

Seasons: July through September.

Fees and permits: Northwest Forest Pass and Indian Heaven Wilderness Permit.

Parking and trailhead facilities: There is parking for several cars, rest rooms, and a few campsites at the Crest Camp trailhead. The trailhead on Forest Road 24 has only a few parking spots.

Maps: USDA Forest Service Pacific Crest National Scenic Trail Washington Southern Portion and USDA Forest Service Indian Heaven and Trapper Creek Wilderness. Both of the Forest Service maps have some small inaccuracies in spots. USGS Gifford Peak and Lone Butte quads also cover this area.

If you plan to camp in the Blue Lake area, you also will need the USDA Forest Service brochure *Indian Heaven Wilderness Helpful Hints For Camping in Designated Sites.* This brochure contains a map of the designated sites.

Trail contacts: Gifford Pinchot National Forest, Wind River Ranger District, Mile Post 1.26 Hemlock Road, Carson, WA 98610; (509) 427–5645.

Mount Adams Ranger District, 2455 Highway 141, Trout Lake, WA 98650; (509) 395–3400; www.fs.fed.us/gpnf.

Finding the trailhead: Drive east from Portland on I–84 to the Cascade Locks (exit 44). Leave the freeway and cross the Bridge of the Gods over the Columbia River. Turn right at the north end of the bridge (east) onto State Route 14. Drive east on SR 14 for about 7 miles to the junction with Wind River Road, signed TO CARSON.

If you are coming from the east on I–84, leave the freeway at Hood River (exit 64). Cross the bridge over the Columbia River and turn west onto SR 14. Follow SR 14 west for 15 miles to the junction with Wind River Road.

Turn north and drive 1 mile to Carson. Head north from Carson on Wind River Road for 4.8 miles to the junction with Forest Road 65, signed TO PANTHER CREEK CAMPGROUND. Turn right onto FR 65 and in a short distance turn left, staying on FR 65 and following the signs toward Panther Creek Campground, which you will pass in about 2 miles. You will reach a four-way junction with Forest Road 60 a little more than 11 miles from Wind River Road. This junction is called "Four Corners."

Turn right onto FR 60 and drive east for 2 miles to Crest Camp trailhead, at 3,500 feet elevation.

To reach the trailhead on FR 24 where this hike ends, first backtrack to the junction with FR 65. Turn right (north) onto FR 65 and follow it for 8.2 miles to the junction with Forest Road 6507. Forest Road 65 turns to gravel 1.9 miles north of Four Corners.

Blue Lake

Turn left onto FR 6507 and drive 4.2 miles to the junction with Forest Road 30 (Wind River Road). Turn right onto FR 30 and go 9 miles northeast to the junction with FR 24. Turn right onto FR 24 and in 0.6 mile you will reach the trailhead where the PCT crosses FR 24.

Special Considerations

Mosquitoes are terrible in July and early August.

The Hike

Heading north from Crest Camp, the PCT crosses FR 60 and climbs very gently through the forest of western hemlock and fir. The well-maintained course crosses several streambeds before reaching Sheep Lake, at 4,020 feet elevation, 1.6 miles from Crest Camp. Sheep Lake is just a small, grass-choked pond on the west side of the trail. Slightly more than 1 mile past Sheep Lake, the trace passes Green Lake, which is on the right (east) side of the path. Green Lake, at 4,250 feet elevation, is larger than Sheep Lake. Beyond Green Lake the trail crosses a meadow and then wanders through the woods to reach the signed junction with Shortcut Trail 171A, 3.2 miles from Crest Camp. Shortcut Trail turns left (west) to join Racetrack Trail 171 at the Indian Racetrack a little less than a mile away.

Bear right (straight ahead) at the junction and continue to climb gently for about another 0.4 mile north. The route then makes a switchback as it begins to ascend the northern end of Berry Mountain. The trail climbs the south-facing, semi-open slopes covered with huckleberries, juniper, and small lodgepole pine. Climb several ascending switchbacks before reaching the crest of Berry Mountain at about 4,800 feet elevation. As you climb, Red Mountain and Mount Hood come into view to the south. The route generally follows the crest of Berry Mountain north for 1.8 miles, crossing the ridgeline several times and reaching nearly 5,000 feet elevation at one point. Looking to the northeast from the viewpoints along the ridge, Mount Adams rises above the forested hills.

The tread then descends the north end of Berry Mountain to reach the junction with the route to Tombstone Lake on the shore of Blue Lake. Tombstone Lake is to the right (east). The area around Blue and Tombstone Lakes is a "designated campsite zone"; you must either find a designated campsite in the area or camp elsewhere. The Forest Service publishes a brochure with aerial photograph maps showing the designated sites. If you plan to camp here, pick up one of these brochures from a ranger station before you begin your hike.

Just past the Tombstone Lake Trail, you will reach the junction with Thomas Lake Trail 111, at 4,650 feet elevation, 7.4 miles from Crest Camp.

Bear right at the junction, hike northeast, and soon pass a side path to the left, which leads a few yards to a large pond. A short distance farther along, there are a couple of side paths to the right leading downhill to another larger pond. The track climbs gently, reaching 4,920 feet elevation as it crosses a small, rounded ridgeline on the west side of East Crater, 0.9 mile from Blue Lake. You then traverse the western and northern slopes of East Crater before descending to the junction with East Crater Trail 48, at Junction Lake. Around the shoreline of Junction Lake, at 4,730 feet elevation, are several campsites and lots of flower-covered meadow.

The PCT continues north from the junction and crosses a wooden bridge in a few yards. Just after crossing the bridge, and 9.1 miles from Crest Camp, Lemei Lake Trail 179 turns to the right. Hike north from the junction, crossing a meadow before entering the timber. The track crosses a rough, steep streambed 0.3 mile from the Lemei Lake Trail and then contours along a wooded slope for another 0.3 mile to cross Rush Creek. Rush Creek is the outlet stream from Lemei Lake. It usually has water, but some years it may be dry in late summer and fall.

Bear Lake comes into view 0.4 mile after crossing Rush Creek. Just before reaching the lake, the Elk Lake Trail leaves the PCT and heads northwest to Elk Lake. Bear Lake, at 4,740 feet elevation and 10.2 miles from Crest Camp, has a few campsites along its south shore. The trail heading north-northeast from near this junction is an abandoned section of the old Cascade Crest Trail.

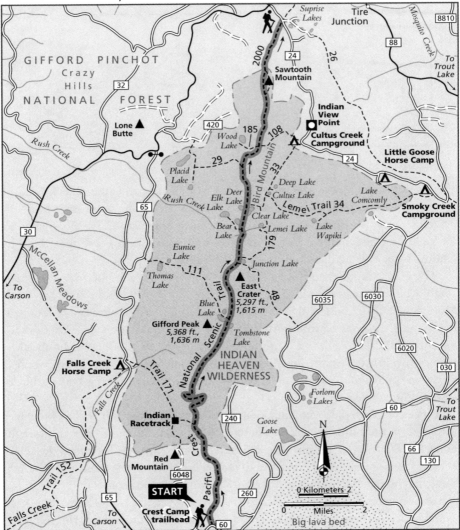

The PCT heads north above the eastern shore of Bear Lake and then traverses a west-facing slope for 0.6 mile, passing above and east of Deer Lake to the junction with Indian Heaven Trail 33. From this junction at 4,900 feet elevation, the Indian Heaven Trail heads east to join Lemei Lake Trail. Slightly more than 1 mile farther north, the PCT crosses a wooden bridge and reaches the junction with Placid Lake Trail 29. From this junction at 5,010 feet elevation, Placid Lake Trail descends west to Placid Lake and Forest Road 420.

One-half mile after passing the junction with Placid Lake Trail, a path bears to the left off the PCT. This path is a shortcut to Wood Lake, and it joins the Wood Lake Trail in a short distance. The main trail then contours around a hillside, well

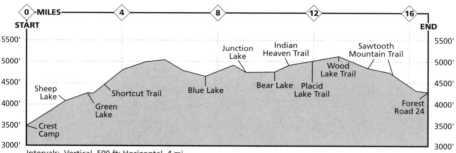

Intervals: Vertical, 500 ft; Horizontal, 4 mi.

above a pond, and reaches the junction with Wood Lake and Cultus Creek Trails in another 0.4 mile. From the junction, at 5,130 feet elevation, Wood Lake Trail 185 descends to the left (southwest then northwest), reaching Wood Lake in 0.6 mile. To the right (northeast) Cultus Creek Trail 108 climbs over a ridge and then drops to Cultus Creek Campground on FR 24 in 1.6 miles.

The PCT continues north from the junction, first along a forested slope and then along a broad timbered saddle for 1.2 miles to the first junction with Sawtooth Mountain Trail 107. Sawtooth Mountain Trail is a more scenic alternate to the PCT for the next 1.2 miles. Sawtooth Mountain Trail is also more strenuous than this section of the PCT. To continue north on the PCT, bear left (nearly straight-ahead to the north-northwest) at the junction (elevation 4,850 feet) and traverse the wooded west slope of Sawtooth Mountain. Along the more open parts of this traverse, huckleberries line the route.

Once you reach the second junction with Sawtooth Mountain Trail, at 4,610 feet elevation on the northern end of Sawtooth Mountain, the route starts to descend. Soon the PCT leaves Indian Heaven Wilderness. As you lose elevation the forest becomes more open. Mountain ash and huckleberry bushes cover much of the landscape, and lupine blooms between the bushes. Mount Adams comes into view to the east as you enter the famous Sawtooth Huckleberry Fields. Native Americans have gathered berries here for centuries, and the tradition continues today. You reach the trailhead, at 4,270 feet elevation, on FR 24, 1.2 miles after passing the northern junction with Sawtooth Mountain Trail.

Options

It is possible to continue north on the PCT, past Steamboat Lake, to the PCT trailhead on Forest Road 521, for a 15.5-mile extension of this hike.

Miles and Directions

0.0 Crest Camp trailhead (GPS 45 54.552 N 121 48.130 W).

2.7 Green Lake.

3.2   Junction with Shortcut Trail 171A (GPS 45 56.755 N 121 48.750 W). Continue straight on the PCT.

7.4   Blue Lake and junction with Thomas Lake Trail 111 (GPS 45 59.051 N 121 47.715 W). Stay right (northeast).

9.1   Junction Lake and junction with East Crater Trail 48 (GPS 46 00.309 N 121 47.342 W). Continue north on the PCT. Junction with Lemei Lake Trail 179. Stay left (north).

10.2   Bear Lake and junction with Elk Lake Trail 176. Stay right (north) on the PCT.

10.8   Junction with Indian Heaven Trail 33 (GPS 46 01.526 N 121 47.182 W). Stay left (north).

11.9   Junction with Placid Lake Trail 29 (GPS 46 02.284 N 121 47.161 W). Stay right (north).

12.8   Junction with Wood Lake Trail 185 and Cultus Creek Trail 108 (GPS 46 02.800 N 121 46.675 W). Continue north on the PCT.

14.0   First junction with Sawtooth Mountain Trail 107 (GPS 46 03.663 N 121 46.441 W). Continue straight (north-northwest). **Option:** For a more scenic and more strenuous route, stay right over Sawtooth Mountain.

15.2   Second junction with Sawtooth Mountain Trail 107 (GPS 46 04.697 N 121 46.318 W). Continue straight (north).

16.4   Pacific Crest Trail 2000 trailhead on FR 24 (GPS 46 05.505 N 121 45.960 W).

15 Sawtooth Mountain Trail 107

Hike near the open crest of Sawtooth Mountain as an alternate to a fairly boring section of the Pacific Crest Trail (PCT).

Start: Junction of Sawtooth Mountain Trail and the Pacific Crest Trail; nearest trailhead is the PCT trailhead on Forest Road 24.
Distance: 1.2-mile internal alternate for the PCT; 2.4 miles one-way from the PCT trailhead on FR 24.
Difficulty: Strenuous.
Seasons: Mid-July through September.
Fees and permits: Indian Heaven Wilderness Permit. Depending on where your car is parked, you may also need a Northwest Forest Pass.

Maps: USDA Forest Service Trapper Creek and Indian Heaven Wilderness or Lone Butte USGS quad.
Trail contacts: Gifford Pinchot National Forest, Wind River Ranger District, Mile Post 1.26 Hemlock Road, Carson, WA 98610; (509) 427-5645.
Mount Adams Ranger District, 2455 Highway 141, Trout Lake, WA 98650; (509) 395-3400; www.fs.fed.us/gpnf.

Finding the trailhead: This description of the Sawtooth Mountain Trail is from north to south. To reach the trail junction where this hike begins, drive east from Portland on I-84 to the Cascade Locks (exit 44). Leave the freeway and cross the Bridge of the Gods over the Columbia River. Turn right at the north end of the bridge (east) onto State Route 14. Drive east on SR 14 for about 7 miles to the junction with Wind River Road, signed TO CARSON.

If you are coming from the east on I-84, leave the freeway at Hood River (exit 64). Cross the bridge over the Columbia River and turn west onto SR 14. Follow SR 14 west for 15 miles to the junction with Wind River Road.

Turn north through Carson and follow Wind River Road for 30.2 miles to Lone Butte Sno-park. From the sno-park, head northeast on Forest Road 30 for another 7.8 miles to the junction with FR 24. Turn right onto FR 24 and follow it 0.6 mile southeast to the trailhead at the point where the PCT crosses the road. Hike south on the PCT for 1.2 miles to the junction with the Sawtooth Mountain Trail. The junction, which has no sign, is at the point where the PCT turns west. The elevation at the junction is 4,610 feet.

Special Considerations

The side trip to the summit of Sawtooth Mountain requires rock-climbing skills to be done safely. There is no water available along the Sawtooth Mountain Trail.

The Hike

As you leave the PCT, the Sawtooth Mountain Trail climbs to the south through small timber. Between the trees mountain ash and huckleberry bushes cover much of the terrain. Avalanche lilies grow in the spots not covered by brush and trees. The track makes two switchbacks and reaches the northern ridgeline of Sawtooth

Sawtooth Mountain

Mountain 0.4 mile after leaving the PCT. You then switchback several more times as you climb the ridge, with Mount Adams in view to the northeast. Two-tenths of a mile farther along, the course begins to traverse the western slope of Sawtooth Mountain. These semi-open slopes dotted with subalpine fir and hemlock offer some great views to the west. A short path leads to the right to the top of an outcrop, where the view is even better. Mount St. Helens stands above the foothills in the distance.

In a short distance, the route again reaches the ridgeline of Sawtooth Mountain. Here a poor path turns to the left. This path leads up the ridge to the rocky 5,330-foot-high pinnacle that is the south peak of Sawtooth Mountain. To reach the very top, it is necessary to make a short class 3 climb over nearly vertical, unstable rock, with some exposure. This is not the place to let children climb. Even without climbing the rock at the top, this is a worthwhile side trip. Near the top rocks, hot pink penstemon bloom in mid-July, and most of the open slopes are covered with a variety of other flowers.

After passing the path to the south peak, the track makes a couple of switchbacks as it descends a red cinder–covered slope. You then continue down the ridge, where

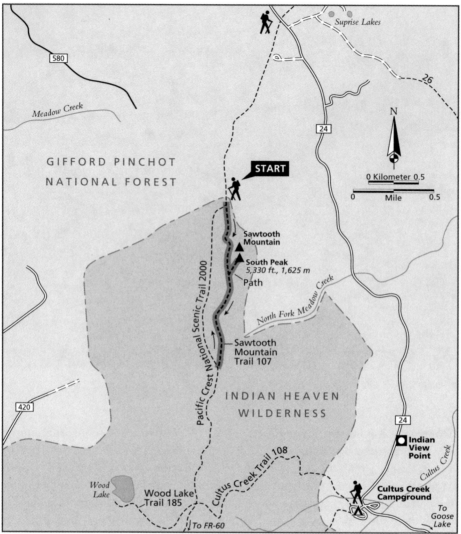

the path is sometimes overgrown with huckleberries, to the junction with the PCT, at 4,850 feet elevation.

Options

Make a lollipop loop by hiking from FR 24 on the PCT to the junction with Sawtooth Mountain Trail. Then follow Sawtooth Mountain Trail as described above and return north on the PCT.

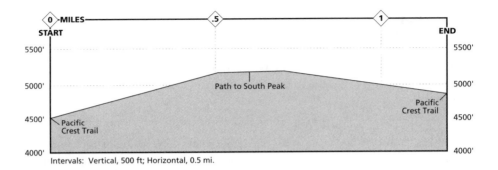

Intervals: Vertical, 500 ft; Horizontal, 0.5 mi.

Miles and Directions

0.0 Junction of PCT and the Sawtooth Mountain Trail (GPS 46 04.697 N 121 46.318 W).

0.7 Path to the south peak.

1.2 Junction with PCT (GPS 46 03.663 N 121 46.441 W).

16 Cultus Creek Trail 108

Cultus Creek Trail offers lots of flowers and an excellent view of Mount Adams as well as the shortest access route to the Pacific Crest Trail (PCT) in the Indian Heaven Wilderness.

Start: Cultus Creek trailhead.
Distance: 3.2-mile out-and-back day hike or backpack.
Difficulty: Strenuous.
Seasons: Mid-July through September. Snow may linger into late July in places.
Fees and permits: Northwest Forest Pass and Indian Heaven Wilderness Permit.
Parking and trailhead facilities: There is a campground, rest rooms, and adequate parking at the trailhead.

Maps: USDA Forest Service Indian Heaven and Trapper Creek Wilderness or Lone Butte USGS quad.
Trail contacts: Gifford Pinchot National Forest, Wind River Ranger District, Mile Post 1.26 Hemlock Road, Carson, WA 98610; (509) 427-5645.
Mount Adams Ranger District, 2455 Highway 141, Trout Lake, WA 98650; (509) 395-3400; www.fs.fed.us/gpnf.

Finding the trailhead: Take I-84 east from Portland to exit 64, at the east edge of Hood River. Leave the freeway and head north across the Columbia River. At the junction with State Route 14 just north of the bridge, turn left and drive west for 1.6 miles to the junction with State Route 141 Alternate, signed TO MOUNT ADAMS RECREATION AREA. Turn right at the junction onto SR 141 Alt and drive north for about 2.1 miles to the junction with State Route 141. Turn left at the junction and continue north on SR 141 for 18.9 miles to Trout Lake.

From Trout Lake drive west then southwest, staying on SR 141. After 5.8 miles SR 141 becomes Forest Road 24 at the Gifford Pinchot National Forest boundary. Continue southwest on FR 24 for 2.2 more miles to Peterson Prairie and the junction with Forest Road 60. Turn right (north) at the junction and stay on the now-gravel-surfaced FR 24. Nine miles from Peterson Prairie, Cultus Creek Campground and trailhead will be on your left.

Cultus Creek Trail starts at the northeast end of Cultus Creek Campground, near FR 24. This is not the same starting point as Indian Heaven Trail, which begins at the southwest end of the campground. The elevation at the trailhead is 4,000 feet.

Special Considerations

Mosquitoes are terrible in July and early August.

The Hike

Leaving the Cultus Creek Campground, the trail climbs through mixed fir and hemlock forest. Huckleberry bushes encroach on the tread as it gains altitude. A small metal sign lets you know you are entering Indian Heaven Wilderness 0.2 mile

Leopard lily

from the trailhead. Lupine, paintbrush, phlox, and avalanche lilies bloom in the openings in mid-July, and occasionally leopard lilies pop up, adding their festive orange color.

About 1.2 miles from the trailhead, the woods open up and allow a view to the northeast of the huge, bulky, humped form of Mount Adams. You cross a ridgeline at about 5,200 feet elevation 1.5 miles from the trailhead. This ridge is the summit of the Cascade Mountains. The course then descends for 0.1 mile to a junction with the Pacific Crest Trail.

Options

To make a loop, combine this hike with a section of the PCT and Indian Heaven Trail. Turn left (south) onto the PCT and hike for 2 miles to the junction with the Indian Heaven Trail. Turn left onto the Indian Heaven Trail and hike 3.2 miles northeast, back to the Cultus Creek Campground and trailhead.

Cultus Creek Trail 108

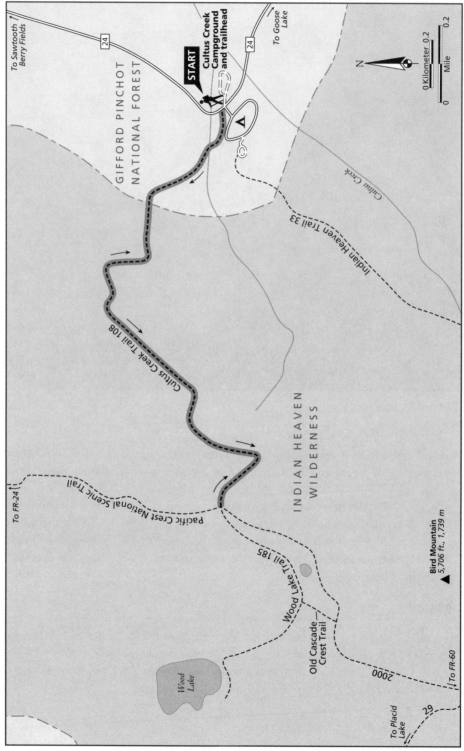

GIFFORD PINCHOT NATIONAL FOREST

START
Cultus Creek Campground and trailhead

To Sawtooth Berry Fields

24

To Goose Lake

24

Cultus Creek

Indian Heaven Trail 33

INDIAN HEAVEN WILDERNESS

Cultus Creek Trail 108

Bird Mountain
5,706 ft., 1,739 m

Pacific Crest National Scenic Trail

To FR-24

Wood Lake Trail 185

Old Cascade Crest Trail

Wood Lake

2000

To FR-60

29

To Placid Lake

N

0 Kilometer 0.2
0 Mile 0.2

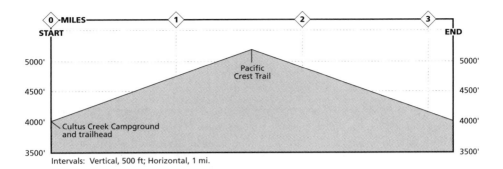

Intervals: Vertical, 500 ft; Horizontal, 1 mi.

Wood Lake makes a good destination if you are not making the loop hike. The trail to Wood Lake starts directly across the PCT from where you reached it via Cultus Creek Trail.

Miles and Directions

0.0 Cultus Creek trailhead (GPS 46 02.878 N 121 45.334 W).

1.6 Junction with Pacific Crest Trail 2000 (GPS 46 02.800 N 121 46.675 W). Turnaround point.

3.2 Cultus Creek trailhead.

17 Wood Lake Trail 185

A short side trip to a pretty little mountain lake.

Start: Junction of Wood Lake Trail and the Pacific Crest Trail (PCT); nearest trailhead is Cultus Creek trailhead on Forest Road 24.
Distance: 1.2-mile out-and-back day hike or backpack from the junction of Wood Lake Trail and the PCT; 4.4 miles round-trip from Cultus Creek trailhead.
Difficulty: Easy.
Seasons: Mid-July through September.
Fees and permits: A Northwest Forest Pass is required for parking at most of the trailheads with trails leading into Indian Heaven Wilderness. You also need an Indian Heaven Wilderness Permit.

Maps: USDA Forest Service Indian Heaven and Trapper Creek Wilderness, or Lone Butte USGS quad. The Forest Service map shows the junction of the Pacific Crest and Wood Lake Trails somewhat incorrectly.
Trail contacts: Gifford Pinchot National Forest, Wind River Ranger District, Mile Post 1.26 Hemlock Road, Carson, WA 98610; (509) 427-5645.
Mount Adams Ranger District, 2455 Highway 141, Trout Lake, WA 98650; (509) 395-3400; www.fs.fed.us/gpnf.

Finding the trailhead: The Wood Lake Trail begins at a junction with the Pacific Crest Trail 3.6 miles south of FR 24. This junction with the PCT is shared with the Cultus Creek Trail coming up from Cultus Lake. The closest way to reach the beginning of the Wood Lake Trail is to drive to Cultus Creek Campground and trailhead and then hike Cultus Creek Trail for 1.6 miles to the junction with the PCT and Wood Lake Trail, at about 5,100 feet elevation. Following the PCT south from FR 24 is an easier but longer hike.

Drive east from Portland on I-84 to exit 64 at the east edge of Hood River. Leave the freeway and head north across the Columbia River. At the junction with State Route 14 just north of the bridge, turn left and head west for 1.6 miles to the junction with State Route 141 Alternate, signed TO MOUNT ADAMS RECREATION AREA. Turn right at the junction onto SR 141 Alt and drive north for about 2.1 miles to the junction with State Route 141. Turn left at the junction and continue north on SR 141 for 18.9 miles to Trout Lake.

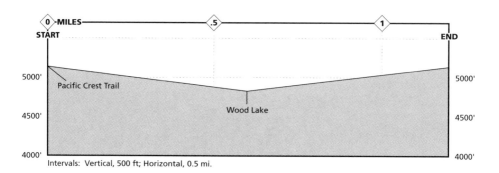

Avalanche lilies

From Trout Lake drive west then southwest, staying on SR 141. After 5.8 miles SR 141 becomes FR 24 at the Gifford Pinchot National Forest boundary. Continue southwest on FR 24 for 2.2 miles to Peterson Prairie and the junction with Forest Road 60. Turn right (north) at the junction and stay on the now-gravel-surfaced FR 24. Cultus Creek Campground and trailhead will be on your left 9 miles from Peterson Prairie.

Special Considerations

Mosquitoes are terrible in July and early August.

The Hike

The Wood Lake Trail descends from the PCT, heading southwest to a meadow that contains a melt pond. Early in the season (late July) the route may be under water as it passes the pond. The water can be avoided by passing the meadow on the right. Next to the pond the trail makes a hard right turn to head northwest. Another path

Wood Lake Trail 185

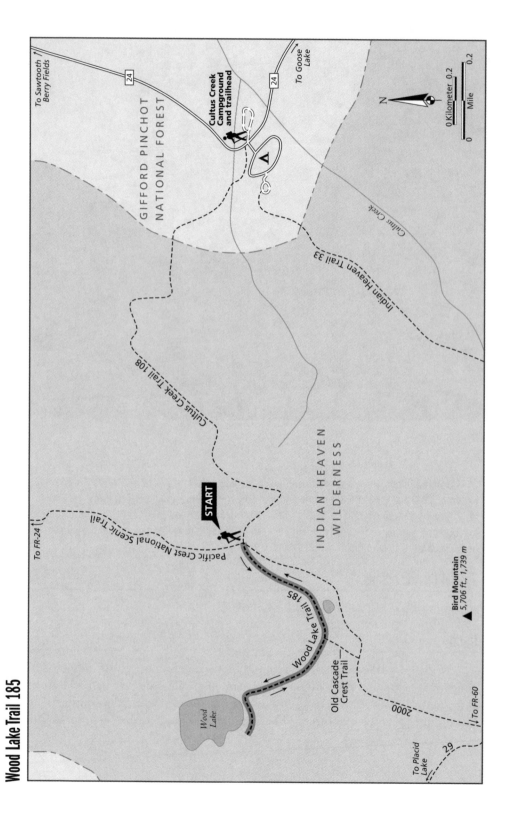

(part of the old Cascade Crest Trail) continues southwest to rejoin the PCT. Turn right and hike the 0.4 mile to Wood Lake.

Wood Lake, at 4,860 feet elevation, makes a good out-of-the-way campsite while hiking the PCT. Avalanche lilies bloom along the shore in late July and August.

Options

Combine the Wood Lake Trail with Cultus Creek Trail for an excellent out-and-back day hike.

Miles and Directions

0.0 Junction of Wood Lake Trail and the PCT (GPS 46 02.800 N 121 46.675 W).

0.6 Wood Lake (GPS 46 02.885 N 121 47.129 W). Turnaround point.

1.2 Junction of Wood Lake Trail and the PCT.

18 Placid Lake Trail 29

Without losing or gaining much elevation, hike to Placid Lake. Then climb the moderate grade to the views and flower-covered meadows next to the Pacific Crest Trail (PCT).

Start: Placid Lake trailhead.
Distance: 5.6-mile out-and-back day hike or backpack.
Difficulty: Moderate.
Seasons: Mid-July through September.
Fees and permits: Northwest Forest Pass and Indian Heaven Wilderness Permit.
Parking and trailhead facilities: There is adequate parking and a couple of campsites available at the trailhead.

Maps: USDA Forest Service Indian Heaven and Trapper Creek Wilderness or Lone Butte USGS quad.
Trail contacts: Gifford Pinchot National Forest, Wind River Ranger District, Mile Post 1.26 Hemlock Road, Carson, WA 98610; (509) 427-5645.
Mount Adams Ranger District, 2455 Highway 141, Trout Lake, WA 98650; (509) 395-3400; www.fs.fed.us/gpnf.

Finding the trailhead: On I-84 drive east from Portland to Cascade Locks. Get off the freeway at exit 44 and cross the Bridge of the Gods over the Columbia River. Turn right (east) at the north end of the bridge onto State Route 14. Follow SR 14 for about 7 miles to the junction with Wind River Road, signed TO CARSON.

If you are coming from the east on I-84, leave the freeway at Hood River (exit 64). Cross the bridge over the Columbia River and turn west onto SR 14. Follow SR 14 west for 15 miles to the junction with Wind River Road.

Turn north through Carson and follow Wind River Road for 30.2 miles to Lone Butte Sno-park. From the sno-park head northeast on Forest Road 30 for 2.3 miles to the junction with Forest Road 420. Turn right (east) onto FR 420 and follow it 1.2 miles to Placid Lake trailhead. The elevation at the trailhead is 4,100 feet.

Special Considerations

Take your bug repellent, because mosquitoes can be very thick during July and early August. If you plan to camp, be sure you have a bug-proof tent.

The Hike

The wide, smooth Placid Lake Trail crosses a wooden bridge as it leaves the trailhead. The Indian Heaven Wilderness boundary is quickly passed as you hike southwest through the fir and hemlock forest. Soon the route begins to descend very gently. The trail forks 0.5 mile from the trailhead, at 4,040 feet elevation. The fork to the right (nearly straight-ahead) crosses a tiny meadow and reaches Placid Lake's northwest corner in a few yards. Turn left at the fork and soon come to another fork.

Placid Lake

Bear left at the second fork and head northeast. Soon the track crosses a small stream and climbs gently south to the junction with Chenamus Lake Trail (elevation 4,180 feet). Hiking straight ahead at the junction will take you to Chenamus Lake. See Options for the details.

Turn left at the junction and climb to the east. The track climbs 510 feet in the next 0.9 mile, where there will be a pond on your left. The course crosses the top of a talus slope with a view to the west of Mount St. Helens in another 0.4 mile. After crossing the talus the path soon crosses a small stream then flattens out at about 4,900 feet elevation as it crosses a meadow. Once across the meadow you climb a few feet to reach the junction with the Pacific Crest Trail at 4,970 feet elevation, 2.8 miles from the trailhead.

Options

Hike the 0.5 mile to Chenamus Lake as a side trip from the Placid Lake Trail, or make it your destination. The trail is smooth and nearly flat to start. It then crosses a

Placid Lake Trail 29

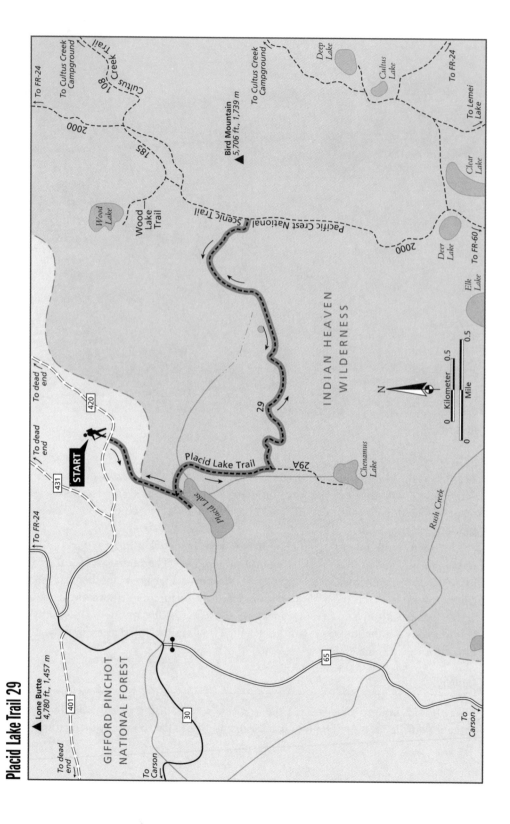

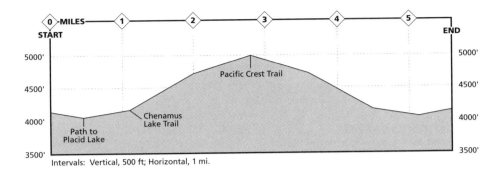

Intervals: Vertical, 500 ft; Horizontal, 1 mi.

creek and becomes rough and rocky for a few yards before entering a wet meadow next to the lake. Beargrass and avalanche lilies line the trail most of the way. Watch for Roosevelt elk around the lake.

Miles and Directions

0.0 Placid Lake trailhead (GPS 46 02.926 N 121 48.549 W).

0.5 Path to Placid Lake (GPS 46 02.636 N 121 48.933 W). Turn left at the fork. Bear left at a second fork and head northeast.

1.1 Junction with Chenamus Lake Trail 29A (GPS 46 02.228 N 121 48.517 W). Turn left and climb to the east.

2.8 Junction with Pacific Crest Trail 2000 (GPS 46 02.284 N 121 47.161 W). Turnaround point.

5.6 Placid Lake trailhead.

19 Indian Heaven Trail 33

Mountain views and pristine meadows dotted with alpine flowers await you as you hike into Indian Heaven Wilderness via Indian Heaven Trail.

Start: Cultus Creek trailhead
Distance: 6.4-mile out-and-back day hike or backpack.
Difficulty: Moderate.
Seasons: Mid-July through September.
Fees and permits: Northwest Forest Pass and Indian Heaven Wilderness Permit.
Parking and trailhead facilities: There is a campground and adequate parking at the trailhead.

Maps: USDA Forest Service Indian Heaven and Trapper Creek Wilderness or Lone Butte USGS quad.
Trail contacts: Gifford Pinchot National Forest, Wind River Ranger District, Mile Post 1.26 Hemlock Road, Carson, WA 98610; (509) 427-5645.
Mount Adams Ranger District, 2455 Highway 141, Trout Lake, WA 98650; (509) 395-3400; www.fs.fed.us/gpnf.

Finding the trailhead: Drive east from Portland on I-84 to exit 64 at the east edge of Hood River. Leave the freeway and head north across the Columbia River. At the junction with State Route 14 just north of the bridge, turn left and head west for 1.6 miles to the junction with State Route 141 Alternate, signed TO MOUNT ADAMS RECREATION AREA. Turn right at the junction onto State Route 141 Alt and drive north for about 2.1 miles to the junction with State Route 141. Turn left at the junction and continue north on SR 141 for 18.9 miles to Trout Lake.

From Trout Lake drive west then southwest, staying on SR 141. After 5.8 miles SR 141 becomes Forest Road 24 at the Gifford Pinchot National Forest boundary. Continue southwest on FR 24 for 2.2 miles to Peterson Prairie and the junction with Forest Road 60. Turn right (north) at the junction and stay on the now-gravel-surfaced FR 24. Cultus Creek Campground and trailhead will be on your left 9 miles from Peterson Prairie. The trailhead is at 4,030 feet elevation at the southwest end of the campground. This is not the same trailhead as Cultus Creek Trail 108, which begins at the northeast end of the campground.

Special Considerations

Mosquitoes may be very aggressive in July and early August.

The Hike

Hike southwest from the parking area at the southwest corner of Cultus Creek Campground. The route crosses a creek and a little farther along begins to climb at a moderate rate. Soon views of Mount Adams appear through the trees to the northeast. Cultus Creek rushes over a small waterfall to your left 0.8 mile from the trailhead. The route then climbs above the creekbed. At a switchback, 1 mile into the hike, there is an excellent viewpoint at 4,800 feet elevation on the right side of the

Cultus Lake

trail. Mount Adams is close by to the northeast, and to its left Goat Rocks are in the distance. To the north, craggy, ice-sheathed 14,410-foot-high Mount Rainier lifts its blunt dome far above the surrounding terrain.

The tread climbs west leaving the viewpoint and then turns south to traverse the meadows below Bird Mountain. You reach the junction with Deep Lake Trail 33A 2.3 miles from the trailhead, at 5,060 feet elevation. Deep Lake Trail is to the left (east) at the junction. The route then follows the western shore of Cultus Lake to the junction with Lemei Trail 34, which also heads east. There are several campsites around Cultus Lake.

Bear right at the junction with Lemei Trail and hike first west then southwest for 0.3 mile to the junction with Lemei Lake Trail 179. Lemei Lake Trail turns left (south-southeast) at the junction to descend to Lemei Lake. Just after the junction the Indian Heaven Trail passes Clear Lake, crossing a talus slope above its north shore. Pikas inhabit these rocks and may make their shrill call as you pass. Soon after passing Clear Lake, the path descends to meet the Pacific Crest Trail at 4,900 feet elevation and 3.2 miles from Cultus Creek Campground and trailhead.

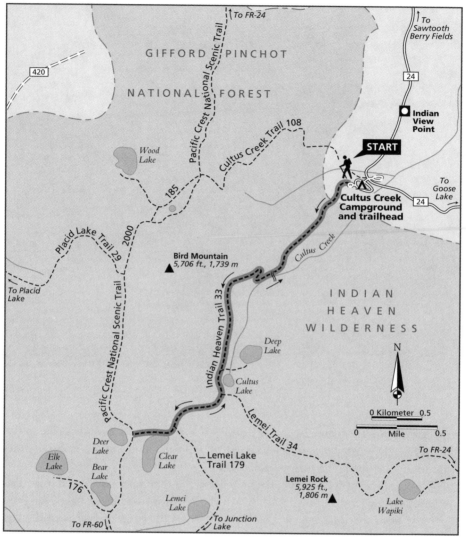

Options

Make a loop by hiking north for 2 miles on the PCT to the junction with Cultus Creek Trail and then following it back to Cultus Creek Campground.

Another option is to take the side trip to Deep Lake. Mount Adams towering over Deep Lake makes an excellent photo.

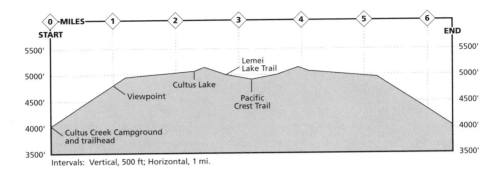

Intervals: Vertical, 500 ft; Horizontal, 1 mi.

Miles and Directions

0.0 Cultus Creek trailhead (GPS 46 02.804 N 121 45.398 W).

1.0 Viewpoint.

2.3 Junction with Deep Lake Trail 33A.

2.4 Cultus Lake.

2.5 Junction with Lemei Trail 34 (GPS 46 01.687 N 121 46.443 W).

2.8 Junction with Lemei Lake Trail 179 (GPS 46 01.526 N 121 46.744 W).

3.0 Clear Lake.

3.2 Junction with Pacific Crest Trail 2000 (GPS 46 01.526 N 121 47.182 W). Turnaround point.

6.4 Cultus Creek trailhead.

20 Deep Lake Trail 33A

A short side trip to a beautiful lake that often mirrors Mount Adams on its still surface.

Start: Junction of Indian Heaven Trail 33 and Deep Lake Trail 33A; nearest trailhead is Cultus Creek trailhead on Forest Road 24.
Distance: 0.4-mile internal out-and-back day hike or backpack; 5.0 miles round-trip from Cultus Creek trailhead.
Difficulty: Easy.
Seasons: August through September.
Fees and permits: Indian Heaven Wilderness Permit. A Northwest Forest Pass is required if you are parking at most trailheads around the perimeter of Indian Heaven Wilderness.

Maps: USDA Forest Service Indian Heaven and Trapper Creek Wilderness or Lone Butte USGS quad.
Trail contacts: Gifford Pinchot National Forest, Wind River Ranger District, Mile Post 1.26 Hemlock Road, Carson, WA 98610; (509) 427-5645.
Mount Adams Ranger District, 2455 Highway 141, Trout Lake, WA 98650; (509) 395-3400; www.fs.fed.us/gpnf.

Finding the trailhead: Drive east from Portland on I-84 to exit 64 at the east edge of Hood River. Leave the freeway and head north across the Columbia River. At the junction with State Route 14 just north of the bridge, turn left and head west for 1.6 miles to the junction with State Route 141 Alternate, signed TO MOUNT ADAMS RECREATION AREA. Turn right at the junction onto SR 141 Alt and drive north for about 2.1 miles to the junction with State Route 141. Turn left at the junction and continue north on SR 141 for 18.9 miles to Trout Lake.

From Trout Lake drive west then southwest, staying on SR 141. After 5.8 miles SR 141 becomes FR 24 at the Gifford Pinchot National Forest boundary. Continue southwest on FR 24 for 2.2 miles to Peterson Prairie and the junction with Forest Road 60. Turn right (north) at the junction and stay on the now-gravel-surfaced FR 24. Cultus Creek Campground and trailhead will be on your left 9 miles from Peterson Prairie. The trailhead is at 4,030 feet elevation at the southwest end of the campground. This is not the same trailhead as Cultus Creek Trail 108, which begins at the northeast end of the campground.

Hike southwest on Indian Heaven Trail for 2.3 miles to the junction with Deep Lake Trail near Cultus Lake.

Special Considerations

Mosquitoes are terrible in July and early August.

The Hike

Hike northeast from the junction across a small meadow. Shortly you cross a wooden bridge over Cultus Creek as the creek emerges from the northern end of

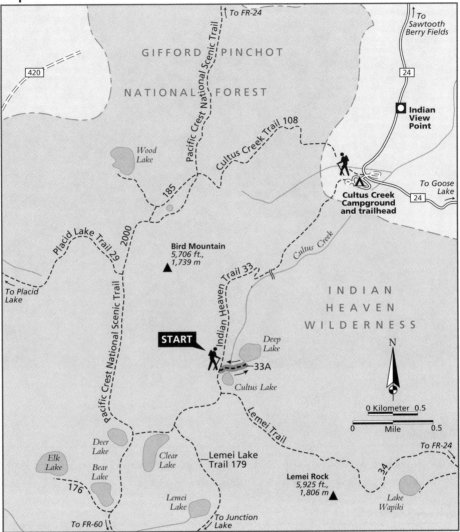

Cultus Lake. The route then climbs over a little rise before descending for a few yards to the shore of Deep Lake.

Avalanche lilies cover the open spots next to the lake between the hemlocks that guard the shore. Huckleberry bushes hug the groups of trees and rock outcroppings. Looking northeast across the water, Mount Adams silhouettes itself against the sky. Fish jump from the clear waters as if waiting for an angler's fly. The rises above the lake make beautiful campsites.

Deep Lake

Options

Hike to Deep Lake as a side trip while you are heading up the Indian Heaven Trail, or make camp and explore the surrounding lakes from there.

Miles and Directions

0.0   Junction of Indian Heaven and Deep Lake Trails (GPS 46 01.822 N 121 46.437 W).

0.2   Deep Lake (GPS 46 01.873 N 121 46.286 W). Turnaround point.

0.4   Junction of Indian Heaven and Deep Lake Trails.

21 Lemei Trail 34

Hike across flower-covered slopes and meadows and past rugged Lemei Rock to a junction with Indian Heaven Trail near Cultus Lake.

Start: Lemei trailhead.
Distance: 10.4-mile out-and-back day hike or backpack.
Difficulty: Moderate.
Seasons: August through September.
Fees and permits: Northwest Forest Pass and Indian Heaven Wilderness Permit.
Parking and trailhead facilities: There is parking for a couple of cars at Lemei trailhead but no other facilities. Little Goose Horse Camp has plenty of parking, rest rooms, and campsites.

Maps: USDA Forest Service Indian Heaven and Trapper Creek Wilderness or Sleeping Beauty and Lone Butte USGS quads.
Trail contacts: Gifford Pinchot National Forest, Wind River Ranger District, Mile Post 1.26 Hemlock Road, Carson, WA 98610; (509) 427-5645.
Mount Adams Ranger District, 2455 Highway 141, Trout Lake, WA 98650; (509) 395-3400; www.fs.fed.us/gpnf.

Finding the trailhead: Drive east from Portland on I-84 to exit 64 at the east edge of Hood River. Leave the freeway and head north across the Columbia River. At the junction with State Route 14 just north of the bridge, turn left and head west for 1.6 miles to the junction with State Route 141 Alternate, signed TO MOUNT ADAMS RECREATION AREA. Turn right at the junction onto SR 141 Alt and drive north for about 2.1 miles to the junction with State Route 141. Turn left at the junction and continue north on SR 141 for 18.9 miles to Trout Lake.

From Trout Lake drive west then southwest on SR 141. After 5.8 miles SR 141 becomes Forest Road 24 at the Gifford Pinchot National Forest boundary. Continue southwest on FR 24 for 2.2 more miles to Peterson Prairie and the junction with Forest Road 60. Turn right (north) at the junction and stay on the now-gravel-surfaced FR 24. Five miles from Peterson Prairie, the Lemei trailhead will be on your left. The elevation at the trailhead is 3,650 feet.

To reach Little Goose Horse Camp where Filloon Trail, the alternate start for this hike, begins, continue another 1.5 miles northwest on FR 24. Then turn left and drive south 0.2 mile to the trailhead. The GPS coordinates at Little Goose Horse Camp are 46 02.037 N 121 42.941 W.

Special Considerations

Mosquitoes may be thick in July and early August.

The Hike

From the trailhead Lemei Trail climbs very gently west along an abandoned roadbed for the first 0.2 mile. A trail sign marks the place where the route leaves the roadbed. Just after leaving the roadbed, there is a spring on the left side of the trail. Past the spring the tread climbs along a poorly defined, rounded ridgeline through dense woods. Western white pine, Douglas fir, and western hemlock make up the forest

Lemei Rock

canopy, while vine maple and huckleberry bushes cover the forest floor. A few leopard lilies grow beside the track, adding spots of orange color. You reach the junction with Filloon Trail 102 0.9 mile from the trailhead, at 3,960 feet elevation. At the signed junction the Filloon Trail turns to the right and heads for Little Goose Campground and trailhead. See Options for a description of Filloon Trail.

Leaving the junction the Lemei Trail continues to climb to the west, quickly passing the Indian Heaven Wilderness boundary. In 0.4 mile the path crosses a streambed that may be dry. It then begins to climb at a steeper grade. Watch for blacktail deer and elk as you hike through the now-thinner timber. Two miles after passing the Filloon Trail junction is the junction with the Lake Wapiki Trail 34A, at 5,020 feet elevation. Lake Wapiki Trail turns to the left and contours around the slope to Lake Wapiki.

As you hike above the Lake Wapiki Trail junction, watch for a view of Mount Adams to the northeast. In late July when the snow leaves this area, avalanche lilies bloom in profusion. If you are here in late August, you will find ripe huckleberries beside the trail. A little farther along on really clear days, Mount Rainier can be seen to the north. The sometimes rough and eroded trail crosses small meadows and then

Lemei Trail 34

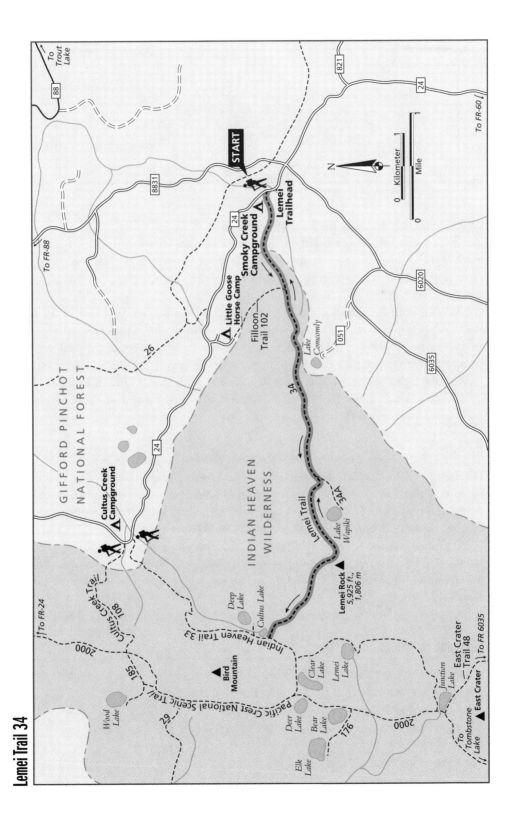

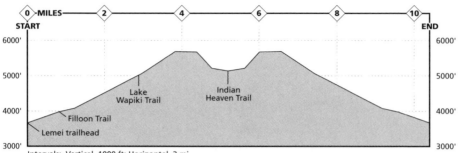

Intervals: Vertical, 1000 ft; Horizontal, 2 mi.

climbs to a ridge overlooking Lake Wapiki. Along the ridge there are several great viewpoints a few feet to the left of the trail. The trace crosses a sandy slope and reaches the phlox-covered ridgeline 0.9 mile from the junction with the Wapiki Lake Trail. Just before crossing the ridge, you are at the highest point reached along this trail, at 5,650 feet elevation.

After crossing the ridgeline the course traverses a slope to a saddle. Lemei Rock is the high point to the left as you make this traverse. Cross through the saddle and begin to descend to the northwest. The path makes two switchbacks and crosses several small streams before reaching a beautiful grassy meadow. Shortly, Cultus Lake comes into view to the right, just before you reach the junction with Indian Heaven Trail 33.

Cultus Lake, at 5,080 feet elevation, as well as nearby Deep Lake have several good campsites around their shores. Please don't camp in the meadows however.

Options

Hiking the Filloon Trail 102 from Little Goose Horse Camp is an alternate way to begin this hike. The slightly shorter Filloon Trail joins Lemei Trail 0.9 mile from the trailhead. From Little Goose Horse Camp (elevation 4,040 feet), hike southeast and quickly pass the Indian Heaven Wilderness boundary. Lupine, spirea, and huckleberry bushes line the route as you hike beneath the white pines, Douglas firs, and hemlocks. The path crests the top of a rise at 4,090 feet elevation, 0.3 mile from the horse camp, and then descends slightly in the remaining 0.5 mile to the junction with Lemei Trail.

Another option is to backpack to Lake Wapiki for an overnight or longer stay.

Miles and Directions

0.0 Lemei trailhead (GPS 46 01.720 N 121 41.153 W).

0.9 Junction with Filloon Trail 102 (GPS 46 01.606 N 121 42.265 W).

3.0 Junction with Lake Wapiki Trail 34A (GPS 46 01.318 N 121 44.507 W).

5.2 Junction with Indian Heaven Trail 33 (GPS 46 01.687 N 121 46.443 W). Turnaround point.

10.4 Lemei trailhead.

22 Lake Wapiki Trail 34A

Hike the short distance off the Lemei Trail, to a beautiful alpine lake.

Start: Junction of Lake Wapiki Trail and Lemei Trail; nearest trailhead is the Lemei trailhead on Forest Road 24.

Distance: 0.8-mile internal out-and back-day hike or backpack; 6.8 miles round-trip from Lemei trailhead.

Difficulty: Easy.

Seasons: Mid-July through September.

Fees and permits: Indian Heaven Wilderness Permit. A Northwest Forest Pass is also required if you are leaving a car at Lemei trailhead.

Maps: USDA Forest Service Indian Heaven and Trapper Creek Wilderness or Sleeping Beauty USGS quad.

Trail contacts: Gifford Pinchot National Forest, Wind River Ranger District, Mile Post 1.26 Hemlock Road, Carson, WA 98610; (509) 427–5645.

Mount Adams Ranger District, 2455 Highway 141, Trout Lake, WA 98650; (509) 395–3400; www.fs.fed.us/gpnf.

Finding the trailhead: Drive east from Portland on I–84 to exit 64 at the east edge of Hood River. Leave the freeway and head north across the Columbia River. At the junction with State Route 14 just north of the bridge, turn left and head west for 1.6 miles to the junction with State Route 141 Alternate, signed TO MOUNT ADAMS RECREATION AREA. Turn right at the junction onto SR 141 Alt and drive north for about 2.1 miles to the junction with State Route 141. Turn left at the junction and continue north on SR 141 for 18.9 miles to Trout Lake.

From Trout Lake drive west then southwest, staying on SR 141. After 5.8 miles SR 141 becomes FR 24 at the Gifford Pinchot National Forest boundary. Continue on FR 24 for 2.2 more miles to Peterson Prairie and the junction with Forest Road 60. Turn right (north) at the junction and stay on the now-gravel-surfaced FR 24. The Lemei trailhead will be on your left, 5 miles from Peterson Prairie. The elevation at the trailhead is 3,650 feet.

Hike west from the trailhead on Lemei Trail for 3 miles to the junction with Lake Wapiki Trail.

Special Considerations

Bring your bug spray; mosquitoes can be bad in July and August.

The Hike

From the junction with Lemei Trail, at 5,020 feet elevation, hike southwest through the medium–size fir and hemlock forest. In 0.4 mile, after climbing slightly more than 200 feet in elevation, you will reach Lake Wapiki.

In late July shooting stars bloom throughout the grassy, wet meadows that partially surround the lake. On the rises between the short trees, heather shows its pink flowers and huckleberries flourish. There are several campsites nearby; please don't camp in the meadows or too close to the lakeshore. If you brought your fishing rod,

Lake Wapiki Trail 34A

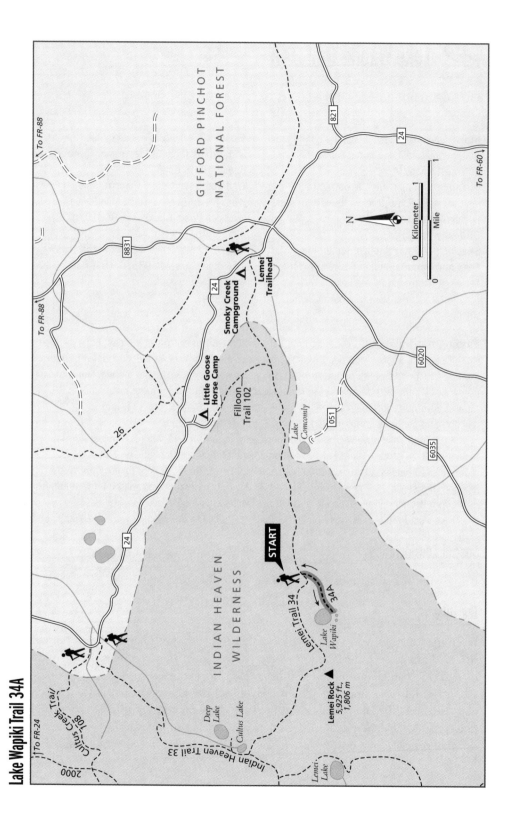

Heather

you may want to try for the many trout that swim in the lake. Expect patches of snow to linger near the lake into late July.

Options

Make the hike to Lake Wapiki as a side trip or to camp when you are hiking the Lemei Trail.

Miles and Directions

0.0 Junction of Lake Wapiki and Lemei Trails (GPS 46 01.318 N 121 44.507 W).

0.4 Lake Wapiki (GPS 46 01.166 N 121 44.885 W). Turnaround point.

0.8 Junction of Lake Wapiki and Lemei Trails.

23 East Crater Trail 48

Hike into the heart of Indian Heaven Wilderness.

Start: East Crater trailhead.
Distance: 5.2-mile out-and-back day hike or backpack, or an easy access route to the Pacific Crest Trail (PCT).
Difficulty: Easy, but the tread may be deeply eroded in a few spots.
Seasons: Mid-July through September.
Fees and permits: Indian Heaven Wilderness Permit.
Parking and trailhead facilities: There is roadside parking for three or four cars at the

trailhead and a single unimproved campsite but no other facilities.
Maps: USDA Forest Service Trapper Creek and Indian Heaven Wilderness, or Gifford Peak and Lone Butte USGS quads.
Trail contacts: Gifford Pinchot National Forest, Wind River Ranger District, Mile Post 1.26 Hemlock Road, Carson, WA 98610; (509) 427-5645.
Mount Adams Ranger District, 2455 Highway 141, Trout Lake, WA 98650; (509) 395-3400; www.fs.fed.us/gpnf.

Finding the trailhead: Drive east from Portland on I-84 to the Cascade Locks (exit 44). Leave the freeway and cross the Bridge of the Gods over the Columbia River. Turn right at the north end of the bridge (east) onto State Route 14. Drive east on SR 14 for about 7 miles to the junction with Wind River Road, signed TO CARSON.

Turn north and drive 1 mile to Carson. Head north from Carson on Wind River Road for 4.8 miles to the junction with Forest Road 65, signed TO PANTHER CREEK CAMPGROUND. Turn right onto FR 65 and in a short distance turn left, staying on FR 65 and following the signs toward Panther Creek Campground, which you will pass in about 2 miles. You will reach a four-way junction (Four Corners) with Forest Road 60 slightly more than 11 miles from Wind River Road.

Turn right (east) onto FR 60 and drive east and north for 7 miles to the junction with Forest Road 6040. The junction is 0.5 mile past Goose Lake Campground. Turn left onto FR 6040 and head north, passing Forlorn Lakes, for 3.5 miles to the junction with Forest Road 6035. Bear left onto FR 6035 and drive 2.2 miles to the East Crater trailhead. The trailhead is on the left side of the road at 4,080 feet elevation.

Roads FR 6040 and 6035 are rough and may require a high-clearance vehicle at times. The trailhead can also be reached from Trout Lake via State Route 141, FR 60, and FR 6035.

Special Considerations

Mosquitoes can be very thick in July and August.

The Hike

From the trailhead the tread climbs very gently through dense forest. Large firs and hemlocks line the route as you hike the first 0.3 mile to a creek crossing. After

Junction Lake

crossing the creek the path crosses three small wooden bridges before reaching the Indian Heaven Wilderness boundary half a mile from the trailhead.

The course crosses another creek on a wooden bridge 0.4 mile past the wilderness boundary. A bit farther along you will cross a tiny stream on a bridge made of rocks. The trace, which may be deeply eroded in spots, flattens out in a small meadow a quarter mile after crossing the rock bridge. You will pass a couple of ponds and cross four more wooden bridges as you work your way through the meadows to Junction Lake.

Junction Lake is on the right side of the trail at 4,730 feet elevation. The trail follows the south shore of Junction Lake to the junction with the Pacific Crest Trail, 2.6 miles from the trailhead. There are several possible campsites in the trees around Junction Lake. When I hiked this trail in mid-July, the ground was still about 50 percent snow-covered, but avalanche lilies were blooming thickly between the remaining snowdrifts.

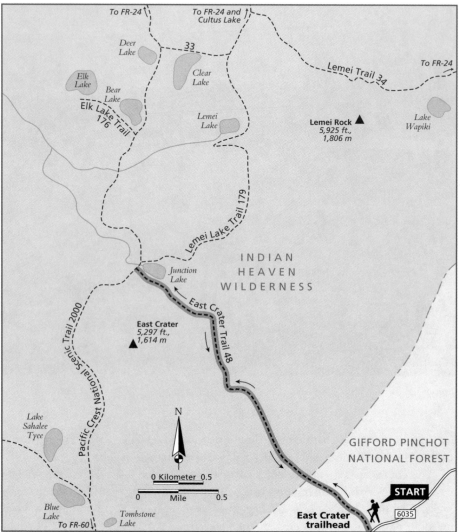

Options

A few yards north of the junction (across the wooden bridge to the right) on the PCT is the junction with Lemei Lake Trail 179. Lemei Lake is about 1 mile to the northeast and makes an excellent side trip. A loop can be made by hiking the Lemei Lake Trail past the lake to the junction with Indian Heaven Trail 33 and then turning left onto the Indian Heaven Trail and following it west to the PCT. On the PCT turn left again and hike back south to Junction Lake.

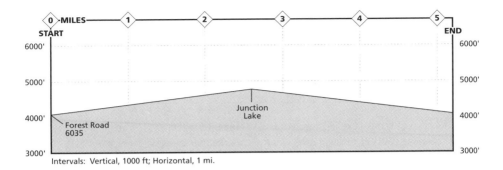

Intervals: Vertical, 1000 ft; Horizontal, 1 mi.

Miles and Directions

0.0 East Crater trailhead (GPS 45 58.881 N 121 45.479 W).

0.5 Indian Heaven Wilderness boundary.

2.6 Junction Lake and junction with the Pacific Crest Trail 2000 (GPS 46 00.309 N 121 47.342 W). Turnaround point.

5.2 East Crater trailhead.

24 Lemei Lake Trail 179

Hike across vibrant meadows and descend to the shore of Lemei Lake before climbing to the junction with Indian Heaven Trail.

Start: Junction of Lemei Lake Tail and the Pacific Crest Trail (PCT) at Junction Lake; nearest trailhead is East Crater trailhead on Forest Road 6035.
Distance: 1.5-mile one-way internal connector day hike or backpack; 4.1 miles one-way from East Crater trailhead.
Difficulty: Moderate.
Seasons: July through September.
Fees and permits: Indian Heaven Wilderness Permit.

Maps: USDA Forest Service Indian Heaven and Trapper Creek Wilderness or USGS Lone Butte quad.
Trail contacts: Gifford Pinchot National Forest, Wind River Ranger District, Mile Post 1.26 Hemlock Road, Carson, WA 98610; (509) 427–5645.
Mount Adams Ranger District, 2455 Highway 141, Trout Lake, WA 98650; (509) 395–3400; www.fs.fed.us/gpnf.

Finding the trailhead: The Lemei Lake Trail begins at the junction with the Pacific Crest Trail 9.1 miles north of Forest Road 60 and 7.3 miles south of Forest Road 24 at Junction Lake. The closest way to reach Junction Lake is to hike from the East Crater trailhead.

To reach the East Crater trailhead, drive east from Portland on I–84 to the Cascade Locks (exit 44). Leave the freeway and cross the Bridge of the Gods over the Columbia River. Turn right at the north end of the bridge (east) onto State Route 14. Drive east on SR 14 for about 7 miles to the junction with Wind River Road, signed TO CARSON.

Turn north and drive 1 mile to Carson. Head north from Carson on Wind River Road for 4.8 miles to the junction with Forest Road 65, signed TO PANTHER CREEK CAMPGROUND. Turn right onto FR 65 and in a short distance turn left, staying on FR 65 and following signs toward Panther Creek Campground, which you will pass in about 2 miles. You will reach a four-way junction (Four Corners) with FR 60 slightly more than 11 miles from Wind River Road.

Turn right (east) onto FR 60 and drive east and north for 7 miles to the junction with Forest Road 6040. The junction is 0.5 mile past Goose Lake Campground. Turn left onto FR 6040 and head north, passing Forlorn Lakes, for 3.5 miles to the junction with FR 6035. Bear left onto FR 6035 and drive 2.2 miles to the East Crater trailhead. Roads FR 6040 and FR 6035 are rough and may require a high-clearance vehicle at times. The trailhead is on the left side of the road at 4,080 feet elevation (GPS 45 58.881 N 121 45.479 W).

From the East Crater trailhead, hike northwest on East Crater Trail for 2.6 miles to Junction Lake and the junction with the PCT. Turn right (north) onto the PCT and cross a wooden bridge to the junction with Lemei Lake Trail. The elevation at the junction is 4,730 feet.

Special Considerations

Mosquitoes can be a problem in July and early August.

Lemei Lake

The Hike

Leaving the PCT, Lemei Lake Trail crosses the meadow at the northwest end of Junction Lake. Soon you come to a fork in the trail. Turn left at the fork. The right fork is a use path that follows the north shore of Junction Lake. Shortly the tread begins to climb the timbered slope. The rough and eroded track makes several switchbacks as it climbs about 150 feet to a plateau. On the plateau at about 4,900 feet elevation, the course flattens and heads northeast through meadows and patches of hemlock and fir woods. The trail crosses several small streams as it makes its way north-northeast, climbing slightly, to the edge of the plateau.

At the edge of the plateau 0.8 mile from Junction Lake, the route begins to descend. Hike down the slope, make a couple of switchbacks, cross a meadow, and head northeast to the meadows on the eastern shore of Lemei Lake, at 4,830 feet elevation. These meadows look inviting, but please don't camp in them. Once across the meadows the tread climbs gently to the north-northwest, gaining 200 feet of elevation in the 0.5 mile to the junction with Indian Heaven Trail 33.

Lemei Lake Trail 179

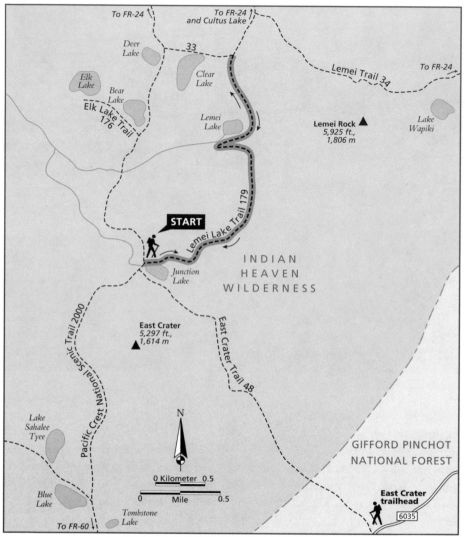

Options

To make an 8.8-mile lollipop loop hike, take East Crater Trail 48 for 2.6 miles from East Crater trailhead to Junction Lake and the junction with the Pacific Crest Trail 2000. Turn right onto the PCT and walk across the wooden bridge to the junction with the Lemei Lake Trail 179. Turn right and hike the Lemei Lake Trail for 1.5 miles, as described earlier. When you reach the junction with the Indian Heaven Trail 33, turn left and follow it for 0.4 mile to the junction with the PCT. Turn left onto the PCT and hike 1.7 miles south to Junction Lake and the junction with the

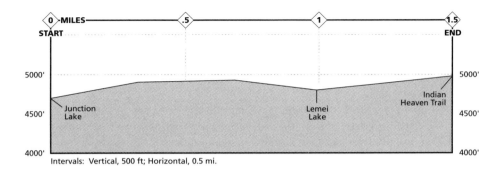

Intervals: Vertical, 500 ft; Horizontal, 0.5 mi.

East Crater Trail. Turn left again on the East Crater Trail and retrace your steps back to East Crater trailhead.

Miles and Directions

0.0 Junction of Lemei Lake Trail and the PCT at Junction Lake (GPS 46 00.316 N 121 47.315 W).

1.0 Lemei Lake (GPS 46 01.072 N 121 46.540 W).

1.5 Junction with Indian Heaven Trail 33 (GPS 46 01.526 N 121 46.744 W).

25 Elk Lake Trail 176

A short side trip, with little elevation gain or loss, to a tree-lined mountain lake.

Start: Junction of Elk Lake Trail and the Pacific Crest Trail (PCT) at Bear Lake; nearest trailhead is East Crater trailhead on Forest Road 6035.
Distance: 1.2-mile internal out-and-back day hike or backpack; 8.6 miles round-trip from East Crater trailhead.
Difficulty: Easy.
Seasons: Mid-July through September.
Fees and permits: Indian Heaven Wilderness Permit.

Maps: USDA Forest Service Indian Heaven and Trapper Creek Wilderness or Lone Butte USGS quad.
Trail contacts: Gifford Pinchot National Forest, Wind River Ranger District, Mile Post 1.26 Hemlock Road, Carson, WA 98610; (509) 427–5645.
Mount Adams Ranger District, 2455 Highway 141, Trout Lake, WA 98650; (509) 395–3400; www.fs.fed.us/gpnf.

Finding the trailhead: Elk Lake Trail begins at a junction with Pacific Crest Trail 2000, at the south end of Bear Lake. This junction is 10.2 miles north of Forest Road 60 and 6.2 miles south of Forest Road 24. The closest way to reach the junction is via East Crater Trail and the PCT.

To reach the East Crater trailhead, drive east from Portland on I-84 to the Cascade Locks (exit 44). Leave the freeway and cross the Bridge of the Gods over the Columbia River. Turn right at the north end of the bridge (east) onto State Route 14. Drive east on SR 14 for about 7 miles to the junction with Wind River Road, signed TO CARSON.

Turn north and drive 1 mile to Carson. Head north from Carson on Wind River Road for 4.8 miles to the junction with Forest Road 65, signed TO PANTHER CREEK CAMPGROUND. Turn right onto FR 65 and in a short distance turn left, staying on FR 65 and following signs toward Panther Creek Campground, which you will pass in about 2 miles. You will reach a four-way junction (Four Corners) with Forest Road 60 slightly more than 11 miles from Wind River Road.

Turn right (east) onto FR 60 and drive east and north for 7 miles to the junction with Forest Road 6040. The junction is 0.5 mile past Goose Lake Campground. Turn left onto FR 6040 and head north, passing Forlorn Lakes, for 3.5 miles to the junction with FR 6035. Bear left onto FR 6035 and drive 2.2 miles to the East Crater trailhead. Roads FR 6040 and FR 6035 are rough and may require a high-clearance vehicle at times. The trailhead is on the left side of the road at 4,080 feet elevation (GPS 45 58.881 N 121 45.479 W).

Hike East Crater Trail for 2.6 miles northwest to Junction Lake. Turn right onto the PCT at Junction Lake and hike 1.1 miles north to Bear Lake and the junction with Elk Lake Trail, at 4,790 feet elevation. At the junction, the Elk Lake Trail appears to cross the PCT. The trail to the east is an abandoned section of the old Cascade Crest Trail.

Elk Lake

Special Considerations

Mosquitoes are terrible in July and early August.

The Hike

Hike west from the junction with the PCT, along the south shore of Bear Lake. In a short distance you cross the outlet stream from Bear Lake and come to a campsite. The route soon leaves Bear Lake, heading northeast and passing a melt pond. The south shore of Elk Lake, elevation 4,685 feet, is reached 0.2 mile after passing the pond. The country surrounding this clear mountain lake is thickly timbered with western hemlock and silver fir. Hike along the southern shore of the lake to its southwest corner, where there are a couple of campsites.

Options

Use Elk Lake as an out-of-the-way campsite when hiking the PCT.

Elk Lake Trail 176

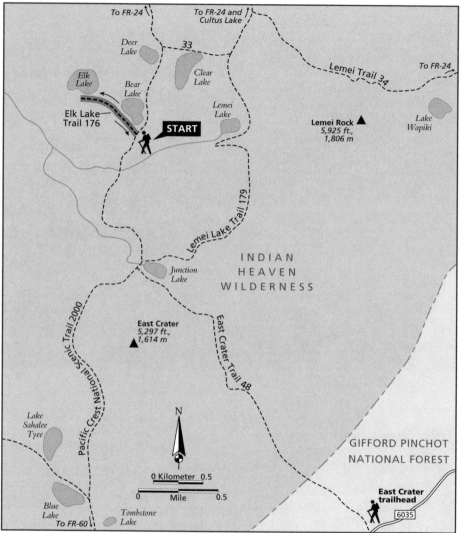

Miles and Directions

0.0 Junction of Elk Lake Trail and the PCT at Bear Lake.

0.6 Elk Lake. Turnaround point.

1.2 Junction of Elk Lake Trail and the PCT at Bear Lake.

26 Thomas Lake Trail 111

Hike into the heart of Indian Heaven Wilderness from the west, passing several lakes along the way.

Start: Thomas Lake trailhead.
Distance: 7.6-mile out-and-back day hike or backpack.
Difficulty: Moderate.
Seasons: July through September.
Fees and permits: Northwest Forest Pass and Indian Heaven Wilderness Permit.
Parking and trailhead facilities: There is adequate parking and a rest room at the trailhead.

Maps: USDA Forest Service Indian Heaven and Trapper Creek Wilderness or Lone Butte and Gifford Peak USGS quads.
Trail contacts: Gifford Pinchot National Forest, Wind River Ranger District, Mile Post 1.26 Hemlock Road, Carson, WA 98610; (509) 427-5645.
Mount Adams Ranger District, 2455 Highway 141, Trout Lake, WA 98650; (509) 395-3400; www.fs.fed.us/gpnf.

Finding the trailhead: Drive east from Portland on I-84 to exit 44 at Cascade Locks. Leave the freeway and cross the Bridge of the Gods over the Columbia River. Turn right (east) onto State Route 14 at the north end of the bridge. Head east on SR 14 for about 7 miles to the junction with Wind River Road, signed TO CARSON.

If you are coming from the east on I-84, leave the freeway at Hood River. Cross the bridge over the Columbia River and turn west onto SR 14. Follow SR 14 west for 15 miles to the junction with Wind River Road.

Turn north and drive 1 mile to Carson. Head north from Carson on Wind River Road for 4.8 miles to the junction with Forest Road 65, signed TO PANTHER CREEK CAMPGROUND. Turn right onto FR 65 and in a short distance turn left, staying on FR 65 and following the signs toward Panther Creek Campground, which you will pass in about 2 miles. You will reach a four-way junction (called Four Corners) with Forest Road 60, a little more than 11 miles from Wind River Road. Go straight ahead (north) at the junction and drive another 8.7 miles to Thomas Lake trailhead. The trailhead is on the right side of the road, at 4,090 feet elevation. There is a great view of Mount St. Helens from the Thomas Lake trailhead.

Special Considerations

If you plan to camp in the Thomas Lake or Blue Lake areas, you will also need the USDA Forest Service brochure *Indian Heaven Wilderness Helpful Hints For Camping in Designated Sites.* This brochure contains a map of the designated sites.

Mosquitoes can be terrible in July and early August; take plenty of repellent.

The Hike

Leaving the trailhead, hike southeast through an old clear-cut where huckleberry bushes cover the ground between the small fir trees. After hiking a short distance,

Thomas Lake

you leave the clear-cut and walk between the larger firs and hemlocks. Beargrass covers much of the ground as the tread begins to climb gently. The route makes a couple of switchbacks and passes the Indian Heaven Wilderness boundary before flattening out as it nears Thomas Lake. Soon there are lakes on both sides of the trail. On the right is Thomas Lake and on the left are Dee and Heather Lakes. Thomas Lake, at 4,290 feet elevation, has a good supply of brook trout.

Thomas Lake and vicinity is a "designated campsite zone." You must either find one of the six designated campsites in the area or camp elsewhere. The Forest Service publishes a brochure with aerial photograph maps showing the designated sites. If you plan to camp here, pick up one of these brochures from a ranger station before you begin your hike.

Cross the bridge over the stream connecting Heather and Thomas Lakes. Just past the bridge a path turns to the right. This path is an anglers' trail along the east side of Thomas Lake. A few yards farther along, the trail forks. To the left a short trail leads to Eunice Lake, which also has fish to be caught. Bear right at the fork and climb, making a switchback. Two-tenths of a mile past the trail to Eunice Lake, a path to the left leads a few feet to a viewpoint. The viewpoint overlooks Eunice Lake with Mount St. Helens in the background. You then hike past a wet meadow and cross a wooden bridge. If you walk off the trail to the right 150 yards after crossing the bridge, you will reach Brader Lake in 100 yards. The trail soon makes two more switchbacks as it climbs to about 4,750 feet elevation before flattening out.

Two miles from the trailhead, the course passes Naha Lake and crosses a meadow to a trail junction. This junction is with an old and now not-maintained section of the Cascade Crest Trail. Straight ahead a short distance is Rock Lake. Turn right at the junction and hike south, passing several ponds. In a little less than a mile, you will reach another trail junction. Bear right at this junction (elevation 4,770 feet) and cross a tiny stream; the trail to the left is no longer maintained. Another 0.3 mile brings you to Lake Sahalee Tyee (elevation 4,680 feet), which is on the left side of the trail. Shortly, as you cross a streambed that may be dry, Blue Lake comes into view below to the south. The route descends to the shore of Blue Lake and the junction with Pacific Crest Trail 2000 at 4,630 feet elevation.

Blue Lake and vicinity (including Lake Sahalee Tyee) is also a "designated campsite zone," so you must either camp in one of the nine designated campsites or leave the zone to camp. Check the Forest Service brochure mentioned earlier to locate the designated sites.

Options

For a short backpack with children, hike the 0.5 mile to Thomas Lake to camp and fish.

From Blue Lake at the end of this hike, it's a short trip to the southeast to Tombstone Lake, which is also part of the Blue Lake designated campsite zone. To reach Tombstone Lake, first hike a few yards south on the PCT to the southeast corner of Blue Lake. Turn southeast off the PCT, following a poor path. Pass along the north side of a pond and descend southeast to Tombstone Lake. The distance between Blue Lake and Tombstone Lake is only about 0.2 mile.

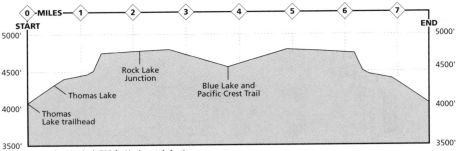

Intervals: Vertical, 500 ft; Horizontal, 1 mi.

Thomas Lake Trail 111

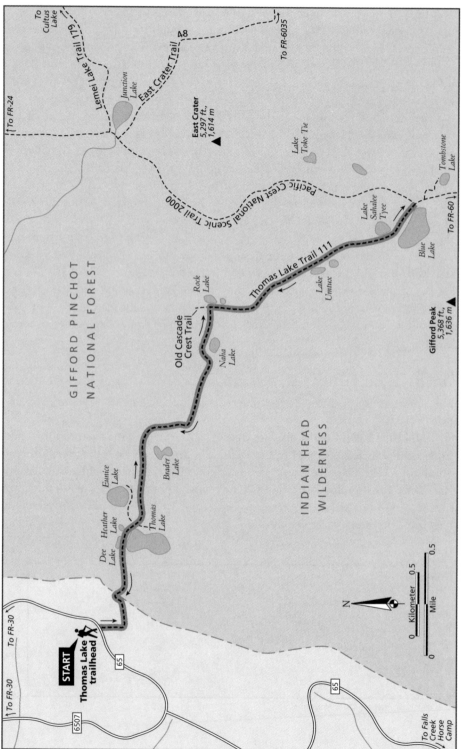

To Cultus Lake

To FR-24

To FR-30

To FR-30

Lemei Lake Trail 179

Junction Lake

East Crater Trail

48

To FR-6035

East Crater
5,297 ft.,
1,614 m

GIFFORD PINCHOT
NATIONAL FOREST

Lake
Toke Tie

Pacific Crest National Scenic Trail 2000

Lake
Sahalee
Tyee

Tombstone
Lake

Rock
Lake

Old Cascade
Crest Trail

Thomas Lake Trail 111

Lake
Umtux

Blue
Lake

To FR-60

Naha
Lake

INDIAN HEAD
WILDERNESS

Gifford Peak
5,368 ft.,
1,636 m

Eunice
Lake

Brader
Lake

Heather
Lake

Dee
Lake

Thomas
Lake

START
Thomas Lake
trailhead

65

6507

To Falls
Creek
Horse
Camp

65

N

Kilometer   0.5

0

Mile   0.5

0

Miles and Directions

0.0 Thomas Lake trailhead (GPS 46 00.349 N 121 50.351 W).

0.5 Thomas Lake.

2.1 Rock Lake junction (GPS 45 59.926 N 121 48.371 W). Turn right and hike south.

3.8 Blue Lake and junction with Pacific Crest Trail 2000 (GPS 45 59.051 N 121 47.715 W). Turnaround point.

7.6 Thomas Lake trailhead.

27 Indian Racetrack Trail 171

Hike across the southern end of Indian Heaven Wilderness to Indian Racetrack, where Native Americans in times past raced their horses. Then, climb to the summit of Red Mountain.

Start: Indian Racetrack trailhead.
Distance: 3.3-mile (shuttle) or 7.0-mile (out-and-back) hike.
Difficulty: Easy to moderate.
Seasons: July through mid-October.
Fees and permits: Northwest Forest Pass and Indian Heaven Wilderness Permit.
Parking and trailhead facilities: There are several campsites and rest rooms at Falls Creek Horse Camp.

Maps: USDA Forest Service Trapper Creek and Indian Heaven Wilderness or Gifford Peak USGS quad.
Trail contacts: Gifford Pinchot National Forest, Wind River Ranger District, Mile Post 1.26 Hemlock Road, Carson, WA 98610; (509) 427-5645.
Mount Adams Ranger District, 2455 Highway 141, Trout Lake, WA 98650; (509) 395-3400; www.fs.fed.us/gpnf.

Finding the trailhead: From Portland head east on I-84 to the Cascade Locks (exit 44). Leave the freeway and cross the Bridge of the Gods over the Columbia River. At the north end of the bridge, turn right (east) onto State Route 14. Drive east on SR 14 for about 7 miles to the junction with Wind River Road, signed TO CARSON.

If you are coming from the east on I-84, leave the freeway at Hood River (exit 64). Cross the bridge over the Columbia River and turn west onto SR 14. Follow SR 14 west for 15 miles to the junction with Wind River Road.

Turn north and drive 1 mile to Carson. Head north from Carson on Wind River Road for 4.8 miles to the junction with Forest Road 65, signed TO PANTHER CREEK CAMPGROUND. Turn right onto FR 65 and in a short distance turn left, staying on FR 65 and following the signs toward Panther Creek Campground, which you will pass in about 2 miles. You will reach a four-way junction (Four Corners) with Forest Road 60 about 11 miles from Wind River Road. Go straight (north) at the junction and drive another 5 miles to Falls Creek Horse Camp. The horse camp is on the left side of the road, and Indian Racetrack trailhead is a few yards farther north on the right. The elevation at the trailhead is 3,540 feet. A path directly across FR 65 from the horse camp also connects with Indian Racetrack Trail.

To reach the trailhead near the summit of Red Mountain where this hike ends, go back to Four Corners, the four-way junction mentioned above. Drive east from the junction on FR 60 for 1.5 miles to the junction with Forest Road 6048. Turn left (north) onto FR 6048 and follow it for 3.2 miles to the trailhead. Forest Road 6048 is often closed well into the summer and requires a high-clearance vehicle to travel safely.

Special Considerations

Mosquitoes are bad in July and early August, so be sure to have insect repellent with you.

Indian Racetrack early in the summer

The Hike

Hike east, leaving the trailhead through mixed conifer woods with an understory of huckleberries and beargrass. In 0.2 mile there is a junction. The path to the right is a spur trail heading back to Falls Creek Horse Camp. Get your wilderness permit at the box next to the junction and then ford Falls Creek. The course, which may be a little rough and eroded in spots, now begins to climb and soon passes the Indian Heaven Wilderness boundary. Glacier lilies bloom along this part of the route in early July.

The grade of the tread eases 1.2 miles from the trailhead, at about 4,300 feet elevation. As soon as the forest thins out, Red Mountain comes into view to the south. In another 1.2 miles you skirt the east side of a small, sometimes dry lake and shortly reach Indian Racetrack and the junction with Shortcut Trail 171A. Shortcut Trail heads east from the junction, first along the racetrack and then through the woods, to join the Pacific Crest Trail (PCT) in about 0.5 mile.

Indian Racetrack is a shallow groove cut across the meadow. Native Americans came to this plateau late each summer to pick and dry the abundant huckleberries.

Indian Racetrack Trail 171

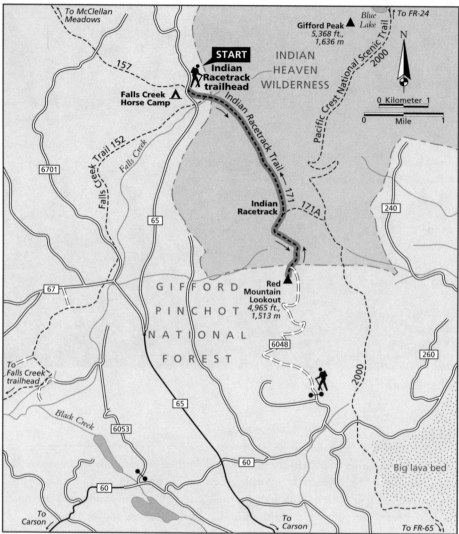

For diversion they wildly raced their horses across this meadow and gambled on the results.

Cross the racetrack and head south-southwest. Soon you begin to climb, quite steeply in spots. Half a mile from the racetrack, there is an excellent view of Mount Adams to the left of the trail. The route then turns south along a semi-open ridge to climb the 200 vertical feet to FR 6048, at 4,810 feet elevation. The section of this hike from the racetrack to FR 6048 may have deep snowdrifts well into July some years.

If FR 6048 is open and you have arranged a car shuttle to here, this is the place to end your hike. If not, turn right onto the road and hike 0.2 mile to Red Moun-

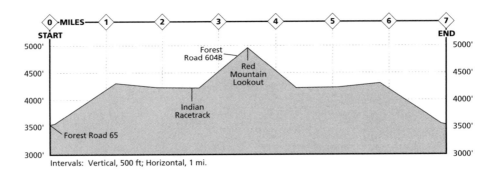

Intervals: Vertical, 500 ft; Horizontal, 1 mi.

tain Lookout. From the summit, at 4,965 feet elevation, the view to the south covers nearly half of the Oregon Cascades. If the day is clear enough, just the tip of the North Sister is visible to the left of Mount Jefferson. Mount Hood, with its sparkling glaciers and jagged rock buttresses, rises above the green Hood River Valley across the Columbia River Gorge. To the northeast the imposing bulk of Mount Adams dominates the landscape. To the north Mount Rainier pierces the thin air above the dark forests of the southern Washington Cascades, and to the northwest the squatty remains of Mount St. Helens is close by.

Options

If FR 6048 is closed to vehicle traffic, you may wish to hike the 3.2 miles down it to the junction with FR 60. Watch for Roosevelt elk if you hike down FR 6048; they are common here.

Miles and Directions

0.0 Indian Racetrack trailhead (GPS 45 58.080 N 121 50.795 W).

2.5 Indian Racetrack (GPS 45 56.805 N 121 49.308 W).

3.3 FR 6048 (GPS 45 56.242 N 121 49.222 W). Turn right (south).

3.5 Red Mountain Lookout (45 56.081 N 121 49.269 W). Turnaround point.

7.0 Indian Racetrack trailhead.

28 Falls Creek Trail 152

Descend through mostly second-growth forest and openings, passing collapsed lava tubes, from near the western edge of Indian Heaven Wilderness to Lower Falls Creek trailhead, deep in the Wind River Canyon.

Start: Falls Creek Horse Camp trailhead.
Distance: 8.9-mile one-way shuttle backpack or day hike.
Difficulty: Moderate, but route-finding skills are required.
Seasons: Mid-June through October.
Fees and permits: A Northwest Forest Pass is required to park at the trailheads at both ends of this trail.
Parking and trailhead facilities: Adequate parking, rest rooms, and a campground are located at Falls Creek Horse Camp. The lower trailhead has only parking.
Maps: There is no single right map for this trail. The Gifford Peak and Termination Point USGS quads cover the area but don't show the trail. The USDA Forest Service Trapper Creek and Indian Heaven Wilderness map

shows the Falls Creek Horse Camp and trailhead and a small amount of this route. The wilderness map has the trail marked incorrectly as Trail 157. The USDA Forest Service Pacific Crest Trail Washington Southern Portion map shows the lower end of the route and the lower trailhead. The USDA Forest Service Gifford Pinchot National Forest map shows the entire route fairly correctly but is too small of a scale to be of much value to the hiker.
Trail contacts: Gifford Pinchot National Forest, Wind River Ranger District, Mile Post 1.26 Hemlock Road, Carson, WA 98610; (509) 427-5645.
Mount Adams Ranger District, 2455 Highway 141, Trout Lake, WA 98650; (509) 395-3400; www.fs.fed.us/gpnf.

Finding the trailhead: From Portland head east on I-84 to the Cascade Locks (exit 44). Leave the freeway and cross the Bridge of the Gods over the Columbia River. Turn right at the north end of the bridge (east) onto State Route 14. Drive east on SR 14 for about 7 miles to the junction with Wind River Road, signed TO CARSON.

If you are coming from the east on I-84, leave the freeway at Hood River (exit 64). Cross the bridge over the Columbia River and turn west onto SR 14. Follow SR 14 west for 15 miles to the junction with Wind River Road.

Turn north and drive 1 mile to Carson. Head north from Carson on Wind River Road for 4.8 miles to the junction with Forest Road 65, signed TO PANTHER CREEK CAMPGROUND. Turn right onto FR 65 and in a short distance turn left, staying on FR 65 and following the signs toward Panther Creek Campground, which you will pass in about 2 miles. You will reach a four-way junction (Four Corners) with Forest Road 60 about 11 miles from Wind River Road. Go straight (north) at the junction and drive another 5 miles to Falls Creek Horse Camp. The horse camp is on the left side of the road, and Indian Racetrack trailhead is a few yards farther north on the right.

To reach the lower trailhead where this hike ends, backtrack to the junction with Forest Road 6517 (Warren Gap Road) near Panther Creek Campground. Turn right (west) onto FR 6517 and drive 2 miles to the junction with Wind River Road. Turn right onto Wind River Road and go 5.5 miles north to the junction with Forest Road 3062. Turn right onto FR 3062 and drive northeast

Small falls next to campsite on Falls Creek

for 2 miles to the road's end at the trailhead. The signs on FR 3062 pointing to this trailhead read UPPER FALLS CREEK TRAIL 152.

Special Considerations

Parties with stock and mountain bikers commonly use this trail. The route crosses several roads both in use and abandoned. It also follows a few roadbeds for short distances. Good route-finding and map-reading skills are necessary to follow this trail.

The Hike

Hike west-southwest from the horse camp on the descending path through fir forest. After about 200 yards the tread passes through a small clear-cut and crosses a small stream (may be dry in late summer). The route soon crosses another clear-cut and then passes through some timber to the third clear-cut. From the third clearcut, Red Mountain can be seen to the southeast. In the clear-cuts between the young white pines, lodgepole pines, and silver firs, huckleberry bushes and vine maple cover the ground, providing great colors for an autumn hike. Watch for Roosevelt elk in the clear-cuts.

Falls Creek Trail 152

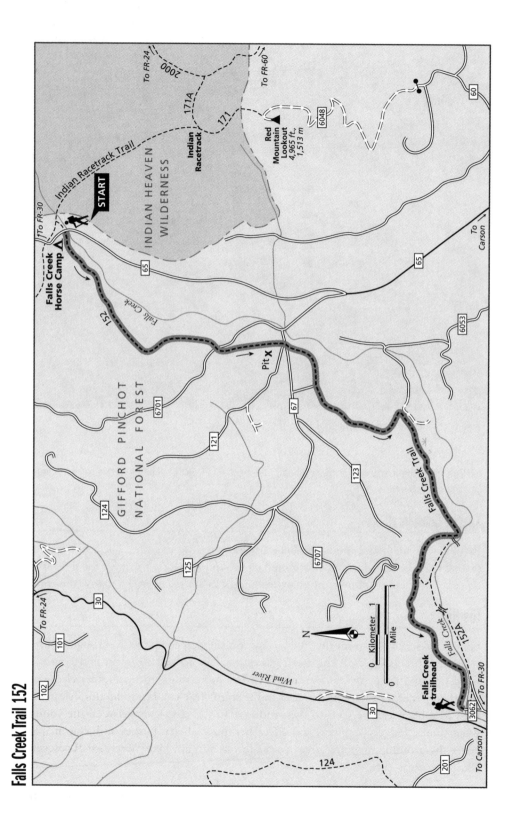

The trail crosses a roadbed 0.8 mile from the trailhead, and 1.2 miles farther along the route becomes a roadbed. Shortly, you reach a junction (roadbeds), bear right, and soon come to another junction. Bear left at this junction. This road is open to motor vehicles. There is a campsite next to this junction. A few yards farther and the route crosses Forest Road 6701. There are signs on both sides of FR 6701 marking the trail. After crossing FR 6701 the route becomes a trail again. Notice the collapsed lava tube next to the path 0.6 mile from FR 6701. Another 0.3 mile brings you to FR 67, at 2,640 feet elevation, 3.2 miles from Falls Creek Horse Camp trailhead. There are signs marking the trail on both sides of FR 67.

Cross the road and head south on a seldom-used roadbed. Before long the road turns to the right to head west. You soon enter a clear-cut, where the roadbed ends and the route again becomes a trail. Just after leaving the clear-cut, the route again turns south (left) onto another roadbed. The GPS coordinates here are 45 55.539 N 121 52.755 W. The roadbed has been bulldozed to prevent auto traffic a short distance ahead. You soon turn west, following the closed road, and climb a little into a sloping clear-cut with a view of Mount Hood in the distance to the south. The trail turns left off the roadbed 0.9 mile after you started following it and 5 miles from Falls Creek Horse Camp. The place where the trail leaves the roadbed is just before the roadbed comes to an end. There is a sign here marking the trail.

Descend for 0.3 mile south and then southeast to the FR 6053 roadbed. This road, which is closed to vehicles, is in a small meadow, at about 2,400 feet elevation. Turn right (west-southwest) onto the roadbed. Soon the roadbed becomes a trail, and you cross a small talus slope with a swamp below to your left. Often there are blue herons in this swamp. Past the swamp the nearly flat tread enters deep forest. In another 0.9 mile the course passes a campsite next to Falls Creek. A short waterfall in the creek, with a sparkling pool below it, makes this an inviting spot to spend some time.

Deep moss carpets the forest floor as you hike away from the campsite. A path bears left off the trail 300 yards after passing the campsite. This 100-yard-long path leads to a viewpoint above the much larger Falls Creek Falls. The view is somewhat obstructed, but the side trip is still worth making. Soon the trail begins to descend along the steep canyon wall. Another path leaves the trail on a small ridgeline 0.7

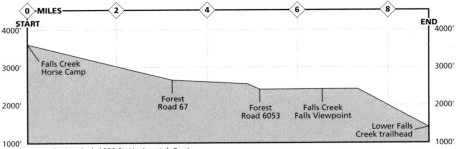

Intervals: Vertical, 1000 ft; Horizontal, 2 mi.

mile past the viewpoint. This rough, steep, unmarked path descends southeast to meet the Falls Creek Falls Trail 152A, next to Falls Creek in the bottom of the canyon.

Continuing southwest, Falls Creek Trail crosses several streambeds. As you hike, notice the large, old-growth Douglas firs, with scars from a long-ago forest fire. One and one-half miles past the path that leads to Falls Creek Falls Trail, you cross a wooden bridge over Falls Creek. Just across the bridge is a trail junction. To the left a trail heads up Falls Creek to join the Falls Creek Falls Trail near Falls Creek Falls trailhead. Turn right and climb a few feet to the Lower Falls Creek trailhead, at 1,350 feet elevation, 8.9 miles from Falls Creek Horse Camp trailhead. For some reason, probably because of its location deep in a canyon, GPS coordinates are very hard to get at this trailhead.

Options

Hike to Falls Creek Falls on the same trip.

Miles and Directions

0.0 Falls Creek Horse Camp trailhead (GPS 45 57.974 N 121 50.747 W).

2.4 Cross FR 6701 (GPS 45 56.636 N 121 52.177 W).

3.0 Lava pits.

3.2 Cross FR 67 (GPS 45 55.988 N 121 52.381 W).

5.2 Reach FR 6053 (closed) (GPS 45 54.869 N 121 53.225 W). Turn right (west-southwest).

6.7 Falls Creek Falls viewpoint.

7.4 Path to Falls Creek Falls Trail, turn right.

8.9 Lower Falls Creek trailhead.

29 Falls Creek Falls Trail 152A

Hike a lowland canyon to one of the best waterfalls to be found.

Start: Falls Creek Falls trailhead.
Distance: 3.4-mile out-and-back day hike.
Difficulty: Moderate.
Seasons: April through November.
Fees and permits: Northwest Forest Pass.
Parking and trailhead facilities: There is parking for six or eight cars at the trailhead but no other facilities.

Maps: Termination Point USGS quad.
Trail contacts: Gifford Pinchot National Forest, Wind River Ranger District, Mile Post 1.26 Hemlock Road, Carson, WA 98610; (509) 427–5645.
Mount Adams Ranger District, 2455 Highway 141, Trout Lake, WA 98650; (509) 395–3400; www.fs.fed.us/gpnf.

Finding the trailhead: From Portland head east on I-84 to the Cascade Locks (exit 44). Leave the freeway and cross the Bridge of the Gods over the Columbia River. At the north end of the bridge, turn right (east) onto State Route 14. Drive east on SR 14 for about 7 miles to the junction with the Wind River Road, signed TO CARSON

If you are coming from the east on I-84, leave the freeway at Hood River (exit 64). Cross the bridge over the Columbia River and turn west onto SR 14. Follow SR 14 west for 15 miles to the junction with Wind River Road.

Turn north and drive 1 mile to Carson. Head north from Carson on Wind River Road for 13.8 miles to the junction with Forest Road 3062. Turn right onto FR 3062 and drive northeast for 1.8 miles to the junction with Forest Road 057. Turn right onto FR 057 and go 0.3 mile to the Falls Creek Falls trailhead, at 1,430 feet elevation.

Special Considerations

This trail is open to mountain bikes as well as hikers. GPS units seem to have a hard time receiving in this canyon.

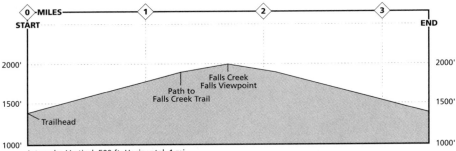

The Hike

Wide, well-maintained Falls Creek Falls Trail heads east-northeast from the trailhead through second-growth Douglas fir forest with a vine maple understory. Quickly, the route moves close to Falls Creek, where a path to the left leads downstream 0.5 mile to the Lower Falls Creek trailhead. Turn right at the junction and head upstream along the creek. Soon the track climbs well above the creek, where there are some older fir trees that show the scars of a long-ago forest fire.

You will cross a suspension bridge across Falls Creek 0.4 mile from the trailhead. A sign next to the bridge states that this bridge is closed to all stock traffic and if you are on a bike you must walk it across. Below the bridge Falls Creek drops into a pretty little pool. After crossing the bridge the path soon climbs above the creekbed, passing some large Douglas firs and western red cedars that also show fire scars. The course climbs moderately along a steep side hill and reaches an unmarked junction 1.3 miles from the trailhead. The path that climbs to the left connects with Falls Creek Trail. At this point Falls Creek Trail parallels Falls Creek Falls Trail, about 200 vertical feet up the slope to the north. Stay on the Falls Creek Falls Trail and hike east. In 400 yards the tread crosses another bridge over a usually dry creekbed and then crosses a small talus slope.

Soon the trace traverses below short cliffs to reach the viewpoint near the base of the beautiful, three-stage Falls Creek Falls. The elevation at the viewpoint is about 2,000 feet, and you are 1.7 miles from the Falls Creek Falls trailhead. There is some exposure at the viewpoint so if you have children with you, watch them closely. Moss-covered rocks line the falls, behind the mist, and maidenhair ferns grow from the cracks.

Options

Make this relatively easy trip as a warm up for a longer hike in Trapper Creek Wilderness, which is close by.

Miles and Directions

0.0 Falls Creek Falls trailhead.

0.4 Suspension bridge across Falls Creek.

1.3 Path to Falls Creek Trail 152.

1.7 Viewpoint of falls. Turnaround point.

3.4 Falls Creek Falls trailhead.

◀ *Falls Creek Falls*

Falls Creek Falls Trail 152A

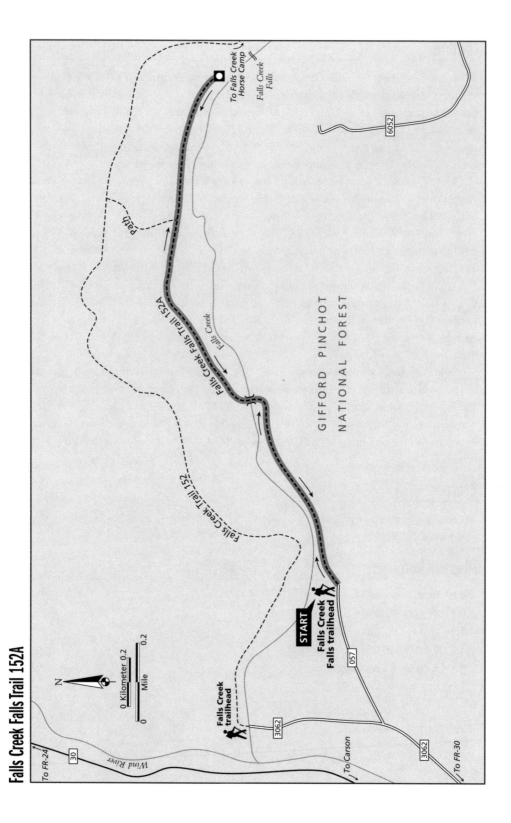

30 Pacific Crest Trail 2000, Wind River Road to Crest Camp

Hike through second-growth forest from Wind River Road through Warren Gap and down to Panther Creek. Then climb to the crest of the Cascade Range and the top of Big Huckleberry Mountain and follow the ridge north to Crest Camp trailhead.

Start: Junction of Wind River Road and the Pacific Crest Trail (PCT).
Distance: 17.6-mile one-way shuttle, long day hike, or backpack.
Difficulty: Moderate.
Seasons: Mid-June through mid-October.
Fees and permits: A Northwest Forest Pass is required to park at the trailhead near Panther Creek and at Crest Camp.
Parking and trailhead facilities: There is roadside parking for only one or two cars on the left (west) side of Wind River Road where the PCT crosses it. Crest Camp trailhead, where this hike ends, has a campground, rest room, and adequate parking.
Maps: USDA Forest Service Pacific Crest Trail Washington Southern Portion or Stabler, Big Huckleberry Mountain, and Gifford Peak USGS quads.
Trail contacts: Gifford Pinchot National Forest, Wind River Ranger District, Mile Post 1.26 Hemlock Road, Carson, WA 98610; (509) 427-5645.
Mount Adams Ranger District, 2455 Highway 141, Trout Lake, WA 98650; (509) 395-3400; www.fs.fed.us/gpnf.

Finding the trailhead: From Portland head east on I-84 to the Cascade Locks (exit 44). Leave the freeway and cross the Bridge of the Gods over the Columbia River. At the north end of the bridge, turn right (east) onto State Route 14. Drive east on SR 14 for about 7 miles to the junction with Wind River Road, signed TO CARSON.

If you are coming from the east on I-84, leave the freeway at Hood River (exit 64). Cross the bridge over the Columbia River and turn west onto SR 14. Follow SR 14 west for 15 miles to the junction with Wind River Road.

Turn north and drive 1 mile to Carson. Head north from Carson on Wind River Road for 8.3 miles to the point where the PCT crosses Wind River Road. This point is a little hard to spot, but there is a crosswalk sign.

To reach Crest Camp where this hike ends, head north from Carson on Wind River Road for 4.8 miles to the junction with Forest Road 65, signed TO PANTHER CREEK CAMPGROUND. Turn right onto FR 65 and in a short distance turn left, staying on FR 65 and following the signs toward Panther Creek Campground, which you will pass in about 2 miles. You will reach a four-way junction (Four Corners) with Forest Road 60 about 11 miles from Wind River Road. Turn right onto FR 60 and drive east for 2 miles to Crest Camp trailhead.

Mount Hood and Columbia River Gorge from Big Huckleberry Mountain

Special Considerations

There is no water along this section of the Pacific Crest Trail after crossing Panther Creek. If you plan on leaving a car where you begin this hike, it may be best to start at Panther Creek. See Options for more information.

The Hike

The Pacific Crest Trail crosses Wind River Road at 1,020 feet elevation. Once across the road the trail winds its way east and climbs gently. Soon you will cross a poorly defined ridgeline and traverse the timbered slope to Warren Gap. In the gap at 1,170 feet elevation and 0.7 mile from Wind River Road, the path crosses Forest Road 6517 (Warren Gap Road). The course then descends through the timber for 1.3 miles to Panther Creek Road (FR 65). There is parking and minimal stock facilities available next to the place where the PCT crosses FR 65. Panther Creek Campground is only a short distance to the left (north).

From Panther Creek Road, at 930 feet elevation, the PCT heads east for 0.2 mile to a wood and concrete bridge over Panther Creek. Just before crossing the bridge, there is a side trail to the left (north). This path leads a short distance to Panther Creek Campground. After crossing the bridge the tread soon begins to climb. The route makes several long switchbacks as it climbs. Due to rerouting of the PCT, the map is not exactly correct in this area. The route crosses the abandoned roadbed of Forest Road 020, 3.6 miles from Panther Creek Road at 2,300 feet elevation. You continue to climb after crossing the abandoned road for another 1.3 miles to the junction with Forest Road 68 at 2,830 feet elevation. There is parking for several cars here next to the trail but no other facilities

The PCT crosses FR 68 6.9 miles from Wind River Road. It then climbs moderately and makes a couple of switchbacks. Soon, as the course crosses a brush-covered slope, the Columbia River Gorge and Mount Hood come into view to the south. The tread passes a viewpoint above a steep, open slope 1.5 miles from FR 68. This spot, at 3,380 feet elevation, offers a great view of Mount Hood.

From the viewpoint to the junction with Big Huckleberry Mountain Summit Trail, 2.4 miles ahead, the USDA Forest Service Pacific Crest Trail map shows the route somewhat incorrectly. The trail makes several switchbacks as it climbs along the ridgeline to the junction with Grassy Knoll Trail 146, at 4,000 feet elevation. The Grassy Knoll Trail descends southeast to another trailhead on FR 68.

A few feet past the junction with Grassy Knoll Trail is the junction with the trail to the summit of Big Huckleberry Mountain. If you can spare a few minutes, the short climb to the summit is well worth the time. To reach the summit, turn right (east) at the junction and climb for 0.3 mile to the top. The open summit, at 4,207 feet elevation, is ringed with silver and other fir trees, as well as a few lodgepole pines. The rocky ground is covered with penstemon, phlox, cat's ear lilies, and many other wildflowers. To the south Mount Hood and Mount Jefferson are in view. Mount Adams is nearby to the northeast and to the north is Mount Rainier. Mount St. Helens is close to the northwest but is obscured by the tall silver firs.

After spending some time admiring the view from the summit, descend back down to the PCT to continue your hike north. Much of the next 3.6 miles of the PCT are shown incorrectly on the USDA Forest Service Pacific Crest Trail map. The trail has been rerouted to make it an easier grade. You will reach an unmarked trail junction 3.6 miles from the junction with Big Huckleberry Mountain Summit Trail. From this junction at 3,250 feet elevation, it is about 0.1 mile west to Forest Road 6801.

Leaving the junction with the unmarked access trail to FR 6801, the PCT heads northeast. The tread soon passes below a clear-cut and reaches the edge of an old lava flow. Watch and listen for pikas in the lava. The path passes a developed campsite with a bench, table, and fire ring 0.4 mile from the unmarked junction. Once past the campsite the route climbs gently and soon bends to the northwest. A little farther along, 1.8 miles from the unmarked junction, the trail bears right (north) and heads across the lava flow. Wind your way across the lava for another 1.3 miles to Crest Camp and the junction with FR 60 at 3,500 feet elevation.

Pacific Crest Trail 2000, Wind River Road to Crest Camp

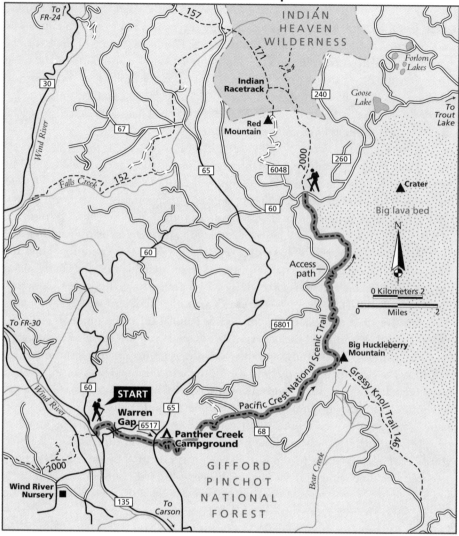

Options

An optional starting point for this hike is the Panther Creek trailhead. To get to Panther Creek trailhead, backtrack south from where the PCT crosses Wind River Road for a short distance to Warren Gap Road. Turn east onto Warren Gap Road and drive 2 miles to the junction with FR 65. Turn right (south) onto FR 65 and you will reach the trailhead in a very short distance. Panther Creek Campground is between the junction with FR 65 and the trailhead.

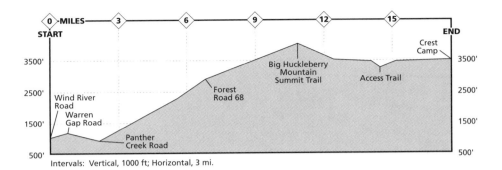

Intervals: Vertical, 1000 ft; Horizontal, 3 mi.

It is possible to continue north on the PCT from Crest Camp through the Indian Heaven Wilderness to the PCT trailhead on FR 24 for a 16.4-mile extension of this hike.

Miles and Directions

0.0   Junction of Wind River Road and the PCT.

0.7   Warren Gap. Cross Warren Gap Road (FR 6517).

2.0   Cross Panther Creek Road (FR 65) (GPS 45 49.069 N 121 52.871 W).

6.9   Cross FR 68 (GPS 45 49.693 N 121 50.150 W).

10.8 Junction with Grassy Knoll Trail and Big Huckleberry Mountain Summit Trail (GPS 45 50.808 N 121 47.207 W). Stay left (north) at both junctions.

14.4 Junction with access trail from FR 6801 (GPS 45 52.847 N 121 47.322 W). Stay right (northeast).

17.6 Crest Camp (GPS 45 54.552 N 121 48.130 W).

Trapper Creek Wilderness and the Region Near the Columbia River Gorge

Being at generally lower elevation than the Mount Adams and Indian Heaven Wilderness areas, the Trapper Creek Wilderness offers lightly used trails through huge old-growth forest. Hike 31, Trapper Creek Trail 192 follows almost the full length of Trapper Creek from near its confluence with the Wind River to its head near Observation Peak and junction with Hike 33, Observation Trail 132. Hike 34, Observation Peak Trail 132A climbs Observation Peak. Challenging Hikes 36, Big Slide Trail 195 and 37, Sunshine Trail 198 descend the northern slopes of Trapper Creek Canyon. Around the southern boundary of the wilderness, Hike 38, Soda Peaks Lake Trail 133 follows the ridgeline close to Soda Peaks and then descends past a beautiful subalpine lake on its way into the depths of Trapper Creek Canyon and a junction with Trapper Creek Trail. Hike 32, Dry Creek Trail 194 is an entirely low-elevation route along a creek bottom thickly inhabited with Roosevelt elk. Black bears are common throughout Trapper Creek Wilderness.

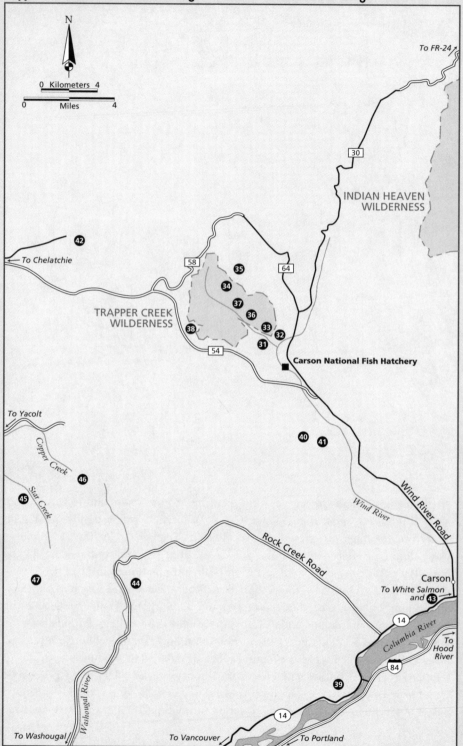

Close to the Columbia River Gorge, Hikes 45, Silver Star Mountain North, Trails 180-1, 180D; 46, Bluff Mountain to Silver Star Mountain Summit, Trails 172, 180-1, 180D; and 47, Silver Star Mountain via the Pyramid, Trails 180F, 180-2, 180D follow open flower-covered ridgelines sometimes within sight of the Portland Metro area. Slightly farther east, Hike 44, Three Corner Rock Trail climbs from the thick green forest deep in the Washougal River Canyon to the ridgetop meadows south of Three Corner Rock and then scrambles to its rocky summit. Far to the east and very close to the Columbia River, Hike 43, Horsethief Butte traverses semidesert tablelands, with early season flowers and views of Mount Hood.

31 Trapper Creek Trail 192

Hike through the magnificent, low-elevation, old-growth forest of Trapper Creek Canyon.

Start: Trapper Creek trailhead.
Distance: 15.2-mile out-and-back day hike or backpack.
Difficulty: Easy up to the Observation Trail, moderate from there to the Big Slide Trail, and then strenuous the rest of the way.
Seasons: May through October to the junction with Sunshine Trail, mid-June through October above there.
Fees and permits: Northwest Forest Pass and Trapper Creek Wilderness Permit.

Parking and trailhead facilities: There is adequate parking at the trailhead but no other facilities.
Maps: USDA Forest Service Trapper Creek and Indian Heaven Wilderness or Bare Mountain and Termination Point USGS quads.
Trail contacts: Gifford Pinchot National Forest, Wind River Ranger District, Mile Post 1.26 Hemlock Road, Carson, WA 98610; (509) 427-5645; www.fs.fed.us/gpnf.

Finding the trailhead: From Portland drive east on I-84 to exit 44 at the Cascade Locks. Pay the 75-cent toll and cross the Bridge of the Gods over the Columbia River. Turn right (east) at the north end of the bridge and follow State Route 14 for about 7 miles to the junction with Wind River Road. At the junction a sign points left to Carson.

If you are coming from the east on I-84, leave the freeway at Hood River (exit 64). Cross the Hood River Bridge over the Columbia River and turn left (west) onto SR 14. Follow SR 14 west for 15 miles to the junction with Wind River Road.

Turn north and drive 1 mile to Carson. Head north from Carson, staying on Wind River Road for 13 miles to the junction with County Road 8c, signed TO GOVERNMENT MINERAL SPRINGS. This junction is just past (north of) the Carson Fish Hatchery. Turn left at the junction and head northwest for 0.5 mile to the junction with Forest Road 5401. Turn right onto FR 5401 and drive north 0.5 mile to the Trapper Creek trailhead, at 1,150 feet elevation.

Special Considerations

The route may be rough and vague in spots past the first junction with Deer Cut-off Trail. Bears are common in Trapper Creek Wilderness; hang your food and keep a clean camp.

The Hike

Fill out your wilderness permit and head north from the parking area. In a few yards you will come to a trail junction with the Dry Creek Trail 194. Turn left at the junction and hike west-northwest through the mixed-age forest of cedar, hemlock, and fir. If you are here in May, trilliums may be blooming beside the path. Yew bushes, vine maple, Oregon grape, and a few dogwood trees form the forest understory.

Trapper Creek

Shortly, the tread begins to climb gently, gaining a little more than 100 feet in elevation before flattening out. Nine-tenths of a mile into the hike, just after passing the Trapper Creek Wilderness boundary, the well-maintained track reaches the junction with the Observation Trail 132. The Observation Trail to the right (north) climbs Howe Ridge to Observation Peak. To the left Trail 132 goes a short distance south to closed FR 5401.

Continue straight ahead (west) at the junction. From this junction onward, the Trapper Creek Trail is closed to all except hikers. A few feet past the junction, the Trapper Creek Trail crosses a wooden bridge and climbs gently. Soon you are on a slope well above the creek bottom. The now-narrower path crosses another wooden bridge over a bubbling unnamed creek 0.7 mile from the junction and soon reaches the junction with Soda Peaks Lake Trail 133. At the junction, elevation 1,380 feet and 1.7 miles from Trapper Creek trailhead, Soda Peaks Lake is to the left (southwest).

In the next mile the route climbs nearly 500 feet in elevation and then descends slightly for another 0.2 mile to the junction with the Big Slide Trail 195. The rough and vague Big Slide Trail climbs to the northeast to join the Observation Trail. Continue west (straight ahead) on Trapper Creek Trail for a few yards to the junction with Deer Cutoff Trail 209. See Options for more information about Deer Cutoff Trail. From this point onward the Trapper Creek Trail is in much poorer condition, and it may be difficult to follow at times.

Turn left at the junction and begin to descend south toward Trapper Creek. The path crosses a small wooden bridge 0.2 mile from the junction. Just past the bridge a side path leads a few yards to the left to Terrace Camp. Terrace Camp is a good camp spot. Past Terrace Camp the Trapper Creek Trail winds on down and soon is fairly close to Trapper Creek. A little farther along the trace crosses Slump Creek on a large but somewhat rotten log in a side draw. If you don't feel comfortable crossing the log, Slump Creek can be forded easily. There are some very large Douglas firs close to the trail here. All of them show the scars of a long-ago forest fire.

The rough trail soon becomes steep as it climbs to the second junction with Deer Cutoff Trail. This junction is 3.8 miles from Trapper Creek trailhead. After passing the second junction with Deer Cutoff Trail, the Trapper Creek Trail climbs to the northwest for 0.2 mile to the junction with the Sunshine Trail 198. The route crosses three tiny streams, which may be dry in late summer and fall, before reaching the Sunshine Trail.

Leaving the junction with the Sunshine Trail, the route continues northwest for 0.1 mile to a very old two-log bridge over Hidden Creek. A short distance past the bridge, a short path leading to a viewpoint of Hidden Creek Falls turns off to the right. Four-tenths of a mile farther along, the trail begins a rugged and sometimes steep climb toward the ridgeline. After making six switchbacks the route crosses another bridge at 2,330 feet elevation. Below the bridge rush the frothing waters of Trapper Creek.

Once across the bridge the path continues its steep climb, making eighteen switchbacks and gaining more than 700 feet in elevation in the next 0.7 mile. Above the switchbacks the trail becomes a little more difficult to follow as it heads north to another crossing of Trapper Creek at 3,240 feet elevation, 6.3 miles from the trailhead. There may be a log crossing about 50 yards upstream from the point where the trail fords Trapper Creek. The trail is marked with tiny, about 1-inch-wide, aluminum diamonds in this area, but you have to look hard to see them very far ahead.

After crossing Trapper Creek the route heads east and crosses a couple of small streams before reaching the junction with the Rim Trail 202. It is 0.7 mile and about a 300-foot climb from the second crossing of Trapper Creek to the Rim Trail junction. The forest here has many large cedars and firs, and the floor is covered with avalanche lilies, beargrass, and huckleberries. At the junction the Rim Trail turns off to the right (southeast) and contours along the slope to join Sunshine Trail. Trapper Creek Trail bears northeast. Soon after passing the junction with the Rim Trail, Trapper Creek Trail turns to the north and climbs to its highest point (elevation 3,790 feet) before descending gently for a short distance to the junction with the Observation Trail 132. The junction, in a saddle on a ridgeline, is 7.6 miles from Trapper Creek trailhead.

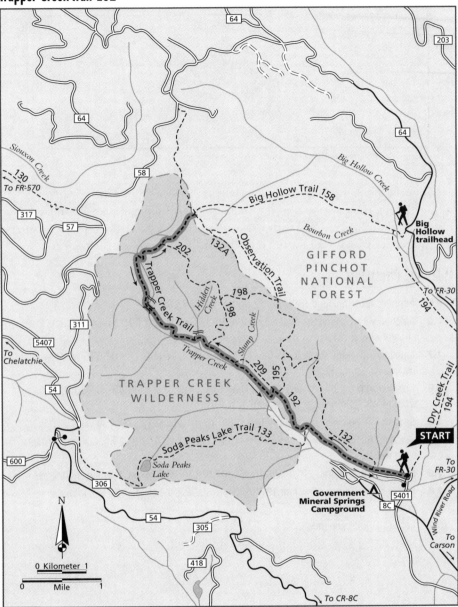

Options

Deer Cutoff Trail is a shortcut for hikers heading up Trapper Creek. The route is narrow, rough, and vague in spots, but it is about 0.2 mile shorter in distance and requires less climbing than following Trapper Creek Trail. You will also need to ford Slump Creek on the cutoff.

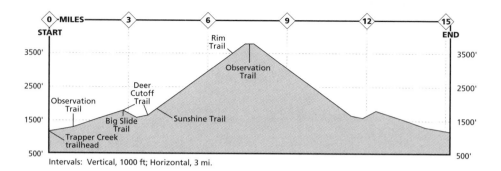

Intervals: Vertical, 1000 ft; Horizontal, 3 mi.

To make a lollipop loop hike, turn right at the second junction with the Observation Trail (at the upper end of the Trapper Creek Trail) and hike 5.5 miles southeast along the Observation Trail to rejoin Trapper Creek Trail. Turn left (east) and follow Trapper Creek Trail for 0.9 mile back to Trapper Creek trailhead.

Miles and Directions

0.0 Trapper Creek trailhead (GPS 45 52.900 N 121 58.790 W).

0.9 Junction with Observation Trail 132 (GPS 45 53.088 N 121 59.721 W). Continue straight ahead (west).

1.7 Junction with Soda Peaks Lake Trail 133 (GPS 45 53.462 N 122 00.410 W). Stay right (west).

2.9 Junction with Big Slide Trail 195 and Deer Cutoff Trail 209 (GPS 45 54.030 N 122 01.034 W). Continue straight (west).

3.8 Second junction with Deer Cutoff Trail (GPS 45 54.246 N 122 01.739 W).

4.0 Junction with Sunshine Trail 198 (GPS 45 54.292 N 122 01.912 W). Continue straight (northwest).

7.0 Junction with Rim Trail 202 (GPS 45 55.367 N 122 02.271 W). Stay left (northeast).

7.6 Junction with Observation Trail 132 (GPS 45 55.788 N 122 02.154 W). Turnaround point.

15.2 Trapper Creek trailhead.

32 Dry Creek Trail 194

Early season hike through dense forest with a good possibility of seeing a band of Roosevelt elk.

Start: Trapper Creek trailhead.

Distance: 4.3-mile one-way shuttle day hike.

Difficulty: Easy unless the streams are high, making crossings difficult.

Seasons: Late April through November.

Fees and permits: A Northwest Forest Pass is required at the trailheads. If you are going to make a side trip into Trapper Creek Wilderness, a wilderness permit is required.

Parking and trailhead facilities: There is adequate parking at the Trapper Creek trailhead

but no other facilities. Big Hollow trailhead has parking for a couple of cars but no other facilities.

Maps: USDA Forest Service Trapper Creek and Indian Heaven Wilderness or Termination Point USGS quad.

Trail contacts: Gifford Pinchot National Forest, Wind River Ranger District, Mile Post 1.26 Hemlock Road, Carson, WA 98610; (509) 427–5645; www.fs.fed.us/gpnf.

Finding the trailhead: From Portland drive east on I–84 to the Cascade Locks (exit 44). Pay the 75-cent toll and cross the Bridge of the Gods over the Columbia River. Turn right at the north end of the bridge (east) onto State Route 14. Drive east on SR 14 for about 7 miles to the junction with Wind River Road, signed TO CARSON.

If you are coming from the east on I–84, leave the freeway at Hood River (exit 64). Cross the bridge over the Columbia River and turn left (west) onto SR 14. Follow SR 14 west for 15 miles to the junction with Wind River Road.

Turn north and drive 1 mile to Carson. Head north from Carson on Wind River Road for 13 miles to the junction with County Road 8c, signed TO GOVERNMENT MINERAL SPRINGS. This junction is just past (north of) the Carson Fish Hatchery. Turn left at the junction and head northwest for 0.5 mile to the junction with Forest Road 5401. Turn right onto FR 5401 and drive north 0.5 mile to the Trapper Creek trailhead. The elevation at the trailhead is 1,150 feet.

To reach the Big Hollow trailhead where this hike ends, go back to Wind River Road and drive north for 2.1 miles to the junction with Forest Road 64. Turn left at the junction and continue north on FR 64 for 2.2 miles to the trailhead.

Special Considerations

Crossing Bourbon Creek and Dry Creek could be difficult during times of high water. Snowdrifts seem to hang on later in the spring in the Wind River drainage than they do in other areas of comparable altitude.

The Hike

The route begins at the north end of the large Trapper Creek trailhead parking area. A short distance into the woods, the trail splits. The tread to the left is Trapper Creek

Dry Creek

Trail 192. Bear right at the junction and hike north-northeast. The moss-hung, second-growth forest here is made up of mostly Douglas fir, with an understory of vine maple. Where you hike close to Dry Creek, big-leaf maple, alder, and western red cedar dominate the canopy. Watch for elk tracks on the trail. If you are hiking early in the morning or in the evening, you may catch a glimpse of these magnificent animals, or you may hear them crashing through the underbrush.

After hiking 3.4 miles through the lush vegetation, you will cross the first of two small wooden bridges. Another half a mile brings you to Bourbon Creek. There is no bridge here, so fording the creek may be necessary. This crossing is usually no problem, but it could be dangerous during times of heavy runoff. A log jam may aid the crossing, but use caution when crossing the logs. Don't ever cross a stream on the upper side of a log jam; you could be swept beneath it. The junction with Big Hollow Trail 158 is reached 0.1 mile after crossing Bourbon Creek.

Bear right (east-northeast) at the junction and walk a short distance to Dry Creek. Dry Creek, which is larger than Bourbon Creek, also has no bridge crossing it. When I hiked this route, there was a log to cross on a few yards upstream from the point where the trail crosses, but getting on and off of it was a little tricky. This crossing could be dangerous during high water.

Dry Creek Trail 194

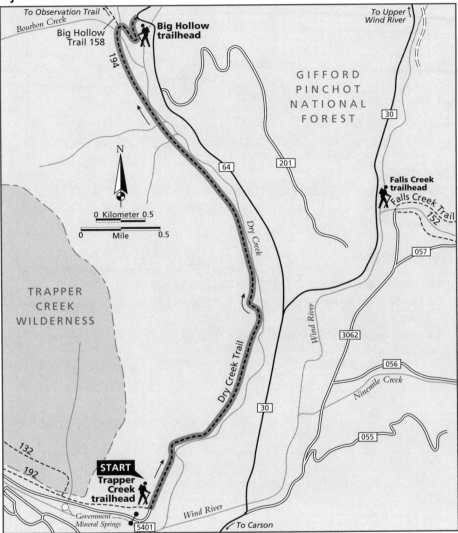

After crossing Dry Creek the track heads southeast for a short distance. It then makes a hard turn to the north and soon reaches Big Hollow trailhead on FR 64, at 1,470 feet elevation.

Options

Dry Creek Trail may be used as part of a loop hike that includes Trapper Creek, Observation, and Big Hollow Trails. To make this 14.7-mile loop, first hike up Trapper Creek Trail to its end at the junction with the Observation Trail. Turn left (northwest) onto the Observation Trail and go 0.1 mile to the junction with the Big

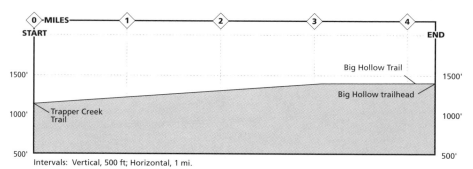

Intervals: Vertical, 500 ft; Horizontal, 1 mi.

Hollow Trail. Turn right onto Big Hollow Trail and descend 2.9 miles to the junction with the Dry Creek Trail. Turn right onto Dry Creek Trail and hike south to the Trapper Creek trailhead.

Miles and Directions

0.0 Trapper Creek trailhead (GPS 45 52.900 N 121 58.790 W).

4.1 Junction with Big Hollow Trail 158 (GPS 45 55.540 N 121 58.990 W). Bear right (east-northeast).

4.3 Big Hollow trailhead (GPS 45 55.599 N 121 58.897 W).

33 Observation Trail 132

Climb from deep in Trapper Creek Canyon to Howe Ridge, and maybe make a short side trip to Observation Peak. Then continue through the old-growth forest to the upper trailhead on Forest Road 58.

Start: Trapper Creek trailhead.
Distance: 8.4-mile one-way shuttle day hike or backpack.
Difficulty: Moderate.
Seasons: July through September.
Fees and permits: Northwest Forest Pass and Trapper Creek Wilderness Permit.
Parking and trailhead facilities: There is adequate parking at the Trapper Creek trailhead but no other facilities. The upper trailhead has parking for a couple of cars but nothing else.
Maps: USDA Forest Service Trapper Creek and Indian Heaven Wilderness or Termination Point and Bare Mountain USGS quads.
Trail contacts: Gifford Pinchot National Forest, Wind River Ranger District, Mile Post 1.26 Hemlock Road, Carson, WA 98610; (509) 427-5645; www.fs.fed.us/gpnf.

Finding the trailhead: From Portland drive east on I-84 to the Cascade Locks (exit 44). Pay the 75-cent toll and cross the Bridge of the Gods over the Columbia River. Turn right at the north end of the bridge (east) onto State Route 14. Drive east on SR 14 for about 7 miles to the junction with Wind River Road, signed TO CARSON.

If you are coming from the east on I-84, leave the freeway at Hood River (exit 64). Cross the bridge over the Columbia River and turn left (west) onto SR 14. Follow SR 14 west for 15 miles to the junction with Wind River Road.

Turn north and drive 1 mile to Carson. Head north from Carson on Wind River Road for 13 miles to the junction with County Road 8c, signed TO GOVERNMENT MINERAL SPRINGS. This junction is just past (north of) the Carson Fish Hatchery. Turn left at the junction and head northwest for 0.5 mile to the junction with Forest Road 5401. Turn right onto FR 5401 and drive north 0.5 mile to the Trapper Creek trailhead, at 1,150 feet elevation.

To reach the upper Observation trailhead where this hike ends, drive back to Wind River Road. Turn left and drive 2.1 miles north on Wind River Road to the junction with Forest Road 64. Turn left at the junction and continue north for 6.1 miles on FR 64 to the junction with FR 58. There is no sign marking this Y intersection at present. Turn left onto FR 58 and drive southwest for 2 miles to the trailhead. The poorly marked trailhead is on the left side of the road at the junction with Forest Road 224. The GPS coordinates at the upper trailhead are 45 56.996 N 122 02.385 W, and the elevation is 3,540 feet.

Special Considerations

There isn't usually any water along the upper 6.5 miles of this trail. There is 3,000 feet of elevation gain hiking the Observation Trail in this direction.

Mount St. Helens from Observation Peak

The Hike

Hike north from the parking area on Trapper Creek Trail 192. In a few yards you will come to a trail junction with the Dry Creek Trail 194. Turn left at the junction, staying on Trapper Creek Trail, and hike west-northwest.

Soon the route climbs gently, gaining a little more than 100 feet of elevation before flattening out. Nine-tenths of a mile from the trailhead, just after entering Trapper Creek Wilderness, you will reach the junction with the Observation Trail 132. Trapper Creek and Observation Trails follow the same route to this point. At this four-way junction, turning left onto Observation Trail 132 will lead you only a short distance to closed road FR 5401.

Turn right (north-northeast) onto the Observation Trail. The route climbs gently for the first 0.2 mile and then turns west to cross a small creek at 1,360 feet elevation. After crossing the stream the tread ascends more steeply along a slope covered with tall, straight Douglas firs and vine maple. The path climbs at a moderate rate for 0.6 mile and then flattens out a little. In May lady slipper orchids grace the sides of the track with their delicate blooms. The large fir trees show the scars of a long-ago forest fire. After crossing a couple more tiny streams, which may be dry by midsummer, the trail reaches another creek crossing. Look above the trail here to the cascading waterfall in the stream. At the creek crossing you are 2.9 miles from the Trapper Creek trailhead, at 2,030 feet elevation. This stream may be the last water source for some distance along this route.

A short distance after crossing the creek, the course crosses another tiny stream. Above the trail here the water splashes and drips over a moss-covered rock outcropping. The path continues to climb and crosses a rounded ridgeline 3.3 miles from the trailhead. Two-tenths of a mile after crossing the ridge is the junction with the Big Slide Trail 195, at 2,470 feet elevation. Rough and steep Big Slide Trail descends to the southwest to join Trapper Creek Trail.

The route continues to climb along Howe Ridge after passing the junction with Big Slide Trail, gaining 1,000 feet in elevation in the mile and a half to the junction with the Sunshine Trail 198. Sunshine Trail is also rough, steep, and hard to follow down to Trapper Creek Trail. From the junction continue heading northwest along the ridgeline. Shortly, the route bears to the right (north) of the ridge to traverse a steep, densely timbered slope. The course regains the ridgeline 1 mile after passing the junction with the Sunshine Trail. On the ridgeline at 3,820 feet elevation, 6 miles from Trapper Creek trailhead, is the junction with the Observation Peak Trail 132A. Observation Peak Trail turns to the left (southeast). After passing the junction with Observation Peak Trail, the tread contours along the wooded slope for another 0.4 mile to its second junction with Trapper Creek Trail.

Continue north from the junction for a short distance to a place called Berry Camp and the junction with Big Hollow Trail 158. Berry Camp, at 3,770 feet elevation, is 6.5 miles from the trailhead. There is a campsite at Berry Camp, and water is sometimes available from a spring near the campsite, but don't count on it.

Heading northwest from Berry Camp, the trail climbs moderately for 0.7 mile to the ridgeline at 4,130 feet elevation. On the ridge a side path turns to the right (north) and leads about 40 yards to a viewpoint. The main route leaves the Trapper Creek Wilderness a short distance after passing the path to the viewpoint. For the next 1.2 miles the trace descends gently through the old-growth fir and hemlock forest of the Sisters Rock Experimental Area to the trailhead on FR 58, at 3,540 feet elevation.

Options

Try to allow enough time to make the side trip to Observation Peak, or make this a 13.2-mile out-and-back hike to the summit of Observation Peak.

To make a 14-mile loop, turn left at the junction with the Trapper Creek Trail 6.4 miles into this hike. Then hike south and southeast along Trapper Creek Trail down into Trapper Creek Canyon and back to Trapper Creek trailhead.

Observation Trail 132

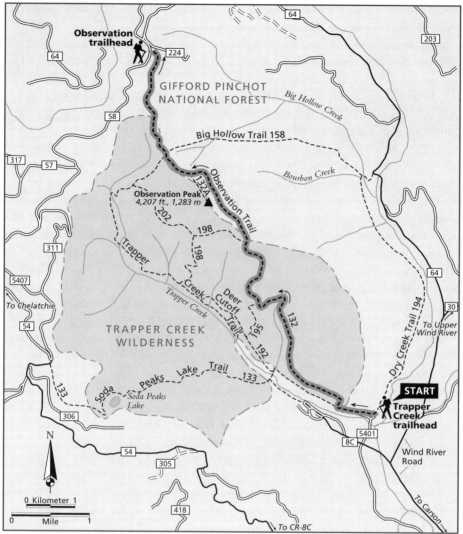

Shorter loop hikes can be made by descending either Sunshine or Big Slide Trails to Trapper Creek Trail. Either of these routes may challenge your route-finding skills.

Miles and Directions

0.0 Trapper Creek trailhead (GPS 45 52.900 N 121 58.790 W). Turn left (west-northwest), onto Trapper Creek Trail 192.

0.9 Junction with Observation Trail 132 (GPS 45 53.088 N 121 59.721 W). Turn right (north-northeast).

3.5 Junction with Big Slide Trail 195 (GPS 45 54.103 N 122 00.768 W). Stay right (north-west).

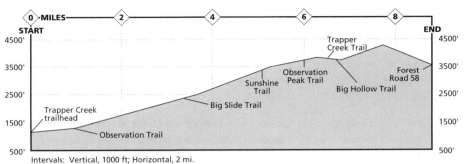

Intervals: Vertical, 1000 ft; Horizontal, 2 mi.

5.0 Junction with Sunshine Trail 198 (GPS 45 55.122 N 122 01.078 W). Stay right (northwest).

6.0 Junction with Observation Peak Trail 132A (GPS 45 55.559 N 122 01.860 W). Continue straight (west).

6.4 Junction with Trapper Creek Trail 192 (GPS 45 55.788 N 122 02.154 W). Continue north.

6.5 Junction with Big Hollow Trail 158 (GPS 45 55.803 N 122 02.148 W). Stay left (northwest).

8.4 Upper trailhead on FR 58 (GPS 45 56.994 N 122 02.386 W).

34 Observation Peak Trail 132A

Hike through old-growth forest to the marvelous view from the open, flower-covered summit of 4,207-foot-high Observation Peak.

Start: Junction of Observation Trail and Observation Peak Trail; nearest trailhead is upper Observation Trail trailhead on Forest Road 58.
Distance: 1.2-mile internal out-and-back day hike; 6.0 miles round-trip from upper Observation Trail trailhead.
Difficulty: Moderate.
Seasons: Mid-June through October.
Fees and permits: Northwest Forest Pass and Trapper Creek Wilderness Permit.

Parking and trailhead facilities: The upper Observation Trail trailhead has parking for a couple of cars but nothing else.
Maps: USDA Forest Service Trapper Creek and Indian Heaven Wilderness or Bare Mountain USGS quad.
Trail contacts: Gifford Pinchot National Forest, Wind River Ranger District, Mile Post 1.26 Hemlock Road, Carson, WA 98610; (509) 427–5645; www.fs.fed.us/gpnf.

Finding the trailhead: From Portland drive east on I-84 to the Cascade Locks (exit 44). Pay the 75-cent toll and cross the Bridge of the Gods over the Columbia River. Turn right at the north end of the bridge (east) onto State Route 14. Drive east on SR 14 for about 7 miles to the junction with the Wind River Road, signed TO CARSON.

If you are coming from the east on I-84, leave the freeway at Hood River (exit 64). Cross the bridge over the Columbia River and turn left (west) onto SR 14. Follow SR 14 west for 15 miles to the junction with Wind River Road.

Turn north and drive 1 mile to Carson. Head north from Carson, staying on Wind River Road for 15 miles to the junction with Forest Road 64. Turn left at the junction and continue north for 6.1 miles on FR 64 to the junction with FR 58. There is no sign marking this Y intersection at present. Turn left onto FR 58 and drive southwest for 2 miles to the upper Observation Trail trailhead. The poorly marked trailhead is on the left side of the road at the junction with Forest Road 224. The GPS coordinates at the upper trailhead are 45 56.996 N 122 02.385 W, and the elevation is 3,540 feet. Hike south and southeast along the Observation Trail for 2.4 miles to the junction with the Observation Peak Trail where this hike begins.

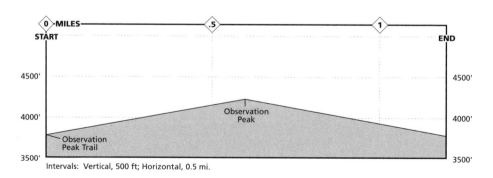

Intervals: Vertical, 500 ft; Horizontal, 0.5 mi.

Soda Peaks from Observation Peak

Special Considerations

Take along all the water you will need, as there may be none along the upper part of the Observation Trail and there is none along the Observation Peak Trail.

The Hike

Observation Peak Trail climbs moderately to the southeast from the junction with the Observation Trail. Thick but mostly open woods line the path and huckleberries abound on the forest floor. After hiking 0.3 mile, a path to the left (north) leaves the trail. The side path climbs 100 feet in a couple of hundred yards to a rocky ridgetop viewpoint at 4,110 feet elevation. Hiking to the viewpoint is well worth the effort. The view includes Mounts St. Helens, Rainier, and Adams, as well as Goat Rocks.

Past the side path the route to Observation Peak climbs more steeply along the ridgeline, heading southeast. As you approach the summit, 0.6 mile from the junction with the Observation Trail, the view opens up in all directions. From the 4,207-foot summit, you can see past Mount Hood and Mount Jefferson as far south as the Three Sisters Mountains, nearly halfway across Oregon. Mount Adams looms high to the northeast, and below to the south is the Wind River Valley and a small section of the Columbia River deep in the Columbia River Gorge. Yellow glacier lilies add spots of cheerful color to the grass-covered summit. Allow plenty of time to enjoy the view.

Observation Peak Trail 132A

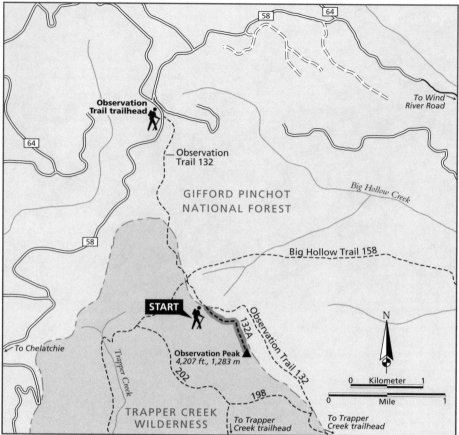

Options

Observation Peak makes a great spot for a bivouac. There is a small flat spot next to the summit that could be used for an overnight stay if you would like to see the sunrise from this beautiful spot. If you do stay here, be sure to practice zero-impact camping. Don't build a fire or trample the flowers. There isn't any water close to the summit, so it must be carried up. Cell-phone service is generally good from the summit.

Miles and Directions

0.0 Junction of Observation Trail 132 and Observation Peak Trail 132A (GPS 45 55.559 N 122 01.860 W).

0.6 Observation Peak (GPS 45 55.238 N 122 01.482 W). Turnaround point.

1.2 Junction of Observation Trail and Observation Peak Trail.

35 Big Hollow Trail 158

Descend this lightly used route from high on a ridgeline into the depths of Dry Creek Canyon.

Start: Junction of Observation Trail and Big Hollow Trail at Berry Camp; nearest trailhead is upper Observation Trail trailhead on Forest Road 58.
Distance: 3.1-mile internal-start shuttle hike; 5.0 miles one-way from upper Observation Trail trailhead.
Difficulty: Moderate.
Seasons: Mid-June through October.
Fees and permits: Northwest Forest Pass and Trapper Creek Wilderness Permit.

Parking and trailhead facilities: There is only limited parking and no other facilities at either of these trailheads.
Maps: USDA Forest Service Trapper Creek and Indian Heaven Wilderness or Bare Mountain and Termination Point USGS quads.
Trail contacts: Gifford Pinchot National Forest, Wind River Ranger District, Mile Post 1.26 Hemlock Road, Carson, WA 98610; (509) 427–5645; www.fs.fed.us/gpnf.

Finding the trailhead: Head east from Portland on I-84 to exit 44 at the Cascade Locks and cross the Bridge of the Gods over the Columbia River. Turn right (east) at the north end of the bridge and follow State Route 14 for about 7 miles to the junction with Wind River Road. At the junction a sign points left to Carson.

If you are coming from the east on I-84, leave the freeway at Hood River (exit 64). Cross the Hood River Bridge over the Columbia River and turn left (west) onto SR 14. Follow SR 14 west for 15 miles to the junction with Wind River Road.

Turn north and drive 1 mile to Carson. Head north from Carson and stay on Wind River Road for 15 miles to the junction with Forest Road 64. Turn left at the junction and continue north for 6.1 miles on FR 64 to the junction with FR 58. There is no sign marking this Y intersection at present. Turn left onto FR 58 and drive southwest for 2 miles to the upper Observation Trail trailhead. The poorly marked trailhead is on the left side of the road at the junction with Forest Road 224. The GPS coordinates at the upper trailhead are 45 56.996 N 122 02.385 W, and the elevation is 3,540 feet.

Hike 1.9 miles south on Observation Trail 132 to the junction with Big Hollow Trail at Berry Camp. The elevation at the junction is 3,770 feet.

To reach the Big Hollow trailhead where this hike ends, head back the way you came on FR 58 for 2 miles to the junction with FR 64. Turn right and follow FR 64 southeast for 3.9 miles to the Big Hollow trailhead.

Special Considerations

Crossing Dry Creek can be difficult at times.

Big Hollow Trail 158

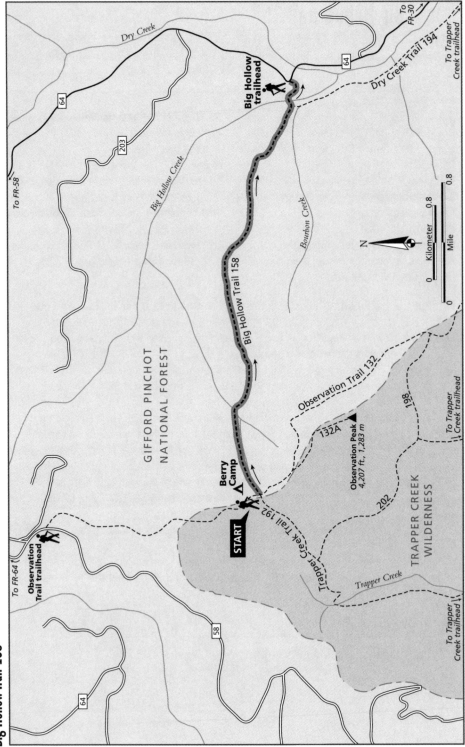

The Hike

From the triangle-shaped junction with the Observation Trail at Berry Camp, the Big Hollow Trail begins its descent to the east. Beargrass, avalanche lilies, trilliums, and huckleberry bushes dot the forest floor beneath the canopy of fir and hemlock. A short distance from Berry Camp, three tiny streams flow from a spring through pipes beneath the trail. The route crosses a creek 0.5 mile after leaving Berry Camp. From here down to the junction with Dry Creek Trail, you will pass many large old-growth Douglas fir trees. Dogwood trees bloom in late June in places, and vine maple adds variety to the forest understory.

The tread maintains a steady moderate-to-steep grade most of the way down. The junction with Dry Creek Trail 194 is reached at 1,380 feet elevation, 2.9 miles from Berry Camp. Along Dry Creek large big-leaf maples make up much of the forest canopy.

Bear left (east-northeast) at the junction and hike a short distance to Dry Creek. There isn't a bridge across Dry Creek, so if no logs are available, you may have to ford its cold waters. During periods of high water, this crossing could be dangerous. After crossing Dry Creek the track heads southeast for a short distance. It then makes a hard turn to the north and soon reaches Big Hollow trailhead on FR 64, at 1,470 feet elevation.

Options

Use Big Hollow Trail and Dry Creek Trail as an alternate return route from either Observation or Trapper Creek Trails.

Miles and Directions

0.0 Junction of Observation Trail 132 and Big Hollow Trail 158 at Berry Camp (GPS 45 55.803 N 122 02.148 W).

2.9 Junction with Dry Creek Trail 194 (GPS 45 55.540 N 121 58.990 W). Bear left (east-northeast).

3.1 Big Hollow trailhead (GPS 45 55.599 N 121 58.897 W).

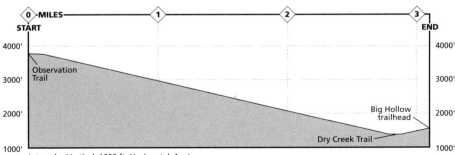

Intervals: Vertical, 1000 ft; Horizontal, 1 mi.

36 Big Slide Trail 195

A short but challenging connecting route on the north slope of Trapper Creek Canyon.

Start: Junction of Big Slide Trail and Observation Trail; nearest trailhead is Trapper Creek trailhead on Forest Road 5401.
Distance: 0.7-mile one-way internal connector day hike; 4.2 miles one way from Trapper Creek trailhead.
Difficulty: Strenuous, with excellent route-finding skills required.
Seasons: June through October.
Fees and permits: Northwest Forest Pass and Trapper Creek Wilderness Permit.

Parking and trailhead facilities: There is adequate parking at the Trapper Creek trailhead but no other facilities.
Maps: USDA Forest Service Indian Heaven and Trapper Creek Wilderness. The USGS Bare Mountain quad covers the area but does not show this trail.
Trail contacts: Gifford Pinchot National Forest, Wind River Ranger District, Mile Post 1.26 Hemlock Road, Carson, WA 98610; (509) 427-5645; www.fs.fed.us/gpnf.

Finding the trailhead: From Portland drive east on I-84 to the Cascade Locks (exit 44). Pay the 75-cent toll and cross the Bridge of the Gods over the Columbia River. Turn right at the north end of the bridge (east) onto State Route 14. Drive east on SR 14 for about 7 miles to the junction with Wind River Road, signed TO CARSON.

If you are coming from the east on I-84, leave the freeway at Hood River (exit 64). Cross the bridge over the Columbia River and turn left (west) onto SR 14. Follow SR 14 west for 15 miles to the junction with Wind River Road.

Turn north and drive 1 mile to Carson. Head north from Carson on Wind River Road for 13 miles to the junction with County Road 8c, signed TO GOVERNMENT MINERAL SPRINGS. This junction is just past (north of) the Carson Fish Hatchery. Turn left at the junction and head northwest for 0.5 mile to the junction with FR 5401. Turn right onto FR 5401 and drive north 0.5 mile to the Trapper Creek trailhead, at 1,150 feet elevation. The GPS coordinates at Trapper Creek trailhead are 45 52.900 N 121 58.790 W.

Hike 0.9 mile west-northwest on Trapper Creek Trail to the junction with Observation Trail. Turn right onto Observation Trail and hike 2.6 miles northwest to the junction with the Big Slide Trail, where this hike description begins. The elevation at the junction is 2,470 feet.

Special Considerations

This is one of the "Mazama Trails"; it is rough and difficult to follow in places. Don't use this vague route unless you or the leader of the party is an expert in route finding. The first time you hike this trail, it is best to follow it from top to bottom as described here. The route is even harder to follow heading uphill.

Big Slide Trail 195

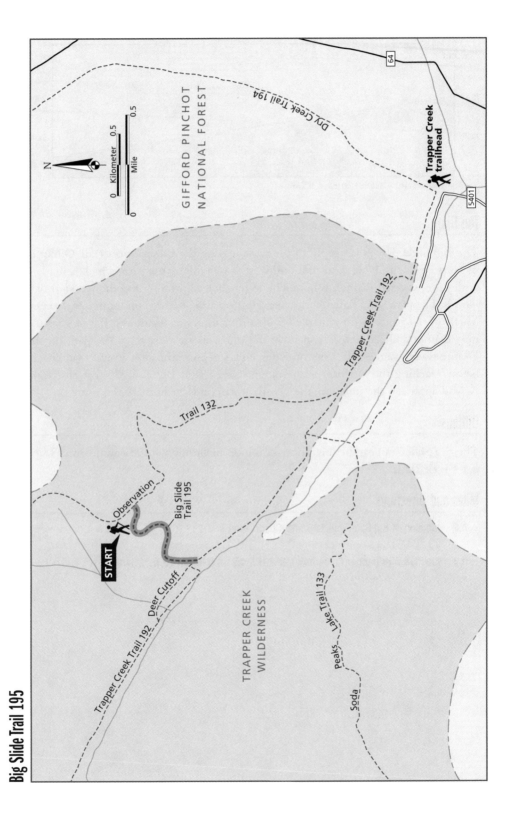

GIFFORD PINCHOT
NATIONAL FOREST

Dry Creek Trail 194

64

Trapper Creek
trailhead

5401

Trapper Creek Trail 192

Trail 132

N

0   Kilometer   0.5

0   Mile   0.5

Observation

Big Slide
Trail 195

START

Deer Cutoff

Trapper Creek Trail 192

TRAPPER CREEK
WILDERNESS

Peaks   Lake Trail 133

Soda

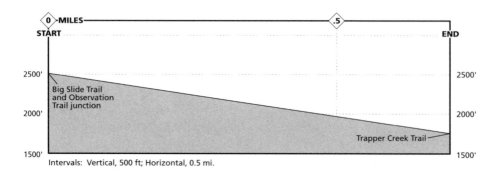

Intervals: Vertical, 500 ft; Horizontal, 0.5 mi.

The Hike

The Big Slide descends steeply to the west, leaving the Observation Trail. Glimpses of Soda Peaks can be seen to the southwest as you follow the path, which is marked with little wooden diamonds here. The letters BST are carved into the wooden diamonds. The path soon flattens and even climbs a little before continuing its descent. Much of the route is now marked with tiny aluminum diamonds. Try to spot the next diamond ahead before you leave the one you are next to, as the path on the ground is very vague here. The route descends steeply and makes several switchbacks before reaching the junction with Trapper Creek Trail 192 at 1,770 feet elevation. As you approach the junction, the wooden diamonds again mark the route.

Options

The Big Slide Trail can be used to make a loop including the Observation and Trapper Creek Trails.

Miles and Directions

0.0 Junction of Big Slide Trail 195 and Observation Trail 132 (GPS 45 54.103 N 122 00.768 W).

0.7 Junction with Trapper Creek Trail 192 (GPS 45 54.030 N 122 01.034 W).

37 Sunshine Trail 198

Descend the challenging Sunshine Trail from the Observation Trail, high on Howe Ridge, to Trapper Creek Trail deep in Trapper Creek Canyon.

Start: Junction of Sunshine Trail and Observation Trail; nearest trailhead is Trapper Creek trailhead on Forest Road 5401.

Distance: 2.4-mile one-way internal day hike; 7.4 miles one way from Trapper Creek trailhead.

Difficulty: Strenuous, with excellent route-finding skills required.

Seasons: Mid-June through October.

Fees and permits: Trapper Creek Wilderness Permit and Northwest Forest Pass.

Parking and trailhead facilities: There is adequate parking at the Trapper Creek trailhead but no other facilities.

Maps: USDA Forest Service Indian Heaven and Trapper Creek Wilderness. The USGS Bare Mountain quad covers the area but does not show this trail.

Trail contacts: Gifford Pinchot National Forest, Wind River Ranger District, Mile Post 1.26 Hemlock Road, Carson, WA 98610; (509) 427-5645; www.fs.fed.us/gpnf.

Finding the trailhead: From Portland drive east on I-84 to the Cascade Locks (exit 44). Pay the 75-cent toll and cross the Bridge of the Gods over the Columbia River. Turn right at the north end of the bridge (east) onto State Route 14. Drive east on SR 14 for about 7 miles to the junction with Wind River Road, signed TO CARSON.

If you are coming from the east on I-84, leave the freeway at Hood River (exit 64). Cross the bridge over the Columbia River and turn left (west) onto SR 14. Follow SR 14 west for 15 miles to the junction with Wind River Road.

Turn north and drive 1 mile to Carson. Head north from Carson on Wind River Road for 13 miles to the junction with County Road 8c, signed TO GOVERNMENT MINERAL SPRINGS. This junction is just past (north of) the Carson Fish Hatchery. Turn left at the junction and head northwest for 0.5 mile to the junction with FR 5401. Turn right onto FR 5401 and drive north 0.5 mile to the Trapper Creek trailhead, at 1,150 feet elevation. The GPS coordinates at Trapper Creek Trailhead are 45 52.900 N 121 58.790 W.

Hike 0.9 miles west-northwest on Trapper Creek Trail to the junction with Observation Trail. Turn right onto Observation Trail and hike 4.1 miles northwest to the junction with the Sunshine Trail. The elevation at the junction is 3,470 feet.

Special Considerations

Like Big Slide Trail, this is one of the "Mazama Trails"; it is rough and difficult to follow in places. Don't use this vague route unless you or the leader of the party is an expert in route finding. The first time you hike this trail, it is best to follow it from top to bottom as described here. The route is even harder to follow heading uphill. An altimeter can be very useful when trying to follow this vague route.

The Hike

At first the Sunshine Trail is nearly level as it leaves the junction with the Observation Trail. Wooden diamonds with the sun carved into them mark the vague path. Soon the trail markers become 1-inch aluminum diamonds as you head west. The course crosses a small gully and climbs steeply out the other side. Continuing to climb slightly, you will cross a couple more small draws, passing some large old-growth Douglas fir trees. After climbing to slightly more than 3,600 feet elevation, 0.4 mile from the junction with the Observation Trail, the route heads down a small ridge.

A couple of hundred yards farther along, there is a sign stating SUNSHINE TRAIL. This spot can be mistaken for the junction with the Rim Trail 202, but that junction is still a short distance ahead. The junction with the Rim Trail is reached 0.6 mile from the junction with the Observation Trail, at 3,440 feet elevation. The junction is signed, but the Rim Trail is vague on the ground. The Rim Trail, which is also marked with aluminum diamonds, heads northwest for about 1 mile to join Trapper Creek Trail. The Trapper Creek and Indian Heaven Wilderness map shows this junction somewhat incorrectly, and the Bare Mountain quad doesn't show these trails at all.

From the junction with the Rim Trail, the Sunshine Trail steepens as it descends to the south along a ridge. About one-fourth of a mile below the junction, the route bears left off the small ridge and soon gains another small ridge at about 3,000 feet elevation. Soon this ridge rounds and broadens out. The route traverses to the right (west-southwest) off the now-rounded ridge and makes a descending traverse. After traversing for a couple of hundred yards, the vague tread makes three small, steeply descending switchbacks. It then winds down another small ridge for a little less than 0.2 mile, passing some large Douglas fir trees.

The route then traverses to the right off the ridge at about 2,400 feet elevation and continues to descend. It heads down another tiny ridge for a short distance and then traverses southwest to a tiny spring, which may be dry by late summer, at about 2,200 feet elevation.

After passing the spring, the course makes three switchbacks as it descends the last quarter of a mile to the junction with the Trapper Creek Trail. This junction, at about 1,850 feet elevation, is 2.4 miles from the junction with the Observation Trail. On the sign marking the junction, someone has scratched in REALLY DIFFICULT, indicating that they may have had trouble negotiating the Sunshine Trail.

Options

Make a loop hike by following the description above and then returning via Trapper Creek Trail.

◀ *Waterfall on Trapper Creek*

Sunshine Trail 198

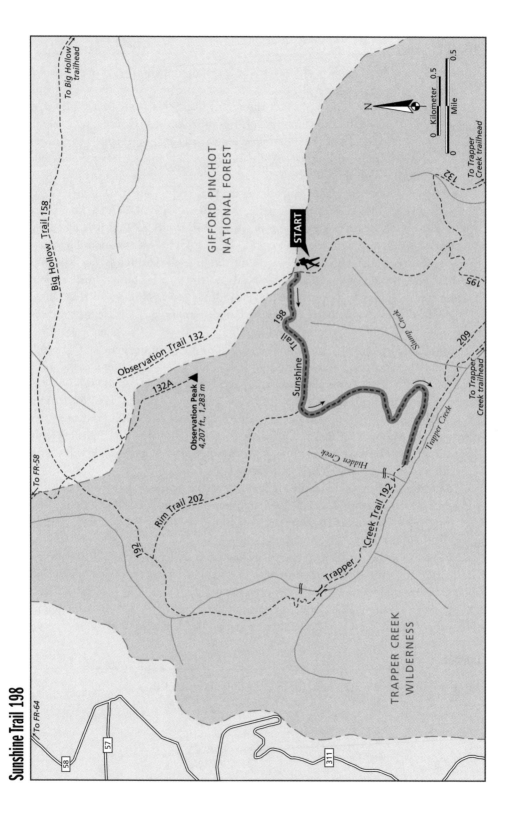

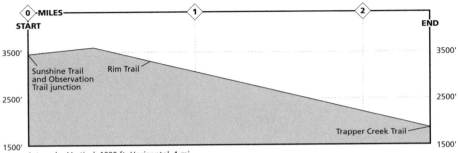

Intervals: Vertical, 1000 ft; Horizontal, 1 mi.

Miles and Directions

0.0 Junction of Sunshine Trail 198 and Observation Trail 132 (GPS 45 55.122 N 122 01.078 W).

0.6 Junction with Rim Trail 202 (GPS 45 54.914 N 122 01.784 W). Stay left (south).

2.4 Junction with Trapper Creek Trail 192 (GPS 45 54.292 N 122 01.912 W).

38 Soda Peaks Lake Trail 133

Hike through old-growth forest to the great views on the ridgeline near Soda Peaks. Then descend past beautiful Soda Peaks Lake to Trapper Creek in the bottom of a canyon.

Start: Soda Peaks Lake trailhead.
Distance: 7.5-mile one-way shuttle day hike or backpack.
Difficulty: Moderate.
Seasons: July through October.
Fees and permits: Northwest Forest Pass and Trapper Creek Wilderness Permit.
Parking and trailhead facilities: There is parking for several cars at both of the trailheads but no other facilities.

Maps: USDA Forest Service Trapper Creek and Indian Heaven Wilderness or Bare Mountain USGS quad.
Trail contacts: Gifford Pinchot National Forest, Wind River Ranger District, Mile Post 1.26 Hemlock Road, Carson, WA 98610; (509) 427-5645; www.fs.fed.us/gpnf.

Finding the trailhead: Drive east from Portland on I-84 to the Cascade Locks (exit 44). Get off the freeway and cross the Bridge of the Gods over the Columbia River. Turn right (east) at the north end of the bridge onto State Route 14. Go east, passing through Stevenson, for about 7 miles on SR 14 to the junction with Wind River Road, signed TO CARSON.

If you are coming from the east on I-84, leave the freeway at Hood River (exit 64). Cross the bridge over the Columbia River and turn left (west) onto SR 14. Follow SR 14 west for 15 miles to the junction with Wind River Road.

Turn north and drive through Carson, staying on Wind River Road. You will reach the junction with Hemlock Road 8.6 miles from SR 14. Turn left onto Hemlock Road and go 0.3 mile west to the junction with Szydlo Road. Turn right (northwest) onto Szydlo Road, which becomes Forest Road 54, and follow it for 13 miles to Soda Peaks Lake trailhead. The trailhead is on the right side of FR 54, at 3,670 feet elevation.

To reach Trapper Creek trailhead where this hike ends, head north from Carson on Wind River Road for 13 miles to the junction with County Road 8c, signed TO GOVERNMENT MINERAL SPRINGS. This junction is just past (north of) the Carson Fish Hatchery. Turn left at the junction and head northwest for 0.5 mile to the junction with Forest Road 5401. Turn right onto FR 5401 and drive north 0.5 mile to the Trapper Creek trailhead, at 1,150 feet elevation.

Special Considerations

Early in the season snow may cover the portion of the route from the ridgeline down to Soda Peaks Lake. In June the last mile of the road leading to the trailhead may be snow-covered and impassable, adding an extra mile to the hike.

Soda Peaks Lake ▶

Soda Peaks Lake Trail 133

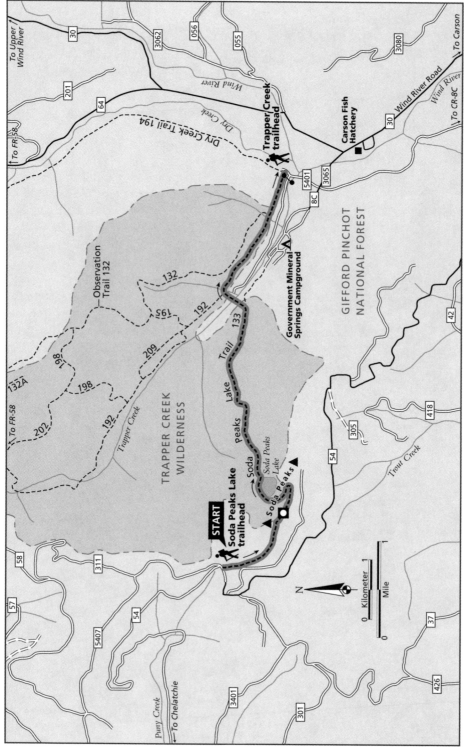

The Hike

Leaving the trailhead the Soda Peaks Lake Trail first climbs south through a clear-cut. Between the stumps and young trees, avalanche lilies grow thickly, to bloom in late June. Shortly, as you reach the upper edge of the cut-over area, you may notice a section of now-abandoned trail turning to the right. The course turns left at the junction with the abandoned section of trail and quickly enters the fir and hemlock forest.

Half a mile from the trailhead, a small logged area to the left of the path allows a view of Mount Adams. The route then climbs fairly steeply for most of the next 0.8 mile, where it comes out on a ridgeline. The view from this ridgetop vantage point is superb. Mount Rainier is in the distance to the north. To the northeast are Goat Rocks, and closer by is Mount Adams. Also to the northeast and below, Soda Peaks Lake sparkles between the green trees and talus slopes. This spot, at 4,370 feet above sea level, is the highest point reached along this trail. Cell-phone service is generally good here.

The tread then follows the ridgeline, descending slightly and passing the Trapper Creek Wilderness boundary. Just past the boundary sign, the trail makes a switchback to the left and begins its descent toward Soda Peaks Lake. The route makes a couple more switchbacks and then traverses around the east side of the cirque that holds Soda Peaks Lake. This section of the trail, in the cirque, may have snowdrifts covering parts of it into mid-July, but the lake is in sight and the route is fairly easy to find. The tread reaches the lakeshore at the north end of the lake, near the outlet stream. Soda Peaks Lake, at 3,760 feet elevation, has several campsites, and a good supply of trout occupy its clear waters.

The trail crosses the outlet stream to continue the descent into Trapper Creek Canyon. Hemlock and some large Douglas firs shade the avalanche lily– and beargrass-covered ground. The tread soon begins to head down along a ridgeline, making twenty-one switchbacks as it descends the next 2.9 miles. As you descend, glimpses of Mount Hood can be had to the south. At the bottom of the ridge, there is an unmarked trail junction. Turn left (northwest) at the junction and cross the alder-covered flats to the bridge across Trapper Creek. The route crosses the bridge and then forks. Bear left (north) at the fork and climb slightly for 0.2 mile to the junction with Trapper Creek Trail, at 1,380 feet elevation, 5.8 miles from the trailhead.

Turn right at the junction and hike 1.7 miles east-southeast to Trapper Creek trailhead along Trapper Creek Trail.

Options

Backpacking to Soda Peaks Lake for an overnight or longer stay is a great way to enjoy the upper part of this trail. The round-trip distance for this backpack is only 4.8 miles, with a total elevation gain and loss of about 1,400 feet.

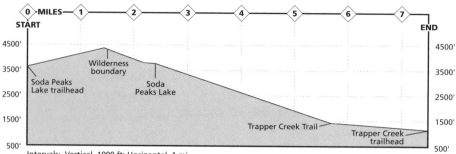

Intervals: Vertical, 1000 ft; Horizontal, 1 mi.

Miles and Directions

0.0 Soda Peaks Lake trailhead (GPS 45 53.439 N 122 03.951 W).

1.5 Trapper Creek Wilderness boundary.

2.4 Soda Peaks Lake.

5.3 Unmarked trail junction, turn left (northwest).

5.6 Trail junction, bear left (north).

5.8 Junction with Trapper Creek Trail 192 (GPS 45 53.462 N 122 00.410 W). Turn right (east-southeast).

7.5 Trapper Creek trailhead (GPS 45 52.900 N 121 58.790 W).

39 Pacific Crest Trail 2000, Columbia River to Wind River Road

Hike from the lowest point on the Pacific Crest Trail (PCT), climbing across two ridges. Then descend down into the Wind River Valley, with countless views of the Columbia River Gorge and the mountain peaks of the southern Washington and northern Oregon Cascades along the way.

Start: Bridge of the Gods trailhead.
Distance: 33.3-mile one-way shuttle backpack.
Difficulty: Moderate.
Seasons: Mid-June through October.
Fees and permits: A Northwest Forest Pass is required at many trailheads.
Parking and trailhead facilities: There is parking for several cars at the Bridge of the Gods trailhead but no other facilities.

Maps: USDA Forest Service Pacific Crest Trail Southern Washington Portion or Bonneville Dam, Beacon Rock, Lookout Mountain, and Stabler USGS quads.
Trail contacts: Gifford Pinchot National Forest, Wind River Ranger District, Mile Post 1.26 Hemlock Road, Carson, WA 98610; (509) 427–5645; www.fs.fed.us/gpnf.

Finding the trailhead: From Portland head east on I-84 to the Cascade Locks (exit 44). Leave the freeway and cross the Bridge of the Gods over the Columbia River. Bridge of the Gods trailhead is approximately 200 yards southwest of the Washington end of the bridge, elevation at 150 feet.

To reach the point where the PCT crosses Wind River Road where this hike ends, turn right (east) at the north end of Bridge of the Gods onto State Route 14. Drive east on SR 14 for about 7 miles to the junction with Wind River Road, signed TO CARSON.

At the junction of SR 14 and Wind River Road, turn north and drive 1 mile to Carson. Head north from Carson on Wind River Road for 8.3 miles to the point where the PCT crosses Wind River Road. This point is a little hard to spot, but there is a crosswalk sign.

Special Considerations

Most Pacific Crest Trail hikers are dropped off at a trailhead to start their hike and picked up at the end of it by someone else. If you are planning to leave a vehicle at the trailhead where you will start this hike, it would be best, because of the limited parking at the Bridge of the Gods trailhead, to use the alternate start at Bonneville trailhead described in Options. If you plan to leave a vehicle at the end of this hike, it would be best, also because of limited parking, to continue your hike another 2 miles to the Panther Creek trailhead. To get to Panther Creek trailhead by road, backtrack south from where the PCT crosses Wind River Road for a short distance to Warren Gap Road. Turn east onto Warren Gap Road and drive 2 miles to the junction with Forest Road 65. Turn right (south) onto FR 65 and you will reach the trailhead in a very short distance.

Numerous Jeep trails, abandoned roadbeds, roads that are in present use, and both abandoned and presently used trails cross this section of the PCT. This would make this hike very confusing if it were not for the small plastic or metal Pacific Crest Trail plates that mark the route. It can be a long distance between water sources along this part of the PCT; be sure to carry enough water to make it to the next "for sure" creek. With more than 5,000 feet of total elevation gain and almost that much loss, this is the most up-and-down section of the PCT described in this book.

The Hike

Leaving the trailhead on SR 14, the Pacific Crest Trail climbs slightly and parallels the highway through the second-growth timber. The route crosses the road to Wauna Lake 0.8 mile from the trailhead. In another 0.5 mile you reach the junction with the Tamanous Trail. Turning left onto the Tamanous Trail will take you to the Bonneville trailhead, next to Bonneville Dam on SR 14, in 0.5 mile.

Hike straight ahead (northwest) from the junction, continuing to side hill through mostly Douglas fir forest. The forest floor is covered with sword ferns and Oregon grape, with vine maple completing the understory. Shortly you pass a steep side path to the left, which leads down to a small, unnamed lake. The PCT crosses an abandoned road 0.9 mile farther along at 310 feet elevation. You then cross a logged area for 0.3 mile. At the far side of the logged area (elevation 350 feet), Beacon Rock comes into view, sticking out of the Columbia River to the southwest.

The route climbs gently to 400 feet elevation and then levels out. About 2 miles from the junction with the Tamanous Trail, the PCT crosses a power-line road and then descends slightly to Gillette Lake, crossing its outlet stream on a log bridge. A side trail leads left to a campsite at the lake. From the stream the tread climbs gently for 0.3 mile to a roadbed, which the route follows west for a short distance, and then passes a pond and descends slightly to cross the bridge over Greenleaf Creek. Look northwest from the bridge for a view of Table Mountain. Fill your water bottles here as there may not be any more water along the route for a considerable distance during the drier times of the year.

After crossing Greenleaf Creek the course climbs, making a couple of switchbacks. It then traverses westward and passes a viewpoint overlooking Bonneville Dam. The route switchbacks up to a rounded ridgetop at 1,140 feet elevation, 1.9 miles after crossing Greenleaf Creek. The route now heads north, climbing along the ridgeline. In 0.4 mile you will come to the first of two unmarked junctions. Hike straight ahead at both of them. Above to your right are Sacaquawea and Papoose Rocks and to the left is Cedar Creek. The tread soon crosses another roadbed. Continue north and recross the roadbed in another 0.3 mile. Before long you will reach

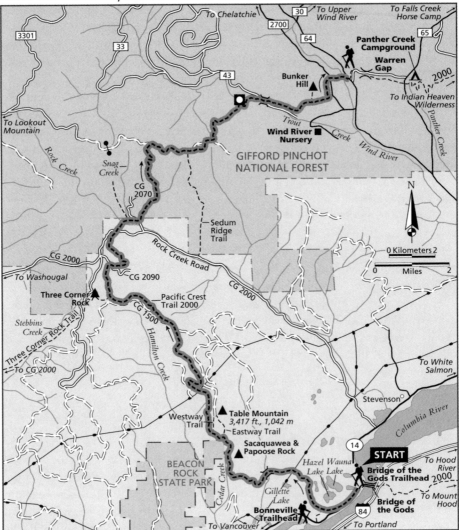

the junction with the Eastway Trail. Eastway Trail to the right (north–northeast) offers a steep route to the summit of Table Mountain. Past the junction with Eastway Trail, the PCT keeps climbing to the northwest for 0.5 mile to the junction with the somewhat-less-steep Westway Trail. This junction is at 1,970 feet elevation and 7.6 miles from the Bridge of the Gods trailhead. Westway Trail also leads to the summit of 3,417-foot-high Table Mountain.

From the junction with the Westway Trail, the PCT descends slightly and then makes an ascending traverse along the west slope of Table Mountain. Along the traverse the route meets and follows an abandoned roadbed for some distance. The views are spectacular along this traverse. The well-marked but fairly steep route eventually leaves the roadbed heading northwest. Soon it passes beneath some power lines and reaches another rocky roadbed at 2,800 feet elevation. The course then turns to the east and climbs to the ridgeline, at 3,120 feet elevation, about 1 mile northwest of Table Mountain.

On the ridgeline the PCT turns to the northwest and climbs along the right side of the crest for 0.7 mile to a saddle at 3,400 feet elevation. The tread crosses the broad saddle and flattens out to make a long traverse of the semi-open southwest-facing slope before regaining the ridgeline and descending to a saddle at 3,020 feet elevation. In the saddle the route meets and then parallels a roadbed to the junction with Roads CG 2028 and CG 1500 in another narrow saddle. This junction is 14 miles from the Bridge of the Gods trailhead, at just more than 3,000 feet elevation.

After crossing the road at the junction, the PCT parallels it for a short distance and then climbs slightly to cross another roadbed before continuing west to the junction with the Three Corner Rock Trail. The Three Corner Rock Trail turns to the left, climbing west and then southwest for 0.3 mile to join a roadbed that continues west another 0.2 mile to the ridgeline just south of Three Corner Rock.

For the next 1.9 miles the PCT winds and switchbacks, descending to the junction with Road CG 2090 in a small saddle at 2,350 feet elevation. The point where the PCT crosses CG 2090 is not marked. There is parking for a couple of cars here, but camping is not allowed. The trail descends east through the timber and then turns north and crosses a clear-cut to the junction with Road CG 2000 at 1,710 feet elevation.

After crossing the road the trail enters larger second-growth forest and descends at a moderate grade. The course winds and switchbacks down for 0.6 mile, losing 320 feet of elevation, to the bridge over Rock Creek. Just as the trail reaches the creek, there is a small but usable campsite on the right. The PCT crosses the wooden bridge over Rock Creek at 1,380 feet elevation, 19.3 miles from the Bridge of the Gods trailhead. The trail then climbs moderately for a few yards before flattening out and heading east. Here the forest contains a few larger Douglas fir trees, some with fire scars. One-third of a mile after crossing Rock Creek is the junction with the Snag Creek Trail. At the junction a Department of Natural Resources sign states that Snag Creek Trail was originally built by the Civilian Conservation Corps in the early 1900s and rebuilt by Boy Scout Troop 317 from Washougal, Washington, in June 1981. A few yards farther along, the PCT crosses a wooden bridge over the rushing waters of Snag Creek. A short distance more and you pass another sign with information about when this section of timber was logged and replanted. Past the sign the track enters smaller timber, and another 0.25 mile brings you to the junction with Road CG 2070. A sign marks the junction.

Cross the road and prepare for a long climb. For the first 0.7 mile, the trail heads up the North Fork of Rock Creek. Then the route crosses a gully and makes several switchbacks as it climbs fairly steeply. After a little more than 3 miles of nearly steady climbing from CG 2070, the PCT turns east, at 2,950 feet elevation, to parallel Forest Road 41. A tank trap closes FR 41 some distance to the west, so you shouldn't see any cars on it. Paralleling the roadbed but usually staying out of sight of it, the route climbs gently to 3,120 feet elevation and then descends slightly to the junction with Sedum Ridge Trail at 2,985 feet elevation. Sedum Ridge Trail to the right drops to the south to meet Road CG 2000. To the left Sedum Ridge Trail climbs a few yards to closed FR 41. The PCT heads east from the trail junction, climbing to 3,140 feet elevation and still paralleling FR 41, for another 0.8 mile. Then you finally cross FR 41 at 2,950 feet elevation, 25.5 miles from the Bridge of the Gods trailhead.

After crossing the roadbed the PCT again parallels FR 41 for a short distance before beginning its descent toward Trout Creek. The tread winds down through thick woods, with only a few openings for views, losing 1,250 feet elevation in the next 2.6 miles. Here the trail makes a switchback to the right, on a ridgetop at 1,700 feet elevation. At the switchback a short path leads left (north) to a viewpoint overlooking Trout Creek Canyon. From the viewpoint looking far below to the east are open fields that are part of the Wind River Experimental Forest. Binoculars may reveal Roosevelt elk feeding in these fields early and late in the day. Far to the northeast Mount Adams can barely be seen past Red Mountain. The route then descends southeast and crosses a couple of wet-weather water courses before turning north and recrossing the same wet-weather water courses. Shortly, the track makes a switchback to the right as you descend through the forest of Douglas fir, western hemlock, and western red cedar. After crossing another small wet-weather stream, the track crosses a rushing tributary of Trout Creek. There is no bridge here and you may get your feet wet early in the season. Past the tributary the grade of the trail moderates. The route descends a short distance along the creek and then turns east and descends very gradually to the bridge over Trout Creek and the junction with Forest Road 43. Just before crossing the bridge, there is a good campsite on the right side of the trail.

The PCT crosses FR 43 at 1,180 feet elevation, 4.1 miles from FR 41 and 29.6 miles from the Bridge of the Gods trailhead. In another 0.9 mile, the nearly flat route crosses Forest Road 417. After crossing the road, the trail follows a game fence for 150 yards east before turning north along the fence for a short distance. The track then bears away from the fence heading east again and crosses a tiny stream, which flows through culverts beneath the trail. You now hike through second-growth forest of Douglas fir with an understory of vine maple and Oregon grape to the junction with Bunker Hill Trail 145. The junction is about half a mile from FR 417 at 1,170 feet elevation.

Past the junction the PCT climbs slightly and heads east. You then descend north to reach County Road 2700 1.6 miles after passing the Bunker Hill Trail junction.

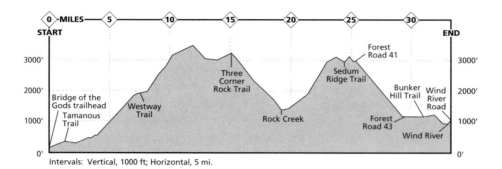

Intervals: Vertical, 1000 ft; Horizontal, 5 mi.

The PCT crosses CR 2700 at 950 feet elevation and descends slightly to the wood and concrete bridge across the Wind River. It then climbs gently, making a switchback along the way, to the Wind River Road at 1,020 feet elevation, 33.3 miles from the Bridge of the Gods trailhead where this hike started.

Options

It is possible to hike north on the PCT, through Warren Gap and past Big Huckleberry Mountain to Crest Camp on FR 60 for a 17.6-mile extension of this hike.

An optional starting point would be the Bonneville Dam trailhead. To do this, drive west on SR 14 from the Bridge of the Gods trailhead for 1.4 miles to the trailhead, which is on the right side of the road. From the Bonneville Dam trailhead, take the Tamanous Trail 0.5 mile northeast to the junction with the PCT. Using the Tamanous Trail will cut 0.8 mile of distance from the hike.

Miles and Directions

0.0 Bridge of the Gods trailhead (GPS 45 39.648 N 121 54.391 W).

1.3 Junction with Tamanous Trail 27 (GPS 45 39.198 N 121 55.564 W). Continue straight (northwest).

3.3 Gillette Lake.

3.5 Greenleaf Creek.

5.8 Two unmarked trail junctions. Continue straight at both.

7.1 Junction with the Eastway Trail. Stay left (northwest).

7.6 Junction with Westway Trail. Stay left.

14.0 Junction of Roads CG 1500 and CG 2028, and the PCT (GPS 45 44.021 N 122 01.407 W).

15.1 Junction with Three Corner Rock Trail. Stay right (north).

17.0 Cross Road CG 2090 (GPS 45 44.952 N 122 02.602 W).

18.7 Cross Road CG 2000 (GPS 45 45.730 N 122 02.423 W).

19.3 Cross Rock Creek.

19.6 Junction with Snag Creek Trail (GPS 45 45.929 N 122 02.039 W). Continue straight (east).

19.9 Cross road CG 2070 (GPS 45 45.914 N 122 01.696 W).

24.6 Cross Sedum Ridge Trail.

25.5 Cross FR 41 near Sedum Point.

29.6 Cross FR 43 (GPS 45 48.685 N 121 57.381 W).

30.5 Cross FR 417 (GPS 45 48.457 N 121 56.440 W).

31.1 Junction with Bunker Hill Trail 145 (GPS 45 48.627 N 121 55.989 W). Continue straight (east).

32.7 Cross CR 2700.

33.3 Wind River Road.

40 Whistle Punk Trail

An interpretive hike through mostly second-growth forest, with signs containing a wealth of information about logging in the past.

Start: Whistle Punk trailhead.
Distance: Short loop, 0.9-mile day hike; long loop, 1.5-mile day hike.
Difficulty: Very easy.
Seasons: April through October; some years, maybe most of the year.
Fees and permits: Northwest Forest Pass.
Parking and trailhead facilities: There is

adequate parking and rest rooms at the Whistle Punk trailhead.
Maps: Check the map on the signboard at the trailhead.
Trail contacts: Gifford Pinchot National Forest, Wind River Ranger District, Mile Post 1.26 Hemlock Road, Carson, WA 98610; (509) 427-5645; www.fs.fed.us/gpnf.

Finding the trailhead: Drive east from Portland on I-84 to the Cascade Locks (exit 44). Leave the freeway and cross the Bridge of the Gods over the Columbia River. At the north end of the bridge, turn right (east) onto State Route 14. Drive east on SR 14 for about 7 miles to the junction with Wind River Road, signed TO CARSON.

If you are coming from the east on I-84, leave the freeway at Hood River (exit 64). Cross the bridge over the Columbia River and turn left (west) onto SR 14. Follow SR 14 west for 15 miles to the junction with Wind River Road.

Turn north and drive through Carson, following Wind River Road for 8.6 miles to the junction with Hemlock Road. Turn left (west) onto Hemlock Road and go 1.3 miles to the junction with Forest Road 43. This junction is just past the Wind River Work and Visitor Information Center. Turn northwest (right) onto FR 43 and drive 0.6 mile to the junction with Forest Road 417. Turn right onto FR 417 and follow it for 0.2 mile to the point where the Pacific Crest Trail crosses the road. The point where the trail crosses the road is just as you reach a high game fence on the right side of the road. Another 0.15 mile along FR 417 is the Whistle Punk trailhead. The elevation at the trailhead is 1,150 feet.

Special Considerations

The trail is barrier-free and nearly flat. Most of the trail is surfaced with crushed rock, and parts of it are boardwalk.

The Hike

Before starting your hike take the time to read the informative signboard. The Whistle Punk Trail heads northeast from the corner of the parking area next to the informational sign. Shortly you will come to a junction. Bear right at the junction and hike through the dense, brushy broadleaf forest of mostly Oregon ash.

The route passes a resting bench 0.2 mile from the trailhead. Here the compo-

Wetland viewing platform ▶

Whistle Punk Trail

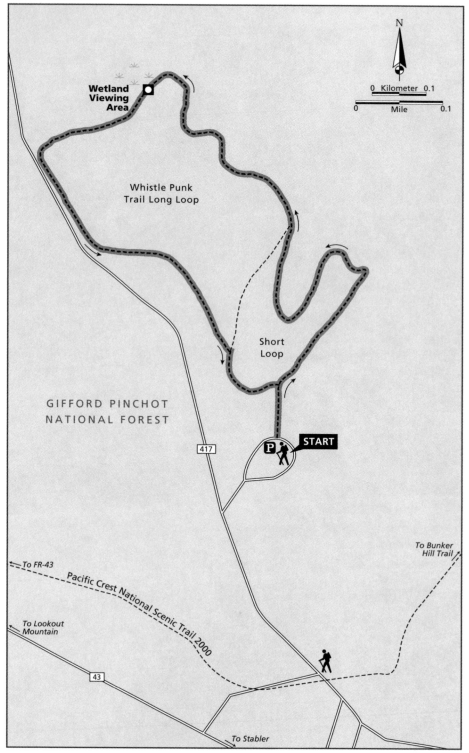

N

0 Kilometer 0.1

0 Mile 0.1

Wetland Viewing Area

Whistle Punk Trail Long Loop

Short Loop

GIFFORD PINCHOT NATIONAL FOREST

417

P START

To Bunker Hill Trail

To FR-43

Pacific Crest National Scenic Trail 2000

To Lookout Mountain

43

To Stabler

sition of the forest changes to second-growth Douglas fir. Shortly you reach a sign on the left side of the trail explaining the job of a "Whistle Punk." The path quickly passes two more signs, one discussing "rusting equipment" and another describing a "smoke stack" and "spark arrestor." Just past the signs is a second bench. Near the bench is another sign about a "portable workshop." A short distance farther is a sign on the left of the trail reviewing "the journey of a big fir." Note the old railroad irons on the ground here.

Just past the sign and 0.4 mile from the trailhead is the junction with the short loop trail. To take the short loop back to the parking area, turn left at the junction. The short loop is a winding boardwalk. To continue on the long loop, hike straight ahead. In 0.1 mile you will reach the third resting bench just before entering an open area covered with bracken ferns. This is a small opening and shortly you will be hiking through more second-growth Douglas firs with an understory of vine maple. The path then passes three chairs that were made from log bolts.

The wooden "wetland viewing platform," with a stump in the middle of it, sits beside the trail 0.8 mile from the trailhead. A little ways farther along, the course crosses a wooden bridge over a swampy area, passes a couple more chairs, and reaches a road. Turn left onto the road and follow it for 0.1 mile to a gate. Bear left off the road, go through the gate, and reenter the woods on a gravel path. In 0.3 mile you will reach the second junction with the short loop trail. Go straight at the junction and walk 0.1 mile to the first junction you came to when you started this hike. Bear right and walk a few more steps to the trailhead and parking area.

Options

Hike the Whistle Punk Trail on the same trip that you hike the Bunker Hill Trail. The trailheads are very close together.

Miles and Directions

0.0 Whistle Punk trailhead.

0.4 First junction with the short loop trail. Continue straight for a longer loop.

0.8 Wetland Viewing Area platform. Turn left.

1.4 Second junction with the short loop trail. Go straight.

1.5 Trailhead and parking area.

41 Bunker Hill Trail 145

A short hike to a high rock outcrop overlooking the Wind River Valley and then on to a long-abandoned lookout site.

Start: Junction of Forest Road 417 and the Pacific Crest Trail (PCT).
Distance: 3.6-mile out-and-back day hike.
Difficulty: Moderate.
Seasons: Mid-April through November.
Fees and permits: Northwest Forest Pass if you park at Whistle Punk trailhead.
Parking and trailhead facilities: There is only limited parking at the point where the PCT crosses FR 417, but at Whistle Punk trailhead

a short distance to the north there is plenty of parking and rest rooms.
Maps: USDA Forest Service Pacific Crest Trail Southern Washington Portion or Stabler USGS quad.
Trail contacts: Gifford Pinchot National Forest, Wind River Ranger District, Mile Post 1.26 Hemlock Road, Carson, WA 98610; (509) 427-5645; www.fs.fed.us/gpnf.

Finding the trailhead: From Portland head east on I-84 to the Cascade Locks (exit 44). Leave the freeway and cross the Bridge of the Gods over the Columbia River. At the north end of the bridge, turn right (east) onto State Route 14. Drive east on SR 14 for about 7 miles to the junction with Wind River Road, signed TO CARSON.

If you are coming from the east on I-84, leave the freeway at Hood River (exit 64). Cross the bridge over the Columbia River and turn left (west) onto SR 14. Follow SR 14 west for 15 miles to the junction with Wind River Road.

Turn north and drive through Carson, following Wind River Road for 8.6 miles to the junction with Hemlock Road. Turn left (west) onto Hemlock Road and go 1.3 miles to the junction with Forest Road 43. This junction is just past the Wind River Work and Visitor Information Center. Turn northwest (right) onto FR 43 and drive 0.6 mile to the junction with FR 417. Turn right onto FR 417 and follow it for 0.2 mile to the point where the Pacific Crest Trail crosses the road. The point where the trail crosses the road is just as you reach a high game fence on the right side of the road. Another 0.15 mile along FR 417 is the Whistle Punk trailhead.

Special Considerations

There is no potable water along the Bunker Hill Trail.

The Hike

The first 0.4 mile of this hike is along the PCT. Leaving the point where it crosses FR 417, at 1,130 feet elevation, the PCT heads east along a fenceline. Shortly the path turns north and soon bears right (northeast) away from the fence. Here you are

Looking down from Bunker Hill ▶

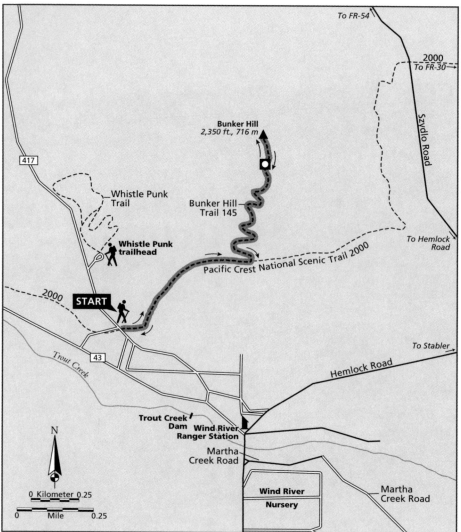

hiking through second-growth Douglas fir forest with an understory of vine maple and a few dogwood trees. Bleeding hearts and Oregon grape line the route as you walk along.

The junction with the Bunker Hill Trail 145 is reached 0.4 mile from FR 417, at 1,210 feet elevation. Turn left (northeast) at the signed junction and begin the climb up Bunker Hill. The well-maintained but fairly steep path makes eleven switchbacks in the next 1.2 miles as it climbs through mixed-age forest with some large Douglas firs. At the eleventh switchback, elevation 2,240 feet, there is a rough and very short path to the right. This path leads to a rock outcropping and the best viewpoint along the Bunker Hill Trail. There is, however, considerable exposure at

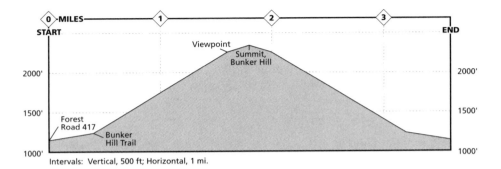

Intervals: Vertical, 500 ft; Horizontal, 1 mi.

the viewpoint, and a dangerous fall could be taken. The Wind River Valley, Mount Hood, and part of the Columbia Gorge are in view from the viewpoint. If you are here in the early morning or in the evening, watch for Roosevelt elk in the fields far below. There is good cell-phone service from this viewpoint.

Past the last switchback the trail continues to climb to the ridgeline of Bunker Hill, where the concrete base blocks that once supported a fire lookout can be found. Dense woods limit the view from the summit, at 2,350 feet above sea level.

Options

Hike the Whistle Punk Trail while you are so close by.

Miles and Directions

0.0 Junction of FR 417 and the Pacific Crest Trail 2000 (GPS 45 48.457 N 121 56.440 W).

0.4 Junction with Bunker Hill Trail 145 (GPS 45 48.627 N 121 55.989 W). Turn left (northeast).

1.6 Viewpoint (GPS 45 48.901 N 121 55.827 W).

1.8 Abandoned lookout site at the summit of Bunker Hill. Turnaround point.

3.6 Junction of FR 417 and the PCT.

42 Siouxon Creek Trail 130

Hike through a lush lowland valley, passing some of the best waterfalls to be found. Then climb to the upper trailhead on Forest Road 58 near the western boundary of Trapper Creek Wilderness.

Start: Siouxon Creek trailhead.
Distance: 9.6-mile one-way shuttle backpack or day hike to reach the trailhead on FR 58, or 8.2-mile out-and-back trip to Chinook Creek.
Difficulty: Easy to Chinook Creek Trail, moderate from there on.
Seasons: Mid-June through October.
Fees and permits: Northwest Forest Pass.
Parking and trailhead facilities: There is adequate parking at the main trailhead but no other facilities. The upper trailhead has very limited parking.

Maps: Siouxon Peak and Bare Mountain USGS quads; both quad maps show parts of this trail incorrectly. The USDA Forest Service Gifford Pinchot National Forest (1999) map shows the trail correctly, but the scale is too small to be very useful to the hiker.
Trail contacts: Mount St. Helens National Volcanic Monument, Monument Headquarters, 42218 NE Yale Bridge Road, Amboy, WA 98601; (360) 449–7800; www.fs.fed. us/gpnf/mshnvm.

Finding the trailhead: Head north from Portland on I–5 to exit 21 (21 miles north of the Columbia River Bridge) at Woodland. Then drive east for 22.5 miles on State Route 503 to the junction with State Route 503 Spur at Jack's Store. Turn right (south) and continue on SR 503 for 6.5 miles to the Chelatchie Prairie General Store and the junction with Healy Road. This junction is a short distance north of (before reaching) the Mount St. Helens National Volcanic Monument Headquarters.

Turn left (east) onto Healy Road, which will become Forest Road 54 in 2.4 miles, and drive 9.3 miles to the junction with Forest Road 57. The pavement on FR 54 ends at this junction. Turn left (east-northeast) onto FR 57 and follow the pavement for 1.2 miles to the junction with Forest Road 5701. Turn left (northwest) onto FR 5701. In three-quarters of a mile, you will reach the first trailhead for the Siouxon Creek Trail. This trailhead, at 1,840 feet elevation, is just after FR 5701 has made a switchback to the right to head east.

To continue to the main Siouxon Creek trailhead (where this hike begins), drive another 3 miles east on FR 5701 to its end. The elevation at the main trailhead is 1,340 feet. The road is paved all the way to the main trailhead, but the roadbed is slipping and settling and quite rough in a few spots.

To reach the upper trailhead where this hike ends, first backtrack along FR 5701 to the junction with FR 57. Turn left (east) onto FR 57 and follow it for about 12 miles to its end at the junction with FR 58. Turn left (northwest) onto FR 58 and go 0.5 mile to the upper trailhead, which will be on the left side of the road. The upper trailhead is not being maintained and may be hard to spot. There is no sign marking this trailhead. The upper 9 miles of FR 57 are gravel and a little rough in spots.

Horseshoe Creek Falls ▶

Special Considerations

This trail is open to hikers, mountain bikers, and stock but closed to motor vehicles. Siouxon Creek Trail is popular with mountain bikers, so hikers should expect to meet many of them, especially on summer weekends.

The Hike

From the main Siouxon Creek trailhead, a path descends gently for a few yards to the north to join the Siouxon Creek Trail. Turn right onto Siouxon Creek Trail and head northeast, descending through Douglas fir and western hemlock forest. Large, tall stumps stand starkly between the medium-age trees, attesting to this area's long-ago destruction by fire. Sword ferns grow thickly between the moss-covered logs on the forest floor. After descending about 200 feet in the first 0.2 mile, the route approaches Siouxon Creek and then climbs a couple of large wooden steps to cross a single log bridge with a handrail over West Creek. To the left of the trail just after crossing West Creek are the first of many campsites along this trail.

After crossing West Creek the tread continues east-northeast for 0.9 mile to the junction with Horseshoe Ridge Trail 140. Horseshoe Ridge Trail climbs southeast for 3.7 miles to reach Forest Road 320. Hike east-northeast from the junction for 0.4 mile. The route then cuts to the right and you climb into Horseshoe Creek Canyon, with Horseshoe Creek Falls to your left. After the short climb the course crosses a wooden bridge above the falls and heads north to the junction with Horseshoe Creek Falls Trail 130B. Trail 130B turns to the left off the Siouxon Creek Trail and descends 0.1 mile to a viewpoint below the falls, passing a campsite along the way.

Siouxon Creek Trail continues northeast from the junction with Horseshoe Creek Falls Trail. In 0.3 mile you reach a viewpoint with a bench. The view is of the first of several large falls in Siouxon Creek. A deep, green pool catches the water below the falls. As you continue along the trail, another falls quickly comes into view. Slightly less than 1 mile past the second falls, you may notice a path descending to the left off the main trail. This path is Wildcat Creek Trail 156, which climbs northwest to meet Trail 129 near Huffman Peak. Hike straight ahead at the junction, staying on Siouxon Creek Trail, and in 0.2 mile there will be another unmarked trail junction with Trail 140, just after you cross a small stream. This trail, which is a continuation of Horseshoe Ridge Trail mentioned earlier, also climbs Horseshoe Ridge. Keep left (straight ahead) at the junction and in another 0.7 mile, just after fording an unnamed creek, you reach the junction with Chinook Creek Trail 130A.

The unsigned Chinook Creek Trail junction is 4.1 miles from the trailhead at 1,500 feet elevation. Chinook Creek Trail turns to the left to cross a wooden bridge over the deep, clear, and slow-moving channel of Siouxon Creek. A short hike to the north along Chinook Creek Trail will take you to a viewpoint below a spectacular falls in Chinook Creek. Chinook Creek Trail fords Chinook Creek below the

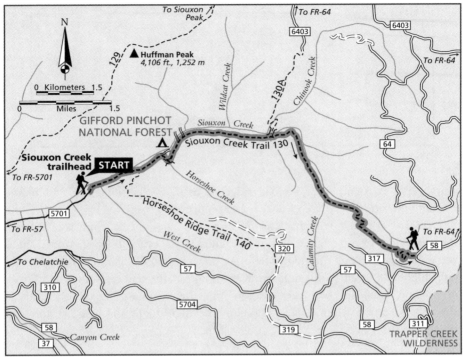

falls and then climbs north to meet Forest Road 6403. There are a couple of nice campsites along Chinook Creek Trail just across the bridge. This is the place to turn around if this is to be an out-and-back trip.

For the next 3.6 miles, the USGS quad map (Bare Mountain quad, 1986 vintage) shows the Siouxon Creek Trail incorrectly. The newest USDA Forest Service Gifford Pinchot map shows this section correctly but is not a topo map, and its small scale limits its use to the hiker.

To head up Siouxon Creek, don't cross the bridge. Once past the junction with Chinook Creek Trail, the track quickly passes another, shorter falls in Siouxon Creek and then climbs, passing a few large, old-growth Douglas firs with scars from the long-ago forest fire. A quarter of a mile past the shorter falls, the route skirts the top of a gorge, with Siouxon Creek rushing far below. This spot could be dangerous for children and pets, as the drop-off is only a couple of steps to the left of the trail and partly concealed by low brush. After passing the gorge the tread descends for a short distance and then climbs again to the top of another large and beautiful waterfall in Siouxon Creek.

Next to the falls you are at 1,580 feet elevation and 4.7 miles from the trailhead. The route continues climbing gradually on the southwest side of Siouxon Creek for another 1.5 miles and then crosses Calamity Creek. About 0.5 mile after crossing Calamity Creek, the track begins to climb more steeply. The path makes several

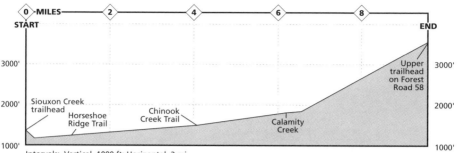

Intervals: Vertical, 1000 ft; Horizontal, 2 mi.

switchbacks as it climbs to a broad ridgeline at 2,660 feet elevation. Just before reaching the ridgeline, the course crosses a semi-open slope.

The trace makes a switchback to the left as it reaches the ridgeline. It then heads southeast close to the edge of a clear-cut. The logged area will be on your right as you climb gently along the ridge. The route stays close to the clear-cut for about 0.4 mile. Eight and seven-tenths miles from the trailhead, the trail crosses the south fork of Siouxon Creek at 2,870 feet elevation. After the creek crossing, the grade steepens. You make five switchbacks as you climb through the fir and hemlock forest to the trailhead on FR 58, at 3,520 feet elevation.

Options

The first 4.1 miles of the Siouxon Creek Trail up to Chinook Creek Trail makes an excellent out-and-back day hike or backpack. The limited elevation gain and the good condition of the trail make this a relatively easy trip. Be sure to allow the time to cross the bridge over Siouxon Creek on Chinook Creek Trail and continue the short distance to the exquisite waterfall in Chinook Creek.

If your plan is to hike the entire length of Siouxon Creek Trail, you might consider starting from the upper trailhead on FR 58 where this hike description ends. This will allow you to hike downhill most of the way.

Miles and Directions

- **0.0** Souixon Creek trailhead (GPS 45 56.792 N 122 10.659 W).
- **1.1** Junction with Horseshoe Ridge Trail 140 (GPS 45 57.112 N 122 09.732 W). Continue straight (east-northeast).
- **4.1** Junction with Chinook Creek Trail 130A (GPS 45 57.604 N 122 07.005 W). Bear right (east). **Option:** Turnaround for an out-and-back hike.
- **6.2** Trail crosses Calamity Creek.
- **9.6** Upper trailhead on FR 58 (GPS 45 55.832 N 122 03.927 W).

43 Horsethief Butte

A great early season hike across flower-covered bench lands to great views of the Columbia River and Mount Hood.

Start: Horsethief Butte trailhead.
Distance: 1.0-mile out-and-back day hike with a short loop in the middle.
Difficulty: Easy on the main trail. The short section through the notch is strenuous but very short.
Seasons: Mid-March through mid-May is the best time for flowers. The route is generally snow-free nearly all year, and it may be very warm in the summer.
Fees and permits: None required, but climbers should register at the trailhead.

Parking and trailhead facilities: There is roadside parking for eight or ten cars on both sides of the road at the trailhead, and a portable rest room is available much of the year. The entrance to Horsethief Lake campground is approximately 1 mile west of the trailhead on State Route 14.
Maps: Stacker Butte USGS quad.
Trail contacts: Washington State Parks and Recreation Commission, P.O. Box 42650, Olympia, WA 98504-2669; information center (360) 902-8844; www.parks.wa.gov.

Finding the trailhead: From Portland drive east on I-84 to exit 87 at The Dalles. Head north from the freeway, cross the bridge over the Columbia River, and drive 3 miles to the junction with State Route 14. At the junction turn right and drive east for 2.2 miles along SR 14 to the trailhead. The trail begins on the right side of the highway at approximately 280 feet elevation.

Special Considerations

There is no water along the route. Poison oak is abundant in the gullies around the butte, and there is the possibility of a rattlesnake anywhere. Ticks are also present in the spring and summer.

The Hike

The trail begins on the south side of SR 14. Take the time to read the informational signs next to the trailhead and then hike south, bearing left at the fork in the trail just past the signs. The unmaintained path to the right goes a short distance across the bench and then becomes overgrown with brush as it descends a draw. Wild irises bloom in early May in the shallow depression next to the fork.

From the fork continue south through patches of Oregon grape and wild roses. In 150 yards you will reach a second fork in the trail. The right fork is the main trail, which is the one to return on. Take the left fork and head southeast toward the band of cliffs that is Horsethief Butte. In a short distance you pass another sign. This one asks that you limit chalk use (chalk is used on the hands to enhance grip when rock climbing) and to avoid climbing in sensitive cultural areas (pictographs).

Horsethief Butte Trail

Past the sign the trail becomes a scrambling route as you climb to a notch that breaks the cliffs of Horsethief Butte. The route climbs to about 350 feet elevation to cross the notch. Beyond the notch the route descends to the southwest, with a view of Mount Hood ahead. Shortly, the rough route becomes a trail again, and you soon reach the second junction with the main trail.

Turn left onto the main trail, hiking southeast and then east on the bench land below the southern side of Horsethief Butte. Below to your right flows the Columbia River. This bench is usually covered with flowers, especially shooting stars in the spring. By mid-May most of the flowers are drying up. About 0.2 mile from the junction, the trail abruptly ends at the top of a gully, which is teeming with poison oak. Turn around here and return to the junction with the trail that you came on through the notch. Bear left (nearly straight ahead to the northwest then north) at the junction and hike on nearly level flower-covered terrain back to the trailhead.

Horsethief Butte

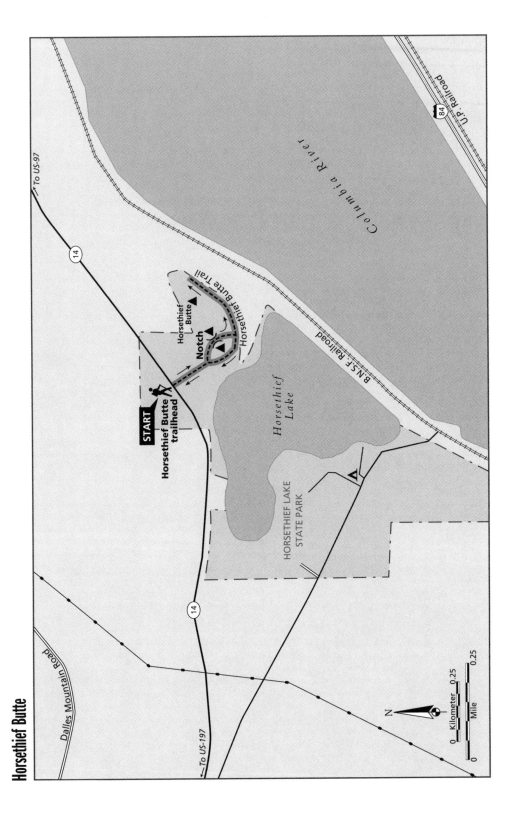

Options

Horsethief Butte is an excellent rock-climbing practice area. Most of the routes can be top roped.

Miles and Directions

0.0 Horsethief Butte trailhead (GPS 45 39.007 N 121 06.015 W).

0.1 Junction with trail to the notch (GPS 45 38.970 N 121 06.002 W). Bear left (southeast).

0.2 The notch (GPS 45 38.922 N 121 05.895 W).

0.3 Rejoin with main trail (GPS 45 38.858 N 121 05.936 W). Turn left (southeast).

0.5 End of trail (GPS 45 38.900 N 121 05.730 W). Turnaround point.

1.0 Horsethief Butte trailhead.

44 Three Corner Rock Trail

Hike from the dense lowland forests along the Washougal River to the open ridgetop meadows near the summit of Three Corner Rock and then scramble the last few feet to the top for a breathtaking view of the southern Washington and northern Oregon Cascade Mountains and the Columbia River Gorge.

Start: Three Corner Rock trailhead.
Distance: 9.3-mile one-way shuttle day hike or backpack or a 0.4-mile round-trip short hike and scramble from the upper trailhead to the summit and back.
Difficulty: Moderate except for the last few feet to the summit, but long.
Seasons: Mid-June through September.
Fees and permits: None.
Parking and trailhead facilities: Roadside parking for three or four cars but no other facilities at either trailhead.
Maps: USDA Forest Service Pacific Crest National Scenic Trail Washington Southern Portion or Beacon Rock USGS quad. Even though this trail is on state land, the USDA Forest Service Gifford Pinchot National Forest map shows the roads to the trailheads correctly; however, they are not numbered on this map. This map is a necessity when trying to find the out-of-the-way upper trailhead.

Finding the trailhead: From State Route 14 at Washougal, take Washougal River Road (State Route 140) northeast for 17.3 miles to the end of the county road (and also the end of the pavement) at a bridge over the Washougal River. Just after crossing the bridge, turn right onto Road 2000. Follow Road 2000 for 3.3 miles northeast to the trailhead, which is on the right side of the road. The elevation at the trailhead is 890 feet. A short distance farther along Road 2000, there is a parking area on the left side. A trail parallels the road on the left side back to the trailhead described above.

To reach the upper trailhead on Road CG 1500A, continue northeast from the trailhead on Road 2000 for another 7.3 miles. Then turn right onto Road CG 1400 and follow it south, passing the point where the trail crosses the road (2.3 miles) for 6.3 miles to the junction with Road CG 1500. Turn left onto CG 1500 and follow it for 0.6 mile to the junction with Road CG 1500A. Turn left onto CG 1500A and drive this rough road for 1.6 miles to the saddle and trailhead. There is a sign marking the trailhead. The GPS coordinates at the upper trailhead are 45 43.908 N 122 02.905 W, and the elevation is 3,450 feet.

Special Considerations

The Three Corner Rock Trail is open to stock and mountain bikes as well as hikers, but is closed to motor vehicles. There may be moderate to heavy mountain-bike use on weekends.

The Hike

Three Corner Rock Trail begins as an abandoned roadbed climbing to the north. After about 100 yards the route turns to the right off the roadbed. There is a sign

Three Corner Rock

at the point where the trail leaves the roadbed. After leaving the road the tread climbs through second-growth timber, making six switchbacks in 0.6 mile, to reach a ridgeline. Sword ferns cover much of the ground on this slope, and vine maple forms an understory beneath the tall conifers. On the ridge, at 1,280 feet elevation, the track makes a hard left turn to head northeast along the north slope of Stebbins Creek Canyon.

Shortly the course begins to descend. Eight-tenths of a mile after crossing the ridgeline, the tread crosses a wooden bridge over a creek at 1,020 feet elevation. The route then begins to climb again, making ten more switchbacks and gaining more than 400 feet in elevation before fording another small creek. Once across the creek the grade moderates but still climbs some and makes a couple of switchbacks before reaching a narrow talus slope at about 1,600 feet elevation, 2.5 miles from the trailhead. A rock cliff looms above the far side of the narrow talus slope. At the base of the cliff, hidden from view by huge boulders and brush, are several shallow caves.

The trail quickly climbs again after crossing the talus, making four switchbacks as it climbs close to the top of the cliff. Past the switchbacks the course contours along the slope to the northeast, climbing slightly. It then makes a couple more switchbacks to cross a spur ridge, at 1,880 feet elevation. You then descend gently to another switchback to the right and a sign pointing out Three Corner Rock in the distance.

The tread makes several more switchbacks and then descends gently to the northeast. Stebbins Creek is reached 3.9 miles from the trailhead at 1,350 feet elevation. The course crosses the creek and then heads east for 0.1 mile before starting up another series of switchbacks. Above the switchbacks the track climbs along a southeast-facing slope for about 0.5 mile and then climbs some more switchbacks to reach a ridgeline at 1,970 feet elevation. You then follow the ridge northeast for 0.4 mile. Here the ridgeline broadens out and the trail climbs along its left side on a northwest-facing slope. The path flattens out 5.5 miles from the trailhead, and it climbs only slightly in the next 0.7 mile. You then climb moderately for the next 0.2 mile to the junction with Road CG 1400 at 2,220 feet elevation.

The trail turns left onto the road and follows it for a few yards, crossing a creek. Then you turn right off the road and climb fairly steeply. The course first climbs along a wooded slope heading north and then makes several switchbacks as it climbs through the timber. After climbing about 1.5 miles through the dense forest, the trace reaches open slopes and the summit of Three Corner Rock comes into view above. You make several more switchbacks as you climb the open flower-covered slopes to the junction with Road CG 1500A in a saddle southeast of the summit. As you reach the road, there will be some radio towers to your right on the top of the ridge. There is good cell-phone service here as well as on the summit.

Turn left onto Road CG 1500A and follow it a short distance to another junction. Turn left onto the rough, rocky road and climb 0.1 mile to its end. From the end of this road a rough path climbs northwest toward the summit. The path has cemented steps that reach within about 10 feet of the summit. From here you must scramble up the slightly exposed rocks if you want to reach the summit of 3,550-foot-high Three Corner Rock.

There are two benchmarks and the remains of a long-abandoned and dismantled lookout on the summit. From the summit there are views of Mounts Hood, St. Helens, Rainier, and Adams. The deep gash of the Columbia River Gorge is to

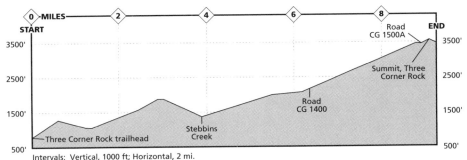

Intervals: Vertical, 1000 ft; Horizontal, 2 mi.

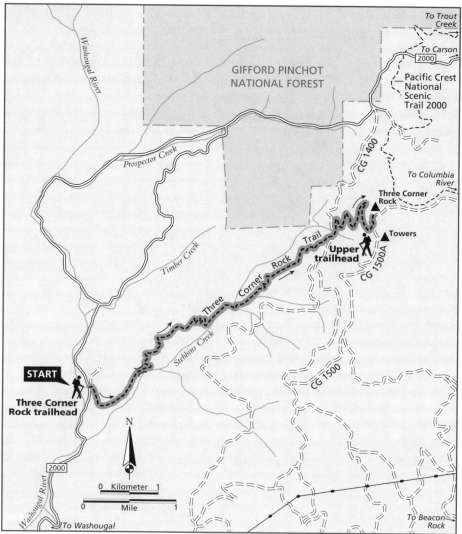

the south, and the river can be seen in a couple of spots. Many blacktail deer inhabit the ridgetop meadows near the summit. They often are easily seen in the morning and evening.

Options

Make this a one-way shuttle hike by driving to the point where the trail reaches Road CG 1500A and hiking down from there, or just make the short hike from there to the summit and back.

Miles and Directions

0.0   Three Corner Rock trailhead (GPS 45 41.990 N 122 07.260 W).

3.2   Sign pointing out Three Corner Rock.

3.9   Trail crosses Stebbins Creek.

6.4   Trail crosses Road CG 1400 (GPS 45 43.728 N 122 03.437 W).

8.9   Junction with Road CG 1500A, in a saddle southeast of summit (GPS 45 43.908 N 122 02.905 W).

9.1   Summit of Three Corner Rock (GPS 45 43.949 N 122 02.986 W).

9.3   Upper Three Corner Rock trailhead.

45 Silver Star Mountain North, Trails 180-1, 180D

Hike through flower-covered ridgetop meadows nearly all the way from the trailhead to the top of Silver Star Mountain. This route is the easiest way to reach the summit. Bears are fairly common in the area.

Start: Silver Star trailhead.
Distance: 4.8-mile out-and-back day hike.
Difficulty: Moderate.
Seasons: Mid-June through October. This route, including part of the road leading to the trailhead, is sometimes used by cross-country skiers and snowshoers during the winter.
Fees and permits: Northwest Forest Pass.
Parking and trailhead facilities: There is adequate parking at the trailhead but no other facilities.
Maps: Gumboot Mountain and Bobs Mountain USGS quads.
Trail contacts: Mount St. Helens National Volcanic Monument, Monument Headquarters, 42218 NE Yale Bridge Road, Amboy, WA 98601; (360) 449–7800; www.fs.fed.us/gpnf/mshnvm.

Finding the trailhead: From Portland drive north on I-205 to exit 30. From the Seattle area drive south on I-5 to the junction with I-205. Then take I-205 to exit 30. From exit 30 on I-205, head east on State Route 500 for 1.1 miles to the junction with State Route 503. Don't turn at the junction but drive straight ahead (north) on SR 503 for 13.5 miles to the junction with Rock Creek Road. Turn right onto Rock Creek Road, which becomes Lucia Falls Road in 2.6 miles. Another 5.7 miles on Lucia Falls Road brings you to the junction with NE Sunset Falls Road. Turn right on NE Sunset Falls Road and go 7.2 miles southeast and east to Sunset Campground.

From the campground head south on Forest Road 41; there is no road sign at this junction. After driving southeast on FR 41 for 3.5 miles, make a hard right turn onto Forest Road 4109 (also no sign). Follow FR 4109 for 2.6 miles to its end at the trailhead, being careful not to bear right onto Tarbell Road, which is at slightly more than a mile after leaving FR 41. The elevation at the trailhead is 3,090 feet. The USDA Forest Service Gifford Pinchot National Forest map can be of great help in finding this trailhead. There is a great view of Mount St. Helens from the trailhead.

Special Considerations

There is usually no water along the trail. This trail is open to mountain bikes and stock as well as hikers. During stormy weather these open ridgetops can be a miserable place to be.

The Hike

The open ridges and vistas in the Silver Star area owe their existence to the 1902 Yacolt Burn that started near Stevenson. The fire burned to the northwest, driven by strong east winds, to stop just short of Longview. The burn is named for the town of Yacolt, which was spared when the fire burned the forest surrounding it.

Mount St. Helens from Silver Star Mountain ▶

The Civilian Conservation Corps (CCC) built fire-access roads and felled snags on the ridgetops to create fire breaks. The area was closed to public use until the early 1960s because of the extreme fire hazard created by the millions of dead snags. Many of the trails in the area today follow the old CCC fire roads.

The trail (not the abandoned roadbed) leaves the parking area heading south along a brush-covered slope. Vine maple and bleeding hearts line the route as it climbs the 0.1 mile to the first switchback. The course makes two more switchbacks and then tops the ridgeline. As you approach the ridge, the brush becomes smaller and Mounts Adams and Rainier come into full, unobstructed view. The track crosses the ridgeline and quickly joins the abandoned roadbed that leads to the summit of Silver Star Mountain and beyond.

Turn right onto the roadbed and soon reach the junction with Ed's Trail 180A, at 3,460 feet elevation, 0.5 mile from the trailhead. See Options for more information about Ed's Trail. Looking south from the junction, there is a view of Mount Hood, rising above the head of Star Creek Canyon. At the junction the route (roadbed) makes a hard turn to the right. The trace continues to climb, recrossing the ridgeline and passing a side trail to the left, before traversing the open slope to the junction with the Chinook Trail 180B. The junction with the Chinook Trail is 1 mile from the trailhead at 3,760 feet elevation. Chinook Trail descends for 2 miles west to join Tarbell Trail.

For the next 0.7 mile, the path generally traverses just to the right (west) of the open, flower-covered ridgeline, reaching it only once in a saddle. Then the trail flattens out and enters the timber at about 4,100 feet elevation. In the timber the track descends slightly to a saddle and then climbs gently for slightly more than 0.1 mile to the junction with the Bluff Mountain Trail 172. The junction is 2 miles from the trailhead at 4,080 feet elevation.

Past the junction with the Bluff Mountain Trail, the tread climbs moderately to the junction with Trails 180-2 and 180D. Turn left at the junction and climb on Trail 180D through the trees to the ridgeline just south of the summit of Silver Star Mountain. As you reach the ridge, the route leaves the woods. The trail, which is still an abandoned roadbed, makes a switchback to the left on the ridge and climbs the last few yards to the summit.

Bare, flower-covered ridges, several with trails on them, radiate from the windswept 4,390-foot-high summit. From here the view is breathtaking in all directions. To the southwest on a clear day, the Columbia River as well as Vancouver and Portland are visible through the haze. To the west are the forest-covered hills of the western Cascades and the Coast Range. To the north is the squat, but still beautiful, remains of Mount St. Helens. Just to the right of Mount St. Helens, far in the distance, is the ice-clad summit of Mount Rainier. To the right of Mount Rainier to the northeast, the jagged peaks that make up Goat Rocks are on the horizon. To the right of Goat Rocks but still to the northeast is the glacier-covered bulk of Mount

Silver Star Mountain North, Trails 180-1, 180D

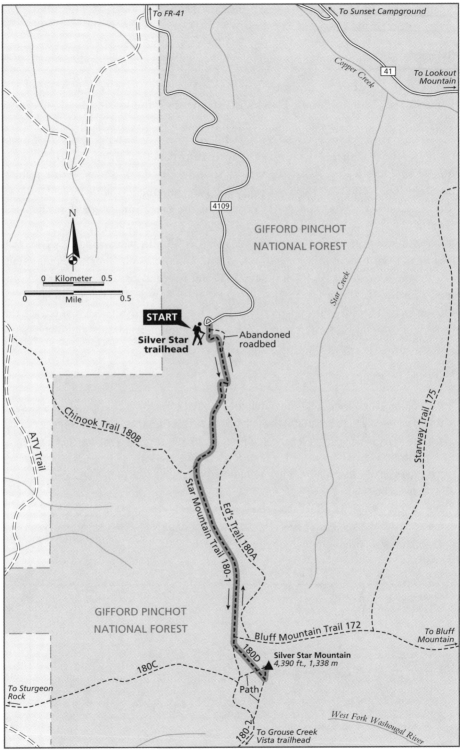

To FR-41

To Sunset Campground

Copper Creek

41

To Lookout Mountain

N

0   Kilometer   0.5

0   Mile   0.5

4109

GIFFORD PINCHOT
NATIONAL FOREST

Star Creek

START

Silver Star trailhead

Abandoned roadbed

Chinook Trail 180B

ATV Trail

Star Mountain Trail 180-1

Ed's Trail 180A

Starway Trail 175

GIFFORD PINCHOT
NATIONAL FOREST

Bluff Mountain Trail 172

To Bluff Mountain

180D

▲ **Silver Star Mountain**
4,390 ft., 1,338 m

180C

To Sturgeon Rock

Path

180-2

To Grouse Creek Vista trailhead

West Fork Washougal River

Adams. Looking southeast the sharp peak of Mount Hood rises high above the green ridges of the Oregon Cascades.

Options

A one-way hike can be made by combining this hike with Trail 180-2 and the Pyramid Trail 180F to Grouse Creek Vista trailhead on the south side of Silver Star Mountain.

To reach the Grouse Creek Vista trailhead by road, first backtrack to Sunset Campground and then drive west on Sunset Falls Road for 5.3 miles to the junction with Dole Valley Road. Turn left (south) onto Dole Valley Road (which becomes Road 1000) and drive for 5.2 miles to the junction with Road W 1200. Turn left onto W 1200 and drive 5 miles on the fairly rough gravel road to the Grouse Creek Vista trailhead.

Another option is to return via Ed's Trail 180A. To hike back along Ed's Trail, first backtrack from the summit for 0.4 mile to the junction with Bluff Mountain Trail. Turn right (east) onto Bluff Mountain Trail and hike a short distance to the junction with Ed's Trail. Turn left onto Ed's Trail and follow it 2 miles north along the canyon wall of Star Creek Canyon to the junction with Trail 180-1. Then retrace the route you came in on for 0.5 mile north back to the trailhead. Ed's Trail is not suitable for mountain bikes or stock.

Miles and Directions

0.0   Silver Star trailhead (GPS 45 46.360 N 122 14.672 W).

0.5   Junction with Ed's Trail 180A (GPS 45 46.046 N 122 14.537 W). Turn right.

1.0   Junction with the Chinook Trail 180B (GPS 45 45.735 N 122 14.746 W). Stay left (south).

2.0   Junction with Bluff Mountain Trail 172 (GPS 45 44.989 N 122 14.528 W). Continue straight (south).

2.1   Junction with Trails 180-2 and 180D. Turn left.

2.4   Summit of Silver Star Mountain (GPS 45 44.864 N 122 14.339 W). Turnaround point.

4.8   Silver Star trailhead.

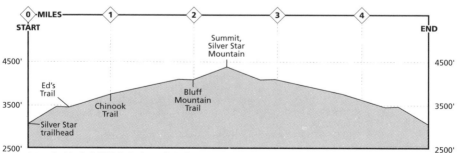

Intervals: Vertical, 1000 ft; Horizontal, 1 mi.

46 Bluff Mountain to Silver Star Mountain Summit, Trails 172, 180-1, 180D

Hike along a mostly open ridgeline with fantastic views and tons of flowers, from a poorly marked trailhead on Forest Road 41 to the summit of Silver Star Mountain.

Start: Bluff Mountain trailhead.
Distance: 13.0-mile out-and-back day hike or backpack.
Difficulty: Moderate.
Seasons: Late June through mid-October. Flowers are best in early July.
Fees and permits: Northwest Forest Pass.
Parking and trailhead facilities: There is plenty of parking but no other facilities at the trailhead.

Maps: Gumboot Mountain and Bobs Mountain USGS quads.
Trail contacts: Mount St. Helens National Volcanic Monument, Monument Headquarters, 42218 NE Yale Bridge Road, Amboy, WA 98601; (360) 449–7800; www.fs.fed. us/gpnf/mshnvm.

Finding the trailhead: From Portland drive north on I-205 to exit 30. From the Seattle area drive south on I-5 to the junction with I-205. Then take I-205 to exit 30. Head east from exit 30 on State Route 500 for 1.1 miles to the junction with State Route 503. Don't turn at the junction but drive straight ahead (north) on SR 503 for 13.5 miles to the junction with Rock Creek Road. Turn right onto Rock Creek Road, which becomes Lucia Falls Road in 2.6 miles. Another 5.7 miles on Lucia Falls Road brings you to the junction with NE Sunset Falls Road. Turn right onto NE Sunset Falls Road and go 7.2 miles southeast and east to Sunset Campground.

From the campground head south on FR 41; there is no road sign at this junction. Forest Road 41 is a gravel road that is usually in fairly good condition, but you may have to ease your vehicle through a few rough spots and around a few rocks. After driving southeast on FR 41 for 9 miles, you will reach the trailhead at 3,550 feet elevation. The trailhead is on the right side of FR 41 as it crosses through a saddle.

Special Considerations

Early in the season steep lingering patches of snow may make this trail difficult and dangerous in spots. The only water along this route is the streams you cross at the head of Copper Creek, about 2.5 miles from the trailhead. Late in the season these streams may not be dependable, so its best to take along all the water you will need. If you get water from the stream, be sure to filter or treat it before drinking. Bears are common here; keep a sharp lookout and you may see one.

The Hike

The first 2.2 miles of this hike follow an old abandoned roadbed. Leaving the trailhead the route heads south-southwest, climbing gently along a brushy slope. Scattered fir trees rise above the vine maple bushes while penstemon and paintbrush add cheer to the trailside. In 0.1 mile the course reaches a saddle in the ridgeline where Mount Hood comes into view to the left. The route then traverses along the right side of the ridgeline for 0.4 mile through a stand of dense small firs. Back on the ridge, at 3,650 feet elevation, the tread crosses to the more-open east slope. Well below and to the left, you may notice a small melt pond. Beargrass and lupine grow in profusion beside the roadbed. Shortly you reach the ridgeline again and, just after crossing it, you reach a junction.

The trail to the right is an abandoned four-wheel-drive road that descends about 3 miles to Copper Creek and a group of mines. From the mines the trail continues another 2 miles to FR 41. Check with the Forest Service before using this trail.

At the junction you are back into patches of stunted fir trees, at 3,610 feet elevation, 0.7 mile from the trailhead. As the trace recrosses the ridgeline 0.6 mile farther along, Mount Jefferson can be seen far to the south, as well as the much closer Mount Hood. Soon the trail turns to the west-southwest and starts to descend from 3,680 feet elevation. The route descends for slightly more than 0.7 mile, losing 350 feet of elevation. A few yards before the roadbed ends, the trail bears to the right to continue its descent another 0.4 mile to a large saddle, making a switchback along the way. This saddle, at 3,120 feet elevation, is the low point of this trail.

Leaving the saddle the trail climbs across talus slopes and below the dark cliffs that are the northwest face of Bluff Mountain. After traversing and climbing around the head of Copper Creek Canyon for 0.7 mile, the track enters a stand of old, fairly large timber. In the timber on the steep north-facing slope, the tread crosses a couple of small streams. If you are here early in the season (June), there may be snow on this slope and in the saddle ahead. On this steep slope, crossing snow can be difficult and in some cases dangerous. Be prepared.

The route reaches the timbered saddle west of Bluff Mountain 0.3 mile after entering the timber, after crossing a mostly brush-covered talus slope. If there is snow in the saddle, head west, climbing just slightly to the left of the ridgeline, and pick up the route as it begins its traverse around the south side of Little Baldy. The south slope of Little Baldy is mostly talus. The trail has been recently maintained here and is in excellent condition. Looking southwest from the open talus slope, the Columbia River and Portland can be seen in the distance through the haze. You reach the ridgeline, at 3,460 feet elevation, on the west side of Little Baldy 0.6 mile after leaving the timbered saddle.

◀ *Silver Star Mountain*

Bluff Mountain to Silver Star Mountain Summit, Trails 172, 180-1, 180D

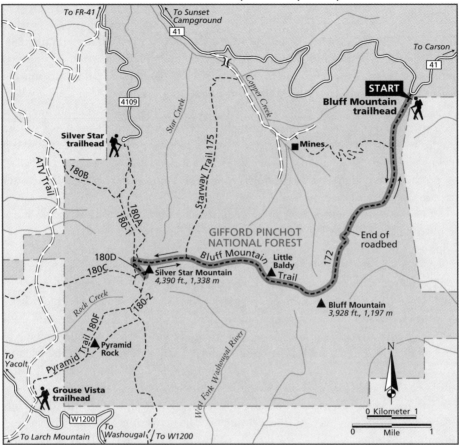

The route now follows the ridge, heading west and climbing for 0.2 mile. Then you traverse, still climbing along the south side of the ridge crest and passing an outcropping before regaining the crest at 3,820 feet elevation, where you will find the junction with Starway Trail 175. This junction is 5.3 miles from the trailhead.

Starway Trail turns to the right (north) and follows the ridgeline for a little more than 2 miles before descending the last 2 miles to Copper Creek and a new bridge that was installed in the summer of 2002. About 0.3 mile before reaching the bridge this route joins the side route described earlier (the one that left Bluff Mountain Trail 0.7 mile from the trailhead). As with the side route described earlier, check with the Forest Service before using this trail.

Past the junction the trail continues to climb the open slope just left (south) of the ridgeline and then traverses the steep, timbered slope north of Silver Star Mountain, passing the junction with Ed's Trail to the junction with Trails 180-1 and 180-2, at 4,080 feet elevation. Ed's Trail and Trail 180-1 are parallel routes leading 2 miles north to the trailhead at the end of Forest Road 4109.

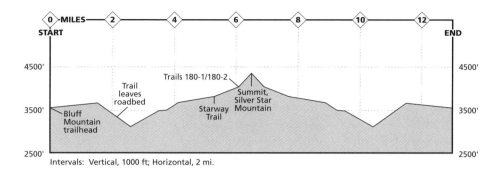

Intervals: Vertical, 1000 ft; Horizontal, 2 mi.

To continue to the summit of Silver Star Mountain, turn left (south) at the junction and climb moderately along Trail 180-2 (which is an abandoned Civilian Conservation Corps fire road) for 0.1 mile to the junction with Silver Star Summit Trail 180D. At this junction, Trail 180-2, which has now become the south-side route to Silver Star Mountain, goes straight ahead (south).

Turn left at the junction and climb on Trail 180D through the trees to the ridgeline just south of the summit of Silver Star Mountain. As you reach the ridge, the route leaves the woods. The trail, which is still an abandoned roadbed, makes a switchback to the left on the ridge and climbs the last few yards to the summit at 4,390 feet elevation.

Options

A one-way hike can easily be made by combining this hike with the Silver Star Mountain North hike. Doing this will shorten the trip by 4.1 miles but will require an 8.1-mile car shuttle.

Another option is to continue south on Trails 180-2 and 180F to the Grouse Creek Vista trailhead on Road W 1200.

Miles and Directions

0.0   Bluff Mountain trailhead (GPS 45 46.800 N 122 10.015 W).

0.7   Trail junction. Continue straight (south).

2.2   Trail leaves roadbed (GPS 45 45.287 N 122 11.056 W).

5.3   Junction with Starway Trail 175. Continue straight (west).

6.1   Junction with Trails 180-1 and 180-2 (GPS 45 44.989 N 122 14.528 W). Turn left (south). Then turn left at the junction with Trail 180D.

6.5   Summit Silver Star Mountain (GPS 45 44.864 N 122 14.339 W). Turnaround point.

13.0   Bluff Meadow trailhead.

47 Silver Star Mountain via the Pyramid, Trails 180F, 180-2, 180D

Hike through the second-growth forest leaving Grouse Creek Vista trailhead to the open flower-covered ridges high above. Then traverse the open slopes to the summit of Silver Star Mountain. The area was burned in the 1902 Yacolt fire, leaving the open slopes that are reforesting only very slowly.

Start: Grouse Creek Vista trailhead.
Distance: 7.6-mile out-and-back day hike.
Difficulty: Moderate grade, but the surface of nearly the entire route is eroded and rocky.
Seasons: June through October. The best flower bloom is in late June and July.
Fees and permits: None.
Parking and trailhead facilities: There is

adequate parking at the trailhead but no other facilities.
Maps: Bobs Mountain USGS quad.
Trail contacts: Mount St. Helens National Volcanic Monument, Monument Headquarters, 42218 NE Yale Bridge Road, Amboy, WA 98601; (360) 449-7800; www.fs.fed.us/gpnf/mshnvm.

Finding the trailhead: Drive north from Portland on I-205. Just after crossing the Columbia River, turn east onto State Route 14 and drive for about 10 miles to the town of Washougal. In Washougal, get on Washougal River Road (State Route 140) and follow it 10.4 miles northeast to the junction with Skye Road. Turn left (north) onto Skye Road and drive 3.7 miles to the junction with Skamania Mines Road. Turn right (north) and follow Skamania Mines Road 2.7 miles to the junction with Road W 1200. You will leave the pavement 1.3 miles before reaching the junction. Bear left (really almost straight ahead) at the junction and follow Road W 1200. In 0.1 mile the road forks; bear left and stay on Road W 1200 heading north. In another 5.6 miles you will reach Grouse Creek Vista trailhead. The elevation at the trailhead is 2,380 feet.

Special Considerations

There may be no water along this trail, so take all you will need. Bears are common here; keep a sharp eye out and you may catch a glimpse of one. If photographing flowers is in your plans, take lots of film.

The Hike

Cross the road from the parking area and walk through an opening in a rail fence. The purpose of the fence is to keep out motor vehicles, which are prohibited on this route. The entire trail was built by the Civilian Conservation Corps as a fire-break road. The tread climbs steeply over large gravel for a few feet and then continues as a good dirt path for 150 yards to a fork. There is no sign at the fork. The left fork is the Tarbell Trail, which can be used as part of a return route from the summit. Bear

Silver Star Mountain summit

right at the fork and climb over the end of a nearly rotted log, which was put here to keep out vehicles.

Past the fork the tread becomes very rocky again and stays that way the rest of the way to the top. The route climbs fairly steeply through the second-growth forest. In places the forest canopy completely covers the course, giving the trail a tunnel effect. In another 0.6 mile the grade moderates for a short distance at 2,860 feet elevation. Quickly you climb steeply again for another 0.2 mile. Here, at slightly more than 3,000 feet elevation, the trace leaves the forest and traverses brushy slopes. Soon the brush becomes shorter; much of the slope is now covered with short huckleberry bushes, beargrass, and paintbrush, as well as many other varieties of flowers. In about another 0.4 mile, the tread passes through two small groves of fir trees at 3,270 feet elevation. Flowers bloom all along these open slopes once the snow has gone; avalanche lilies are among the first to show. Shortly after passing through the second grove, you reach another trail junction.

The trail to the right climbs a few yards to a saddle on the ridgeline, where another trail leaves it to the right to climb to the top of a peak on the ridgeline south of Pyramid Rock. After crossing the saddle the trail heads northeast. There is a view of Mount Hood from the saddle.

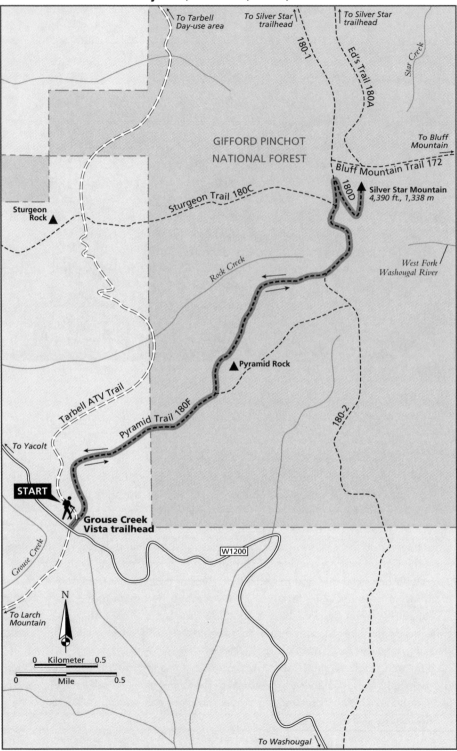

To Tarbell
Day-use area

To Silver Star
trailhead

To Silver Star
trailhead

180-1

Ed's Trail 180A

Star Creek

To Bluff
Mountain

GIFFORD PINCHOT
NATIONAL FOREST

Bluff Mountain Trail 172

Sturgeon Trail 180C

180D

Silver Star Mountain
4,390 ft., 1,338 m

Sturgeon
Rock

Rock Creek

West Fork
Washougal River

Pyramid Rock

Tarbell ATV Trail

Pyramid Trail 180F

180-2

To Yacolt

START

Grouse Creek
Vista trailhead

W1200

Grouse Creek

To Larch
Mountain

N

To Washougal

0   Kilometer   0.5

0   Mile   0.5

From the junction the main trail descends slightly and then crosses a short talus slope before resuming its climb to the north-northeast along the open slope. After crossing the flower-covered slope for 0.8 mile, the track reenters the timber at 3,600 feet elevation. If you are here early in the season, this is where you will hit snow. In another 0.4 mile is the junction with Trail 180-2, at 3,800 feet elevation. Bear left (straight ahead) onto Trail 180-2. Three-tenths of a mile farther along, the trail will be quite close to the ridgeline. If the ground is snow-covered, climb right here to the ridge and work your way up the ridgeline to the summit.

If the trail is clear, follow it for another 0.5 mile, passing the junction with Sturgeon Trail 180C, to the junction with Silver Star Summit Trail 180D. At the junction turn right onto the summit trail and climb to a switchback to the left, on the ridgeline just south of the summit. You will leave the timber just before the switchback. From the switchback climb the last few yards along the ridge to the 4,390-foot-high summit of Silver Star Mountain, where a lookout once stood.

Bare ridges radiate from the summit, most with trails on them. The view sweeps around the compass. Mount Hood is to the southeast, and Three Corner Rock, with a tower next to it, is to the east. To the northeast is Mount Adams and Goat Rocks. Far to the north-northeast is Mount Rainier, and to the north is Mount St. Helens. To the southwest are Vancouver, Portland, and the Columbia River. Cell-phone service is generally good from the summit.

Options

An alternate return may be made by first backtracking to the junction with the Sturgeon Trail and then following the Sturgeon Trail west to the junction with the Tarbell Trail. Turn left onto the Tarbell Trail and hike southeast back to the junction 150 yards from the trailhead.

Another option is to continue on Trails 180-2 and 180-1 along the crest to the trailhead north of Silver Star Mountain. To get to the northern trailhead, follow Road W 1200 north to NE Sunset Falls Road. Go southeast and east to Sunset Campground. From the campground head south on Forest Road 41. There is no road sign at this junction. After driving southeast on FR 41 for 3.5 miles, make a

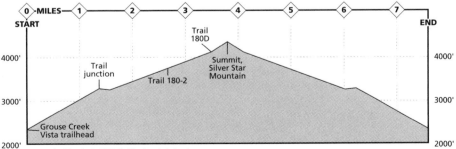

Intervals: Vertical, 1000 ft; Horizontal, 1 mi.

hard right turn onto Forest Road 4109 (also no sign). Follow FR 4109 for 2.6 miles to its end at the Silver Star trailhead. The trailheads are 21.6 miles apart by road.

Miles and Directions

0.0 Grouse Creek Vista trailhead (GPS 45 43.313 N 122 16.168 W).

0.1 Junction with Tarbell Trail. Bear right.

1.4 Trail junction (GPS 45 43.988 N 122 15.257 W). Stay left (north).

2.7 Trail Junction with Trail 180-2 (GPS 45 44.486 N 122 14.556 W). Continue straight (northeast).

3.0 Side path to ridge (use when route is snow-covered).

3.5 Junction with Silver Star Summit Trail 180D. Turn right.

3.8 Summit (GPS 45 44.864 N 122 14.339 W). Turnaround point.

7.6 Grouse Creek Vista trailhead.

Appendix

Glossary

Accumulation zone: The area of a glacier or snowfield where the amount of snowfall exceeds the amount that is melted each year.

ATV: All-terrain vehicle.

Bivouac or bivy: Camp without the benefit of a prepared or other comfortable campsite.

Blacktail deer: A subspecies of mule deer that inhabits the coastal areas of southern Alaska, western Canada, Washington, Oregon, and northern California.

Blaze: A mark on a tree made by cutting away a small section of bark with an ax or hatchet. A blaze may consist of one or two marks. Blazes usually can be seen for some distance ahead while hiking.

Cairn: A stack or pile of rocks that marks the trail or route.

Cirque: A bowl-shaped area where a glacier has eaten its way into a mountain slope and then melted. A cirque is formed at the head of a glacier.

Cinder cone: A volcanic vent from which little or no liquid lava has erupted. Cinder cones are typically fairly steep and smooth-sided and made up of fragments of volcanic rock.

Clear-cut: An area that has been logged of all, or nearly all, its timber.

Cloud cap: A cloud that forms on the top of a ridge or mountain. At times a cloud cap may be the only cloud in the sky.

Columnar basalt: Basalt lava that has cooled in such a way that it has cracked into tight columns.

Crevasse: A crack in an active glacier; it may be narrow or wide enough to swallow a building.

Cross deer: A cross between a blacktail deer and a mule deer.

Exposure: In climbing, the amount of exposure refers to the possibility of falling farther than just to the ground at your feet. In a highly exposed spot, it would be possible to fall several tens to several thousands of feet.

Fire scars: Charred bark, and in some cases wood, on the trunks of living trees, generally caused by a long-ago forest fire.

FR: Forest Road.

GPS: Global Positioning System.

Gray digger: Common name in the northwest for several species of ground squirrels.

Internal trail: A trail that begins and/or ends at a junction with another trail. Internal trails do not reach any trailhead.

Lava flow: A stream of molten rock flowing from a volcano, or a stream of rock after it has cooled and hardened.

Lava tube: An opening beneath or in a lava flow where a stream of molten rock has continued to flow after the outer crust of the lava flow has cooled and hardened and has flowed out, leaving a tube.

Lava tube cave: A lava tube large enough for a person to enter.

Log bolt or just bolt: A log that has been cut in short lengths for the purpose of making shakes. Normally, bolts are cut from cedar.

Mixed forest or mixed woods: A forest made up of several species of trees.

MSHNVM (map): USDA Forest Service Mount St. Helens National Volcanic Monument map. The one with the waterfall on the cover. Also known as the brown line map.

Mule deer: A large-eared deer of the western United States, southwestern Canada, and northern Mexico.

Notch: A naturally carved-out section of a ridge. Smaller than a saddle, with rock outcroppings on both sides.

Old-growth forest: Forest that has never been logged and has not been burned in a fire hot enough to kill the mature trees in the last one hundred years.

ORV: Off-road vehicle.

ORV trail: Off-road-vehicle trail.

PCT: Pacific Crest Trail.

Pika: A small mammal that lives in steep rocky areas or talus slopes. Pikas are related to rabbits and do not hibernate.

Pumice: The solidified froth of volcanic rock. Pumice is a light-colored rock that is light enough to float.

Rock roof: The underneath side of an overhanging cliff. Typically, a roof will stick out at nearly a right angle to the cliff below it.

Saddle: A low point on a ridge, usually with a gentle slope. A saddle is larger than a notch.

Scree or scree slope: Small loose rock on a slope. The rocks are a smaller size than on a talus slope. Scree is very tiring to climb.

Second-growth forest: Regrown forest that has been logged or burned in the last one hundred years.

Signed junction: A junction with a sign next to it indicating direction to a particular point and or the mileage to a point.

Spur ridge: A smaller ridge on the side of a main ridge. Spur ridges may be very steep.

Spur trail: A short side trail.

SR: State Route.

Stock driveway: A trail, usually wide, that is used or was once used to drive stock.

Stratovolcano: A volcanic cone composed of both lava and fragmented material, usually in alternating layers. Stratovolcanoes are also known as composite cones. Mount Adams is a stratovolcano and Goat Rocks is the remains of a very old one.

Sub ridge: Same as spur ridge.

Sun cup: A pattern in melting snow that forms bowl-shaped depressions in its surface. In advanced cases the depressions nearly melt together to form upright spikes of snow. North of the equator these spikes normally lean south to point at the noontime sun.

Switchback: A sharp turn in a trail, usually on a steep slope. Switchbacks allow a trail to ascend a steep slope more easily.

Talus or talus slope: A slope covered with large rocks or boulders.

Tank trap: A large hole dug in a roadbed to prevent the passage of vehicles.

Tarn: A small lake or pond, usually shallow.

Top roped: A rock-climbing technique in which the rope is anchored at the top of the pitch above the climber and belayed by another climber. This is the technique used on indoor climbing walls.

Traverse: The crossing of a slope, climbing or descending but usually in nearly a straight line. The term is also used to describe a route that follows a fairly flat ridgeline.

USDA: United States Department of Agriculture.

USGS: United States Geological Survey.

Understory: Plants, brush, and short trees beneath the canopy of a mature forest.

Vent or volcanic vent: A tube, crack, or other weak spot in the earth's surface, from which lava, ash, and/or volcanic gasses rise, blast, or flow.

Water bar: A bar (may be made of wood, rock, soil, or even used highway guardrail) that drains water off a trail to prevent erosion.

Winter range: The area where migrating animals spend the winter.

About the Author

While growing up in Oregon's Willamette Valley, Fred Barstad developed a keen interest in the Cascade Mountains at an early age. He hiked and fished extensively with his parents in the range, mostly between Mount Hood and Mount Jefferson in Oregon. The high volcanic peaks of the Cascades quickly became of special interest to him.

This interest had become an addiction for the high and remote country by the time he was a teenager in the 1960s. Fred has climbed most of the Cascade volcanoes in Washington and Oregon, including sixty-four climbs of Mount Hood, several of both Mount Rainer and Mount Adams using various routes. He climbed Mount St. Helens eleven times before the 1980 eruption and a couple of times since. Further from home, Fred has ascended Mount McKinley (Denali) in Alaska, Aconcagua in Argentina, and Popocatepetl, Citlaltepetl (Pico de Orizaba), and Iztaccihaatl in Mexico.

Now living in Enterprise, Oregon, at the base of the Wallowa Mountains, Fred devotes as much of his time as possible to hiking, climbing, and snow shoeing when he isn't working on a book.